MISSING IN GREECE

Destinies in the Greek Freedom Fight
1941–1944

H. F. MEYER

MINERVA PRESS
MONTREUX LONDON WASHINGTON

MISSING IN GREECE
Copyright © H. F. Meyer 1995

All Rights Reserved

ISBN 1 85863 355 9

First Published 1995 by
MINERVA PRESS
10 Cromwell Place,
London SW7 2JN

Printed in Great Britain by
Antony Rowe Ltd., Chippenham, Wiltshire.

MISSING IN GREECE

Translated from the German by
Joyce Nelson-Smith

Published in Greece as
Η ΑΝΑΖΗΤΗΣΗ
by Kalendis & Co. Ltd. Publishers
Mavromichali 5, GR-10679 Athens

Originally published in Germany as
*Vermisst in Griechenland, Schicksale im griechischen
Freiheitskampf 1941–1944*
by Verlag Frieling & Partner GmbH, D – 12247 Berlin
(ISBN 3-89009-376-0)

Front cover designed by Alexander Schmitt

About the Author

H. F. Meyer, who was born in Hanover in 1940, worked as a business man and entrepreneur in many countries and continents. He first visited Greece in 1963, and from then until 1991 he carried out intensive research, which led him as far as New Zealand, to discover the fate of his father and those who had disappeared with him. He studied the history of the time, sifting through documents including some unpublished texts in war archives belonging to Germany, Greece and the Allies. He interviewed British and Greek eyewitnesses and visited the families of the missing Germans, some of whom he could not reach until after the Berlin Wall came down. Finally he wrote this documentary which not only describes the destinies of individual people, but gives a general insight into the Greek freedom fight against the German occupation.

People are not shaped by war,
they are, in war, what they truly are.

Jean Giono

For Mother, Liesel, Christian, Philipp
and the families of the missing men

———————

Contents

Table of Illustrations

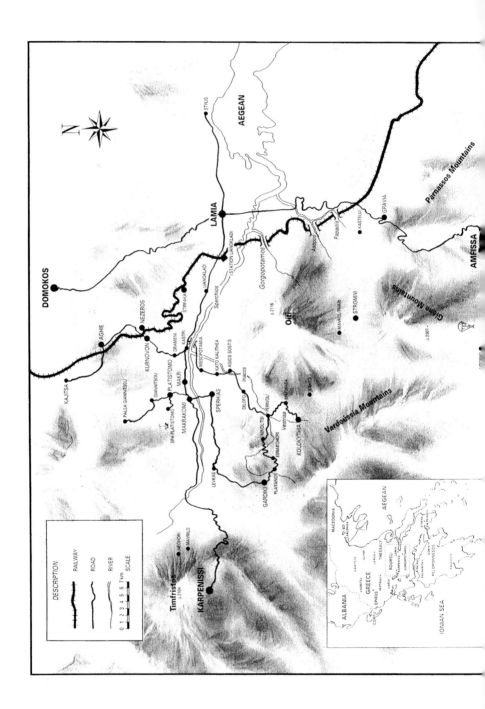

Preface

This documentary is based on my research into German, British, Italian and Greek archives and publications, and on many conversations and interviews which I had with contemporary witnesses in Germany, Italy, Greece, Great Britain and New Zealand. The dialogues quoted in the book were either recorded on tape at the time or written down in notes immediately after each conversation.

Against the background of Greece during the second world war, when it was occupied by German, Italian and Bulgarian troops, I have described the life and fate of my father and thirty-three of his comrades who were reported missing in Greece during the war, in 1943.

My thanks go to Professor Hagen Fleischer whose authoritative book *"Im Kreuzschatten der Mächte"* (In the cross shadow of the great powers) was the basis for my description of how Greece was drawn into the war.

I am also much obliged to the Hon. C. M. Woodhouse, Brigadier E. C. W. Myers and A. Edmonds for their permission to quote from their books and manuscripts. I thank Messrs Meyer and Moritz from the Bundesarchiv - Militärarchiv (Federal and Military archives) in Freiburg; also Oberstleutnant Nöhl, Bundeswehrpionierschule (Army School of Engineers) in Munich; H. Ortstein, Zentralbibliothek der Bundeswehr (Central library of the army) in Düsseldorf; Friedrich, Baron von Falkenhausen, Saarbrücken; Generalleutnant a.D. Hans v. Donat, Honorary Chairman and Werner Johnsdorf, Chairman of the Kameradschaft der ehemaligen Eisenbahnpioniere (Club of former Rail Engineers) in Frankfurt; Professor Richard Clogg, St. Anthony's College, Oxford; Frau Blümert and H. Daniel from WASt, Berlin; H. von Lutzau, Volksbund Deutsche Kriegsgräberfürsorge (German War Graves Commission) in Kassel; Dr. W. Rodehorst, Lüneburg; Dr. Brugioni and Tenente Colonelle Fratolillo, Stato Maggiore dell'Esercito, Rome; Dimitrios Dimitriou and Themistocles Marinos, Athens and Dr Franz Tsagaris, Lamia. They all gave me their help in my research.

My two Greek interpreters, Agapi Maria and her brother John Paspadakis, were a constant source of support during difficult interviews. Vana Papachristou accompanied me on many arduous trips into the mountains and her collaboration was of inestimable value to me.

Above all, I wish to thank my wife Liesel and my sons Christian and Philipp. I am also indebted to Ute Steinbicker, Martine Sacré, Joyce and David Nelson-Smith and the families of the missing men. Without their encouragement and sensitive understanding, I would never have succeeded in completing this book in its present form.

Uccle, Belgium   H. F. Meyer
1995

CHAPTER ONE
Prologue

Excursion to Makrakomi

The Lufthansa Super Constellation rolled slowly to a halt in front of the Olympic Airways building at Athens airport. She was the last to step out of the plane and walk uncertainly down the gangway onto the runway. She was wearing a light summer hat and I could see from afar that she was suffering in the exceptionally humid heat. It was August 1963.

Mother had never been abroad, but for once in her life, she wanted to travel to Greece, because her husband, my father, had been reported missing here while he was an Oberzahlmeister (senior paymaster) in the German Wehrmacht in 1943.

"Abducted into the mountains" were the words used by the Mayor of Mellendorf who telephoned the news through to her. She had reacted violently, totally disbelieving that anything could have happened to her husband far away in Greece. The country was supposed to be "pacified", conquered by the German troops, who had saved their ally Mussolini from shameful defeat after his ill-advised attack on the Hellenic land.

His superior, a certain Captain Christ, had written her this neutral letter in April 1943, which always gave us hope that he would return one day:

On 30 March, your husband Hermann Meyer was attacked and captured by revolutionaries while out driving with three comrades. The Greek revolutionaries have, in previous attacks, freed the German army railway men within a few days, but this has not been the case so far, so we have to assume that they are no longer willing to do so. Your husband has not reported back since the attack and must therefore be declared missing.

There is however no reason to fear, at the moment, that your husband is not alive. We consider it to be our duty simply to prepare you for the worst that could happen owing to the unreliability of the bandits. As soon as we have any news, we shall inform you immediately.

Already in the bus on the way from the airport to the Hotel
Atlantic on Omonia Square, she pulled a small black and white photo
out of her handbag. "One of his comrades sent it to me after the war,"
she said. "He took it from the moving train when the German troops
were leaving Greece."

The picture shows a hilly, wooded landscape with a snow-clad
mountain range in the background. It seemed to have been snapped
from a hill. On the front someone had noted "Makrakomi" which we
took to mean a village, so we decided spontaneously to include in our
tourist programme a visit to the area where her husband had
disappeared.

Fig. 1   *His comrade's photo: "X = Makrakomi"*

"They captured him somewhere on the Olympus with three of his
comrades in the car," she said. "I think that the dotted line marked on
the photo is the road he was driving on in the end. We were never told
any more."

That evening at Athens central railway station, it was confirmed
that there was indeed a village called Makrakomi but that it could only
be reached by train to Lianokladi and then by bus. The early train
leaving at five a.m. would take us to Lianokladi in a good six hours,

and a further hour in the bus would take us to Makrakomi. The village was about two hundred and fifty kilometres north of Athens in the hilly central area, and the return trip could be made in the late afternoon.

"He was really supposed to come home on leave in the beginning of April 1943," she confided in the early morning in the empty train compartment. "I never heard anything more from the German Army, only from that man who sent the photo after the war. He must have been a friend."

I was two and a half years old when the uncertain news of his fate arrived. I have no conscious knowledge of him. She and he had both been national socialists and believed in "building a New Germany". He was a teacher by profession and he volunteered for the army because he did not wish, "when the new Reich had been created", to have to face his sons "without having played his part". It was not until the nineteen fifties that she began to halfway comprehend the extent of the atrocities that she and he, as little cogs in the Hitler-machine, had to take some responsibility for.

Her faith in his return was never shaken after 1945. As he had been declared missing and according to Captain Christ's letter "there was no reason to fear", there was hope and even justification to clutch at every straw. "Those Greeks who took him were apparently Communists. They had good contacts with the Soviets in Moscow.

Fig. 2   *June 1946. Helga, Helmut, Erika Meyer, Hermann: "There is no reason to fear, at the moment, that your husband is not alive."*

Maybe he ended up in a Russian prisoner of war camp," she comforted herself and her children after the war. "Prisoners are still coming back from Russia, he might be one of them."

But this dream, too, faded, when the last German privates returned from the Soviet Union. In 1955 we listened spellbound to the daily radio messages when lists of names were read out. I remember those emotional scenes at the railway station in Friedland when emaciated men hugged their wives, who had meanwhile put on a little post-war weight. The children stood next to them, looking puzzled, for they did not recognise their fathers. But ours was never there.

I pulled the dirty window down. It was already very hot in the morning. The breeze from the open window tugged gently at her new silk blouse. The long train made its way laboriously through the barren hilly landscape, which seemed so unlike what tourists imagine Greece to be. The air was sticky and stagnant in the compartment. At times the view opened up over deep, fertile valleys with olive trees planted in careful rows. In the late afternoon we could make out the blue Aegean Sea on the horizon, floating like a mirage in the shimmering heat. The train wound its way higher into the mountains, thundered through a tunnel and came out on the other side onto a long viaduct. "There's the bridge," she cried suddenly, her excitement shaking me out of my apathy. "That's the one they had to repair!"

There was no doubt in her mind. We twisted our necks to catch a glimpse of the imposing, slightly curved steel construction. I just managed to snap a photo before the train dived into the next tunnel. "I remember it well," she said animatedly. "He sent pictures of it. He belonged to a unit that rebuilt bridges damaged by the fighting. He talked about it on his last leave. He said it was really madness to painstakingly build a bridge, just to have it blown up by partisans."

Many passengers got out at Lianokladi. Acacias grew in front of the station entrance. Clapped out old busses with uncomfortable metal seats were parked in their dappled shade. Most people were taking the bus to the nearby capital of the province, Lamia. We were told to take the other one in the direction of Karpenissi. Makrakomi was a small village on the way there; the driver would tell us in good time where to get out.

The old Mercedes bus trundled along the dusty, pot-holed road, following a long drawn-out valley through which a wide river meandered. There was very little water now, but one could see that in the spring the river would flow well out of its present bed. Mountains rose on either side, wooded on their lower slopes, smooth barren rock above. The fields bordering the river were lined with olive and

Fig. 3   *The imposing railway viaduct before Lianokladi: "There's the bridge!"*

pistachio trees. Peasants were harvesting cotton from low plants which grew lusciously green on the red-brown earth. There were also strips planted with tomatoes and potatoes. Everywhere bee-hives studded the pathways in the midst of low-growing, dry bushes and moorland shrubs, reminiscent of our own heath back home. We passed through a number of small villages where black-clad women boarded the bus.

At last the bus stopped in a fairly large village square, surrounded by low, shabby houses huddled close together. The driver signalled to us that we had reached our destination.

We found ourselves in the middle of the market place in Makrakomi. Tables and chairs stood around haphazardly under the ancient acacia trees. Old men sat at the tables, some with empty coffee cups in front of them. Others were playing a board game. No one seemed to be actually eating or drinking. They all stared at us curiously, supposing that we were foreign and would be needing assistance.

22

"What are you looking for? Can I help you?" asked a friendly looking man. He was wearing a shabby jacket over a checked shirt and he had a greasy old cap with a narrow peak on his head. Instantly, several men and youths surrounded us, all talking animatedly. This was at least a change from the usual village boredom!

Fig. 4   *Hermann Meyer, Senior Paymaster
("Oberzahlmeister")*

"My name is Alex Grivas," he said, presenting himself. Like so many Greeks, he had lived in the USA for a few years and had retired back home.

"We are from Germany. We have come here to see the area where my father went missing in 1943," I replied evenly. "He was with the German Wehrmacht, and a friend of his told us that he had been captured by partisans here. What happened after that, we do not know."

Alex Grivas translated. It seemed as though the whole village had meanwhile assembled around us. We couldn't understand a word. They were discussing violently amongst themselves. Everyone clamoured to see the photo of the German soldier which she had handed out. I knew it all too well. My father in uniform, looking directly into the camera lens, on the left of his chest the sports badge. An idealised picture, typical of the kind taken of every soldier at the time. She had had it copied. A large picture hung in the living-room above his book-case. The same photo appeared in the linen cupboard and stared out of several drawers. He was always present. Each of us children had a copy. Yet another copy stood on her night-table, as though on a shrine.

Two of the men reacted immediately. One of them pushed through the crowd. Alex Grivas translated: "Yes, we know him, that was 'Uffzier'. Of course we knew him. We called him 'Uffzier', that was his nickname. He was stationed somewhere near here. We often saw him at Platistomo Spa, which is a farm estate with a hot-water spring and a hotel which the Germans occupied. They not only farmed here, but they also operated a sawmill in Makrakomi. We used to work there. They were all captured by the partisans and taken away into the mountains."

"On that particular day 'Uffzier' was not in Platistomo but at the German headquarters at Lamia," the other man interrupted him, "and when he went looking with three men for the rest of his crew, he was taken prisoner too. They were three young chaps from Makri who captured them. They stopped his car. On its way into the mountains the car passed through this square and headed off towards Sperhias. One of the young guys was holding a pistol to his head. We never understood why the Germans let themselves be caught by those youths. After all, the Germans were armed and the boys only had an old pistol."

We were thunderstruck. Alex Grivas translated emotionlessly, in the knowledge that he was accomplishing an important task that only he was able to perform in this village community. His sonorous voice boomed out across half the square.

"He was very popular, your father," he said sympathetically. "Whenever the Italians robbed us or stole our pigs or if we had any other difficulties with them, we used to go to 'Uffzier', who then put in a word for us at the headquarters in Lamia. Frequently, he was able to correct the injustice that had been inflicted on us."

We were still standing in exactly the same spot where, barely three minutes earlier, we had stepped out of the bus. Twenty years of uncertainty had just been blown away in one breath by this man in his greasy peaked cap. Someone pushed a plastic chair towards us. My mother sat down in front of an empty coffee cup. Again and again, people asked to see the picture of the German in uniform.

"I used to work in the fields near Platistomo Spa and I carved a little doll's cradle for Christmas which I gave your father for his children, and we also gave him a small container of olive oil," said another man.

I looked at her questioningly. "Yes, that's right," she said remembering in a daze. "That last Christmas, in 1942, he sent us a bottle of olive oil, some raisins and tea and a small wooden toy for you children."

A shudder jerked her body. "What did happen to him?"

"We don't really know," the men said evasively. "Some were apparently shot, but not all. Two men supposedly escaped. Others were said to have joined the partisans."

And almost as though to justify themselves, one of the older men, with a dark unshaven face, added quietly but decisively that Makrakomi had been attacked and destroyed seven times in the war by Italians and Germans. Everybody nodded. Yes, seven times, their village had been sacked by Italians and Germans!

Alex Grivas was of the opinion that these old stories should now be forgotten. He insisted on buying us a cup of tea, which was immediately brought across the road by the inn-keeper who balanced it on his tin tray. It was midday, so according to custom in those parts he invited us into his kitchen to choose a meal. My mother declined. She was sitting bolt upright in the dirty plastic chair.

Alex suggested that we should take the village taxi in the direction of Sperhias. He pointed into the valley. "They drove them off in that direction," he said with an enveloping gesture while the others nodded their affirmation. It was a Mercedes — yes, an authentic black Mercedes. They had not forgotten that.

"Some of the young Greeks were standing on the running boards on both sides. They looked proud and high-spirited when they drove across the market square here," added another man.

We got up, stepped into the taxi which had meanwhile been summoned, and drove down into the valley towards Sperhias. We got out and walked a few yards along the dried-out river bed. She cried when Alex stretched his right arm out and pointed towards the dark, wooded mountains on the other side of the river, saying that that was probably where the Germans had been shot.

"Where exactly?"

"Somewhere there, up in the mountains," said the man gesticulating. "I heard that some of them were able to get away, but I don't know what happened to them. One was wounded and almost reached his garrison. But the partisans apparently caught him just before he got there and killed him."

We drove back to Makrakomi. The acacia trees were full of birds whose twittering was intrusively loud, but they could not be seen. The square was almost empty. "Everyone has gone home to lunch," said Alex, "but I know one of the men who took your father prisoner. Do you want to talk to him?"

"Of course I want to talk to him. Where does he live?"

"In Makri, the small village before Makrakomi. You travelled through it when you came from Lianokladi. We can also visit the house where the Germans were stationed."

Across the fence of his run-down property, we met a sturdy man who looked at us distrustfully. He had thick black hair combed back. His tanned face was deeply lined although it did not look old.

"He is about forty years old," Alex Grivas said. The man was standing in front of his house which was hardly better than a hovel.

Alex spoke without interruption, seemingly haranguing him. The man avoided direct eye contact with us. It was obvious that our visit was disagreeable to him. He seemed afraid that we might somehow take steps against him. I assured Alex that we had only come out of historical interest.

"So, what did happen?" she interrupted Alex's stream of words. The man shrugged. "We were ordered to take the Germans prisoner. We stopped their car here in the square in Makri and then handed them over to the partisans in the mountains. What happened after that, I don't know."

"His name is Yannis Iannacopoulos," Alex added.

"I don't know what happened to them," repeated Yannis without having been asked.

My mother was crying again. "Did they take anything off him, such as maybe his wedding ring?"

"No, no, we never took anything," Yannis replied emphatically, raising his broad labourer's hands defensively in front of him. Alex translated assiduously, savouring the pleasant change this day had brought to the monotony of his life in retirement.

"In Makrakomi we were told that the Germans let themselves be captured although they were armed. Why didn't they put up any resistance? Apparently they had just come from the estate and the damaged hotel. So they knew, they were forewarned that an attack had taken place," I questioned Iannacopoulos.

Fig. 5   *Alex Grivas* (left) *and Yannis Iannocopoulos* (middle) *looking at the picture of the German Officer: "He wanted to join up with his comrades. That's why he had the car stopped"*

"He explained to us later that he wanted to join up with his comrades," Yannis replied laconically. "That's why he had the car stopped."

"So, if he hadn't had the car stopped, then—"

I could not finish the sentence, for Alex interrupted, "Then they would have returned to Lianokladi." Iannacopoulos nodded, still avoiding our eyes, while Alex twirled a green leaf in his right hand which he had plucked off a shrub.

"Well then, let's go," my mother declared abruptly and turned her back on Iannacopoulos without saying goodbye.

"Yes, it's time to go," Alex agreed. "Your bus will soon be returning to Lianokladi."

I took a photo of Iannacopoulos in front of his hut. Alex whispered that Yannis had been jailed after the Civil War and had only been released in 1958, for "crimes committed during the Civil War".

We drove across the small square in Makri back to Makrakomi in the midday sun. The road was narrow and bumpy. The taxi skidded along the sharp camber of the old surface. Poppies gleamed red on the sandy verges.

Shortly before the beginning of the village of Makrakomi, Alex directed the driver to turn right which led us to a large, elongated building standing in an imposing park with beautiful old trees. Above the main entrance large letters read "ASKLEPIOS".

"This is where the Germans lived before they were taken prisoner," he explained. "Many Greeks worked here with the Germans tending the farm. Before the war it used to be a spa. The Athenians loved to come here to bathe in the hot springs."

Just three kilometres to Makrakomi. We were silent as the taxi drove us back. The bus was already waiting at the market square.

"Well, Mr Grivas, I shall come back. We still have to find out what happened to the Germans who were deported. And very many thanks for your help." Alex nodded. I shook his hand. The square was deserted.

We chose seats right at the back of the bus. In front of us silent black-clad women sat indiscriminately apart. Our return trip took us again across the market square in Makri. I turned around and gazed through the dirty rear window at the line of old trees. This is where he was captured. Behind that cypress Iannacopoulos had hidden himself. Why hadn't the Germans put up a fight? They obviously knew that their comrades on the "Asklepios" estate had already been seized on the previous day. Was it true what we had been told by the men in Makrakomi and by his captor Iannacopoulos? What was the teacher and officer in the Wehrmacht, Hermann Meyer doing here anyway? What sort of railway viaduct was it that he had apparently been involved in rebuilding? Who destroyed it? Why had he been declared missing, together with his driver and the men in his car and all those Germans who had been running the farm and the sawmill, when everyone here was patently aware of what really happened? Who was shot? Who was freed? And if that was indeed true, what had happened to the survivors?

I had no inkling then that this holiday trip to Greece was to lead me onto my own Odyssey and a quest for my father spanning many years.

CHAPTER TWO
Operation Harling

It was the end of September 1942. The German troops under Rommel were lying before El Alamein after capturing Tobruk at the end of June 1942. Although the Eighth British Army had succeeded in regrouping in a stable position between the coast and the impassable Qattara Depression, there was still the risk that Rommel might break through with his troops in order to take Cairo, and from there, the Egyptian Nile Delta and the Suez Canal.

The S.O.E., the special branch of the British Secret Service for sabotage and subversive warfare in territories under German occupation, had its headquarters for the Middle East and Greece in Cairo, and as soon as it realised this danger, it quickly assembled twelve British and New Zealand officers who were already active in North Africa and the Middle East.

The purpose of the operation was to destroy at least one of the three main bridges on the railway link North of Athens. These were the Papadia Bridge, the Asopos Viaduct and the Gorgopotamos Bridge, which enabled supplies vital to the North African troops to be transported by railway from the arms manufacturers in Northern Europe down to the Athenian port of Piraeus and from there shipped on to North Africa. Every twenty minutes, in a steady rhythm, the military trains rolled through Prague, Budapest, Belgrade, Salonica and Larissa down to Athens. Enormous quantities of military supplies were loaded daily in Piraeus onto the ships sailing for North Africa.

In September 1942 the S.O.E. had inquired of its secret agent Prometheus II, operating out of enemy-occupied Athens, whether the freedom fighters in central Greece might be able to destroy at least one of these bridges. The reply was received by radio a few days later. A certain Colonel Napoleon Zervas, encamped in the remote hilly area, was allegedly prepared to attempt such an attack. However, he requested help from trained British explosives experts and said that he required arms, military equipment and explosives.

S.O.E. Cairo sent back a message saying that they would consider parachuting in a voluntary team of officers and men equipped with the necessary arms and explosives. Prometheus II confirmed promptly that Zervas was ready, and that on the night of the full moon in September 1942, on a high plateau in central Greece quite close to the Gorgopotamos Bridge, beacons would be lit to guide the plane to the drop. In addition, further information was received from Athens that there was also a certain Major Aris commanding a group of about thirty partisans, who were badly equipped but nevertheless operating in the Greek mountains. It might be possible for the parachute unit to count on his support too.

The men planning the operation in S.O.E. Cairo considered these reports from Greece to be too vague to risk flying the twelve men to Greece in one plane. Reckoning with a fifty-per-cent failure rate, they decided to distribute the twelve volunteers in several aircraft. Three of the expensive, new long-distance Liberator bombers made available by the USA were to be employed. Only with these, thanks to their four engines, would it be possible to fly the long distance to central Greece and back without a stop.

Each team was to operate independently and consist of four men: a leader, a translator speaking fluent Greek, a bomb expert and a radio operator. The men and the load, which was packed in containers, were to be dropped by parachute. Plastic explosives, Sten guns, spares, provisions and specially developed light-weight radio receivers and transmitters with their batteries and harnesses were made ready for transport. Eddie Myers, a thirty-year-old colonel, was appointed leader and made responsible for the expedition; he was to fly in the first plane, together with Captain Denys "Bull" Hamson, Captain Tom Barnes, the New Zealand explosives expert, and Sergeant Len Wilmot, a twenty-one-year-old radio operator who was always ready for a joke. Hamson could speak Greek well and also had some knowledge of Arabic and Italian. He was thirty-five and therefore the oldest member of the mission.

The second plane was to take Myers' second-in-command, Christopher "Chris" Montague Woodhouse, a major in the British army, Captain Arthur Edmonds, a New Zealand technician, and Sergeant Mike Chittis, the radio operator. Captain Nat Barker was the translator for this group. He had spent most of the twenty-six years of his life in Turkey and Greece.

The team in the third plane was to consist of: Major John Cook, an officer in the British Commandos who had just recently been promoted; an explosives expert, Captain Inder Gill, who was only twenty-one and the son of an Indian father and a Scottish mother; Sergeant Doug Philipps, who was to be responsible for communications; and Themie Marinos, the only Greek in the operation, who was to do the translating. He was proud of his British medal for courage, the M.B.E., which had been conferred on him for fighting against the Germans in Crete.

These vastly differing groups met up for the first time on a Saturday morning on a house boat on the Nile near Gezira, after most of them had been put through their first hour of parachute training. The men were introduced to each other only by their first names, because it was traditional to ignore surnames. The less they knew about the private lives of each other, the less likely they would be to put family members at risk of retaliation in the event that they were taken prisoner.

Eddie Myers gave a speech about the aim of the operation. The Commander-in-Chief General Alexander had seen him personally to insist how important it was for the success of the imminent battle against Rommel, that at least one of the three bridges should be destroyed.

Brigadier-General Keble, the commander of "The Firm", as the S.O.E. Headquarters for the Middle East and Greece was called, addressed the men after Myers' briefing. He promised that he would get all twelve of them out of Greece after the operation had succeeded. Keble, who was a specialist in operations of this type in the Balkans, was a "dynamic, tubby" little man who pursued his goals ruthlessly. According to Eddie Myers' second-in-command, Chris Woodhouse, "His eyes almost popped out of his head with lust for killing". He chewed a cigar as he spoke. "First of all, you must realise that you mustn't breathe a word about this operation to anyone outside," he warned. "The target is a railway bridge in Greece, in the Brallos Pass. The Hun is bringing supplies over this line to Athens and is shipping and flying them from there to Rommel in North Africa. The Commander-in-Chief General Alexander considers that cutting this line will throw an effective spanner in Rommel's works and he wants the job to be started immediately. The code-name of the operation is 'Harling'."

Keble then showed the men detailed maps of central Greece so that they could familiarise themselves with the mountainous terrain. Blueprints of the three bridges were handed around, and lists of additional equipment which would be dropped by further parachutes were worked out. The men would make the jump clad in the battle dress of the British Army.

All three bridges were situated on the eastern side of the Oiti mountain, 2,152 metres high, and each one led straight into a tunnel. Myers hoped that it would be at least possible to destroy the Asopos Viaduct. It was a hundred-metre-long steel bridge leading along an almost vertical rock face across a hundred-metre-deep gorge.

"Its destruction would interrupt rail traffic for months," said Colonel Myers, addressing his eleven-man team. "I have been assured that everything will be done to support us materially inside Greece, and I promise to do everything humanly possible to get you out of Greece when the operation has been successfully concluded. At present we believe that we will most likely be picked up by submarine. Are you still ready to come along?" said the colonel, concluding his lecture and casting a questioning look around.

Everyone nodded: not one of the eleven men thought of backing down. They all felt that they were standing at the threshold of the biggest adventure of their lives.

"Go in, go!"

At dusk on the 28 September 1942, the twelve men met at an aerodrome close to Cairo. Eddie Myers was carrying a radio transmitter which was attached to the parachute cords above his head. Everyone was excited and they were streaming with sweat, for, in that African heat, they were wearing battle dress underneath their overalls with the parachute on top. Take off was set at 20.30. Huge quantities of beer, whisky and sandwiches had been devoured in the last twenty-four hours prior to their departure. After all, who knew what the situation was going to be in Greece in terms of provisions? Themie Marinos seemed to be looking forward to returning to his homeland although it was under enemy occupation. Joyfully, he sang a Greek folk-song, and "Bull" Hamson gave an account, to anyone who wanted to hear, of his macho exploits on the last night in the Egyptian whore-houses.

The three Liberator airplanes stood ready for departure, with their engines running, on the tarmac. The twelve men climbed into their allotted planes, through a small hatch underneath the fuselage. It had been decided that the bombers should take off at intervals of a quarter of an hour. They had already been loaded with arms and equipment.

Eddie Myers and his three team-mates squeezed into the cockpit with the pilot. There was a feeling of relief as they rose above Egypt into the cloudless evening sky with its pink and emerald hues. The flight was to steer well clear of Crete to avoid the German air defences, and to fly across the Aegean Sea and the island of Euboea to Roumeli in central Greece.

It was about one o'clock in the morning when Eddie Myers announced that they would be in the area of the drop in another twenty minutes. Parachutes were buckled on, and the floor boards over the hatch were removed. However, when the plane started circling over the jump-off area, Myers was horrified that no beacons could be distinguished although visibility was perfect in the light of the full moon. There were a few fires discernible on the ground but they did not at all correspond to the agreed shape of a cross. The pilot decided to draw larger circles further to the West in the hope of recognising the signals there. But this proved to be in vain.

Disillusioned, the pilot and Eddie decided to return to Cairo. The men were deeply disappointed. They unfastened their parachutes, rolled themselves in their blankets and slept shivering in the cold of the long flight back to Egypt.

The other two planes had already landed when Eddie's aircraft rolled to a standstill in Cairo. He spoke immediately to Keble and they arranged that a second attempt should be made on the following night. They knew that it was their last chance to risk parachuting in, as the moonlight period meant that their next opportunity would not arise until three weeks later. That would effectively mean cancelling the entire project as the wintry conditions in central Greece would by then make it impossible. Thus, the new slogan for the second attempt was: "Beacons or no beacons, go in, go!"

After the ground crew had worked feverishly to make the bombers ready in the short turn-around time, the second departure took place in the evening of 30 September, 1942. After about five hours' flying time they reached the mountain range of Mount Giona in Roumeli. Again, there were small fires, sometimes even in pairs, but no clear signal could be distinguished to indicate that this was indeed the area allocated for the jump.

The plane went on circling until Myers could make out a group of three fires and a relatively flat plain. A short discussion with the pilot led him to decide to parachute into this region. The pilot flew another long loop to swoop into the narrow valley at a height of about a thousand metres. It was a brave undertaking, for he was now holding his huge machine at a level considerably lower than the mountains closely surrounding him.

Eddie Myers was the first to receive the call to jump from the monitor, "Go in, go!" and he jumped into the unknown. The parachute opened promptly and the cords uncoiled smoothly out of his rucksack. But the wireless had slipped slightly out of its harness and rubbed painfully against his head. In the moonlight he could only see the silhouettes of barren mountains around him and deep valleys in which he could not distinguish any details. He tried in vain to recognise the valley with the three fires grouped together which he had seen from the plane.

The wind, which was now blowing with some force, was sweeping him over mountain slopes and valleys and he had the impression that he was well off-course from the target. The terrain below him seemed to be covered with small bushes, but as he sank lower he realised to his horror that the little bushes were turning out to be fully grown pine trees. A huge, forbidding forest was spreading out beneath him and there was not a single fire in sight that he might have aimed for.

With increasingly uncontrollable speed he was now moving straight into the tops of the trees and finally fell into a tall pine, slipped through the canopy, and finally got caught up in the lower branches while his parachute was snarled up in the branches high above. Still in shock, he finally freed himself of the cords, and discovered that fortunately no bones were broken, but he then sensed the immensity of the fearful silence around him.

Denys Hamson, for his part, had got caught by his feet which he had drawn up to his stomach, and had fallen head over heels into the branches of a pine tree. The searing pain on the right side of his chest was accentuated when he breathed deeply. He carefully moved his arms and legs, but apart from a bruised or broken rib, he did not seem to have any further injuries. He felt very lost and lonely as he waited for help, hanging in the tree. He thought of his Chief, Eddie Myers, who must have landed somewhere nearby and whom he could not stand. And then he heard the Liberator bomber flying into the valley for the second time and he saw a number of parachutes with their containers raining down in his vicinity.

A sudden thud and an oath coming from the other side of the rocks gave him the certainty that one of his comrades had landed close by. Soon afterwards, he saw a red flare and a voice called, "Is that you, Denys, hanging up in the tree?"

"Yes, I'm ok," Hamson called back with relief.

"I am coming over to help you," he heard Len Wilmot, the radio operator, shout, and soon afterwards he was cutting him out of his parachute and bringing the good news that Tom Barnes had landed without any problems. They built a fire, rolled themselves into their blankets and fell asleep with exhaustion in spite of the extreme cold.

The next morning they could see down into the valley and distinguish a mule trail. They heard the peaceful tinkle of bells which the sheep wore around their necks. They packed up their belongings and crept through the undergrowth down into the valley, taking care to avoid any possible encounter with the enemy.

When they stepped out into a clearing, they saw a peasant who was riding his donkey up the narrow path. Hiding in the thicket as the man rode past, Denys called to him imperiously to come to them. The man almost fell off his mount with fright but he hurried to comply. Denys presented himself as a British officer who had just landed in Greece and who needed assistance.

"How am I to believe you that you are really English and not German?" asked the Greek, to which Denys responded by whipping open his flying overall and showing him his British uniform. The Greek's joy was overwhelming. He hugged the men, kissed them heartily on both cheeks in true Greek fashion, and told them that they were on the donkey path between Lidoriki and Amfissa.

"My village is called Karoutes, sir, and I shall hurry home to tell my wife that the British are now coming to free us."

"Don't you dare breathe a word to anyone apart from your village elder," Denys hissed at the peasant, "and in particular not to your wife. But now scram, and bring us back something to eat because we are damned hungry."

When the man came back, he reported that some villagers had heard of another parachutist who had landed nearby. Carefully, the peasant shared out some brown bread and dry goat cheese which the men devoured greedily. They did not as yet appreciate the sacrifices that the Greek was imposing on himself and his family by sharing their meagre food with the British.

Return to the Nineteenth Century

Eddie Myers had joined the army as an engineer and had been a staff officer overseas for the last seven years. In two weeks' time he was scheduled to return to England from Cairo, when the call came for him to lead Operation Harling. He had accepted promptly.

Although he did not speak Greek and was not really fit for such a demanding task — he had been working in an office — he was chosen because he had a reputation for excellent work as a staff officer, was an accomplished parachutist, and above all he was professionally able to handle explosives.

In the darkness, on the steep mountain side, he could only vaguely make out the landscape in the moonlight. The wind was still blowing strongly and when he had made sure that no one else was in the vicinity, he tried to grope his way down the slope in order to get a better view of the valley.

He did indeed come across a Greek shepherd on his way into the valley. "*Ime inglesos*. I am English," Myers called out the memorised words. He waited for an answer with his revolver at the ready. A sort of conversation ensued, and by using hands and feet and pointing to the sky, Myers somehow made the shepherd understand that other men had parachuted that night. When he was confident that the shepherd meant him no harm, he gladly let himself be led to his camp fire and he soon fell into a sleep of exhaustion.

Myers was woken before dawn. Someone offered him a handful of black olives which he ate hungrily. It took a good hour for him to lead the shepherds up the mountain to his landing place. His belongings had, however, disappeared. Suddenly Tom Barnes, the New Zealander, emerged from behind some branches. Fortunately he knew the whereabouts of Sergeant Wilmot and Denys Hamson, so that by the afternoon they were all happily re-united. However, no one brought news of their eight comrades who had been dropped by the other two planes, although a number of villagers had come scurrying up the mountain to stare at them like creatures from another planet. The Greeks were able to inform them, however, that there were no

German nor Italian troops in the village and that the nearest Italian garrison was about an hour's march away.

Fig. 6   *Greek freedom fighter. "Dashing figures from another age"*

Nevertheless, a young Greek led the group away from the village that afternoon as a precaution against enemy scouts finding them. "I know an andarte, a freedom fighter, called Dimo Karalivanos, who lives on the other side of the valley and who will certainly be able to help you," he told the British.

The meeting took place the very next day. "I felt as though I had been transported back to the year 1821," Denys Hamson recounted later on. In that year the Greeks conquered the Turks, and so secured their country's freedom. "The andartes might have stepped out of illustrations of books on the Greek Revolution of 1821. They all wore Greek national dress with the baggy trousers of rough dark material, and one wore a bright red fez on his head. Their hair hung down unkempt over their shoulders, their beards nearly to their waists. Their chests were criss-crossed with cartridge belts full of ammunition, and their belts were studded with revolvers and old-fashioned daggers. They wore necklaces of small gold and silver icons and chains."

Their leader, Karalivanos, wore breeches and stockings and "Tsaruha" shoes with their picturesque pom-poms; his jacket was grey and worked in complicated embroidery patterns and multitudinous pleats. Around his waist he wore a wide leather belt, from the front of which hung by pieces of string, which could be snapped by a quick jerk, two hand-grenades; on the right side he carried a heavy pistol with an attractive bone butt. Pushed between the belt and his waist were two large knives in skilfully engraved metal sheaths. Two shoulder straps supporting the weight of this belt of lethal weapons were covered with clips of ammunition for the rifle that he had slung over his shoulder and for his pistol, and the remainder of his broad chest was decorated with fine metal chains from which hung medals and other mementos he had taken from Italians he had killed.

The British gazed in amazement at these dashing figures and only suspended their disbelief when they saw that some of these men were indeed equipped with modern Greek army guns.

While Karalivanos' andartes helped the British erect two wigwams made out of pine branches on a high plateau, Myers described his plan to make contact with the leadership of the partisans in order to blow up one of the three bridges in the Thermopylae. "These bridges are very well guarded," Karalivanos warned the colonel. "I know that the guards were doubled last month. Only a very strong unit would have any chance of attacking these bridges successfully."

It was already rather a shock for the British to find that Karalivanos had only assembled a group of five men around him, who really gave the impression of being brigands rather than freedom fighters. There was no news of Zervas, the guerilla leader whom Myers was to contact, while Aris, the andarte whose name was familiar to Myers from Cairo, was supposedly somewhere north of Karoutes with a small group of men.

Meanwhile, Tom Barnes and Len Wilmot were trying to work the transmitter that they had brought along, in order to ask Cairo where the other two units had landed. "The batteries are flat," young Len declared with desperation. The generator would not work either and one of the pinions was broken and as yet the canister with spares had not been retrieved.

What an utter disaster! There was no guerilla movement worth mentioning, and radio contact with Cairo was out of the question. There was no sign of the other eight men and most of their canisters could not be traced.

On the following day, however, some of the containers were dragged along by the people living in the area, but strangely none with food stuffs were among them, and all the canisters came from the second aircraft in which Chris Woodhouse and his men had been travelling. This did, in fact, give Eddie Myers a glimmer of hope as it indicated that his second-in-command and his comrades must have landed close by.

Finally Karalivanos and two of his men set off to the village to inquire about the remaining containers. After about two hours he returned with a number of villagers who were carrying the major part of the missing material. There were precious explosives, Sten guns, blankets, and clothing which belonged to the second airplane. "I almost had to set fire to a house before the owner finally admitted that most of the equipment had been hidden all over the village," bragged Dimo.

While helping to unpack, he wanted to know what the sticks in plastic bags were.

"Highly explosive bombs," explained Hamson.

"Are they poisonous?" asked the andarte.

"I should think so."

"Then there will be many sick people in the village, because most of the children have been eating them. They thought they were sweets," laughed Dimo gleefully.

One of the andartes appeared with a young man and a dozen apologetic-looking villagers. The young man's hands had been tied behind his back by the guerilla. Apparently he had been the leader of the thieving gang. Dimo then put on a show for the embarrassed British who, however, made no move to intervene. The twenty-year-old youth was brutally beaten. He lay on the ground, and Karalivanos whipped him mercilessly with his short riding crop. The blows tore his face, blood squirted out, and Karalivanos kicked him all over his body and in his genitals. The youth swore he was innocent and begged the men to stop. It was not until his sister came screaming shrilly up the hill and threw herself protectively over his unconscious body that the British finally remonstrated and ordered Dimo to stop the beating.

In the evening the villagers' mules were loaded up with the equipment. A light, cold drizzle had set in. It was wet and windy. All their clothes were sodden. A warning had come through from the village that an Italian unit was combing the area. Dejected and shivering with cold, the caravan set off on their first night march through the wild mountainous terrain to find a reasonably safe haven.

It was well after midnight when Dimo Karalivanos brought the British to a goat hut which was home to his wife and daughter. Eddie Myers was totally exhausted. He was not used to such prolonged marches, and he was constantly worried about the other eight men. There was hardly any food left. The shelter stank of goats and dung, it was crawling with fleas, and the wind howled through the open door made of crude planks. The men lay huddled as close together as possible and slept fitfully till morning.

Yiorgo, one of Dimo's men, appeared at dawn and reported on the movements of the Italians. "They are staying on the mule paths and are not leaving them to comb through the mountains. But they have searched through Karoutes and discovered a few containers. Several men were carried off as punishment and three houses were burnt down."

It was not till the next day that the cold wind died down and the sun broke through the clouds. The men could at last hang their wet clothes out in the warming sun to dry. Although they interrogated every shepherd they met in this high mountain region as to whether they had seen or heard of the British parachutists, the answer was always in the negative. Nevertheless, Myers refused to be disconcerted. He insisted on pushing on because he was keen to get closer to the bridges. From time to time they heard the drone of surveillance planes above the clouds; but they avoided walking through any of the villages as doubtless the Italians were on the look-out for them.

By now, the small ration of tea, tobacco and sugar which each man carried as iron reserves had become more precious than gold. They could only get old bread and some goat cheese from the shepherds. Scrambling through the brushwood and ploughing over the uneven stony paths was exhausting and depressing. They had the feeling that they were making hardly any progress.

On the third day, however, they met a shepherd who confirmed that a group of parachutists had come down in the area and were encamped about an hour's march away. Myers immediately ordered Hamson and Barnes to confirm this report.

Accordingly, the two set out and they did indeed find a British parachute stretched across two rocks to form a shelter. Under it sat the group from the second plane: Chris Woodhouse, their leader, Nat Barker, the interpreter, the New Zealand demolition expert, Arthur Edmonds, and Sergeant Chittis, the radio operator. They had fortunately all landed unhurt on a plateau only about twenty metres away from a three-hundred-metre-deep abyss.

It was an emotional moment for Eddie Myers when he was re-united with his second-in-command Chris Woodhouse. They decided that the next step was to send a messenger to Athens in order to inform the "Firm" in Cairo, via the secret agent Prometheus II, that two of the units from the planes had joined up but that radio contact was impossible because both transmitters had been damaged in the drop. They reckoned with about a week to smuggle a runner over the mountains through to Athens.

Myers was desperately disappointed that the reserve batteries carried by Edmonds and Barker had somehow been drained and become useless in the drop. Wilmot and Chittis persisted in tinkering around helplessly on their radio sets. No one had had the foresight before their departure to familiarise the two men with the mechanics of the sets. Myers was seething with fury and blamed the technicians violently for this lapse.

The colourful Dimo Karalivanos seemed to become more and more tense and unreliable every day. Italians were still scouring the countryside. He reproached the British for being cowardly and for avoiding a fight. He finally told Myers that he would not guide them anymore nor procure food for them. This was a bitter set-back for the British, as Karalivanos was their only contact in this harsh region. Also, they had still hoped that he would lead them to the two elusive partisan leaders Zervas and Aris.

The colonel took stock. The morale of his seven men was battered. The food supply was a shambles. There was no news of the third unit. No contact was possible with Cairo, let alone with any of the Greek partisans. After a week in Greece they had accomplished nothing. The Italians were at their heels and every day, the relentless, depressing rain dripped through the parachutes under which they had set up their makeshift, primitive camp.

Christopher Montague Woodhouse

Eddie Myers lay next to Chris Woodhouse on the soaking tarpaulin and cursed his fate. During the night another Liberator bomber had dropped supplies over the gorge. They had collected wood all day long to build the agreed fire signals. Towards midnight they heard the familiar deep roar of the planes, and soon after lighting their fires they saw the parachutes dropping in the moonlight but the wind pushed them over to the far side of the gorge.

It was 9 October, 1942. Eddie was homesick and didn't mind telling his second-in-command. He would have loved to have been sitting next to that pilot who would be back in a comfortable bed in Egypt in a few hours time!

Chris Woodhouse had a different point of view. This tall, strong, broad-shouldered man had already been active in the underground movement in Crete after it fell to German paratroops. He had organised the escape of the scattered British soldiers who could not be evacuated before the enemy occupation and had subsequently directed the Cretans in their sabotage work against the enemy. His past experience in guerilla warfare and his fluent mastery of the Greek language made him an invaluable companion.

Had the Second World War not broken out, the Englishman would probably have followed an academic career and taught Greek history instead of joining the army. The sudden end to his career at Oxford University in 1940 had been rather a shock for him but it was also a challenge to serve his country. On 11 May, 1940, he was just twenty-three years of age when Hitler's armies overran Western Europe.

Euphoria over serving his country soon dissipated however. Basic military training was mind-numbing and bone-breaking. He started as gunner 949285 at the training base at Aldershot. That first wartime winter consisted of roll calls at six a.m. on the icy parade ground; brutal inspections of the barracks and dormitories where everything had to be in perfect order; interminable, mindless polishing of boots and buttons; monotonous, repetitive exercises with old guns for which there was no ammunition — all this brought the young student Woodhouse to the edge of desperation. He had to suffer insults from superiors who would never be sent to the front in France because they would be likely to be shot in the back by their own people. His sensitive spirit was summarily kicked into understanding what it was to be a soldier. Moral standards and courtesy were shelved. Discipline, responsibility and leadership were the new buzz words which his lips soon learned to form: Woodhouse had become a soldier.

For Chris Woodhouse the actual war started on 28 October, 1940, when Mussolini attacked Greece. The ambitious Duce tried to imitate the German Blitzkrieg tactics although Hitler was strictly against this campaign. As late as August 1940 the "Führer" stressed at a meeting with Count Ciano, Mussolini's Foreign Minister, that "the Balkans must remain at peace". When, however, the German troops "secured" the oil fields near Ploesti in Rumania at the end of September 1940, without informing the "fratelli" beforehand, Mussolini avenged himself by initiating his planned campaign in Greece.

"Hitler always confronts me with a *fait accompli*. I shall give him a taste of his own medicine this time. He shall read in the newspapers that I have marched into Greece. In this way we can redress the balance," blustered the Duce to his son-in-law Count Ciano. "It will all be over in two weeks, anyway," he boasted when Hitler remonstrated furiously.

The German generals in Berlin were horrified by the strategic procedures of the Italians. The attack took place just before the onset of winter in the Greek mountains, and they had not even bothered to include the Navy to secure Crete and other strategic islands beforehand so as to stave off British units stationed in North Africa.

As early as 14 November, 1940, the Greeks staged a successful counter attack, and by December, the Italian Supreme Commander in Albania considered further military action to be hopeless and urged Mussolini to seek help from Hitler. Although Ciano "would have preferred to shoot himself through the head" rather than to ask for help, Mussolini had no other option. Hitler agreed in principle to step in. He supplied forty-nine Ju-52 planes which helped to stabilise the front within Albania in December, so that a total collapse of the Italian troops could be avoided. The Greek groups, badly equipped though they were, fought with such self-sacrificing bravery that they pushed the enemy far back inside Albania.

During that hard winter, when heavy snow fell in December, many soldiers suffered frost-bite. The first victims were taken to the field hospital in Koritsa. They were carried by stretcher between two mules, suffering unspeakable pain in their frozen limbs. Many amputations had to be made in the over-crowded wards. Most of the Greek soldiers only wore light clothing because they had been called up so suddenly that there had been no time to kit them out with woollen clothing.

On 13 December, 1940, Hitler, having the events in the Balkans in mind, issued his directive No. 20 concerning operation "Marita":

> *In view of the menacing situation in Albania, it is particularly important to undermine all English efforts to secure, under the protection of a front in the Balkans, an air base which would be primarily dangerous for Italy, but also for the Rumanian oil reserves. It is therefore my intention,*
>
> *a) to assemble a gradually growing number of forces in Southern Rumania during the next few months*
> *b) to deploy these forces when better weather conditions prevail — presumably in March — via Bulgaria, and if necessary, across all mainland Greece in order to occupy the Northern Aegean coast. It can be expected to receive support from Bulgaria.*

Nonetheless, Hitler hoped through diplomatic channels to persuade Athens to find an agreement with Rome and to "throw out the English". Hitler had a high regard for "this brave little land" which had shown the Italians its teeth. The Greek dictator Metaxas, however, had little inclination to follow Hitler's wish although he knew that the English were hardly in a position to afford him much help in case of a German attack, as they themselves needed every man in the desert war which they were fighting simultaneously in North Africa.

Metaxas died unexpectedly on 29 January, 1941, and King George II appointed the minister for health, Korisis, as the new prime minister, but he proved to be out of his depth. The die was cast on 22 February, 1941, when the British Minister for Foreign Affairs, Eden, together with General Wavell and the British liaison officer, Major-General Heywood, and his adjutant, C. M. Woodhouse, met up in Athens with the Greek King, Korisis, and General Papagos in order to negotiate the deployment of an expeditionary force. Greece had opted for British support in case of an attack by Germany. Just a few days afterwards, the first units of the expedition corps landed in Volos and Piraeus: a British armoured brigade plus one New Zealand and one Australian Division.

There was a *coup d'état* in Belgrade during the night of the 26 and 27 March, 1941. The commander of the air forces, General Bora Mirkovic, arrested Prince Paul and his government who were friendly towards the Germans, and General Simovic took over the leadership of the Government. Hitler's reaction was immediate. His directive No. 25, on 27 March, 1941, ordered a lightning campaign against Yugoslavia and Greece once the support of Italy, Hungary and Bulgaria was secured. On 6 April, 1941, German troops attacked Yugoslavia and Greece without declaring war beforehand.

Immediately before the German invasion an article appeared in the well-known Greek newspaper Kathimerini. The editor, George Vlakhos, had written it in the form of an open letter addressed to Hitler. This was the first indication of a Greek resistance movement:

The Greeks know what to expect, but nothing will deter them from fighting to the last man, even if, in the last resort, they have to mobilise the 20,000 men wounded in the war against Albania. Those men, with the stumps of their arms and legs wrapped in bloodied bandages, shall be expecting the return of the Greek runner who carried the Olympic flame in 1936 to Berlin for the Games. And with this very flame they shall set fire to this country: this country, so small, but so strong, which once gave life to the world, shall now show the world how to die.

Three weeks later, on 27 April, 1941, the swastika flag was hoisted on the Acropolis in Athens. The King fled abroad and Korisis committed suicide. 12,000 soldiers of the British expeditionary force had fallen or been taken prisoner. The German side registered 1,099 dead and 3,500 wounded.

As Crete was still held by British troops, German units now launched an attack on the island at dawn on 20 May. Barely two weeks later, in the evening of 1 June, 1941, General Löhr sent a message to Field Marshal Göring, saying: *"Mission accomplished, Crete free of enemy as of today."*

"Free of enemy" meant: 12,245 English and 2,266 Greeks taken prisoners of war, 1,742 British dead, 1,737 wounded and 1,835 missing, 1,915 Germans fallen, 1,759 missing and 2,200 wounded. The conquest of Crete had cost more human lives than the entire Balkan campaign.

On the 20 of May, 1941, Chris Woodhouse had been evacuated on the *Ulster Prince* from mainland Greece to Crete where he joined a British unit who had to defend the airport of Maleme. At the last moment, when Crete had fallen, he was shipped out to Alexandria and reached Haifa via Cairo where he was to train men as resistance fighters; these were Greeks, Albanians, Yugoslavs and other nationals who had been scattered by the war and recruited by the S.O.E. The aim was to re-introduce them to their home countries as partisan fighters.

The robust and experienced Woodhouse was thus far better prepared to adjust to the hard and dangerous conditions in the Greek mountains than his sensitive and depressed superior who had only been used to desk work. However, things took a turn for the better when Barba Niko appeared at their camp.

Barba Niko? Eddie Myers turned morosely and found himself looking at the broad face of a man in his middle fifties, with a big walrus moustache, twinkling, humorous eyes and a large bulbous nose. His hair was thin, grey and untidy. He was wearing a dark, dirty suit, no socks, just some desperately worn shoes which hardly protected him from being barefoot. His dirt-encrusted feet looked as though they had not been washed for years. A useless old musket was slung over his shoulder and a rusty revolver was stuck in his belt.

"Hello, boys," he called with an indefinable American accent. "How are you, okay?"

His name was Niko Bey, and he came from Lithoriki, a village about eight hours' journey away. He had spent many years in America and had returned to Greece before the war. In spite of his ten years in the USA, his English was rudimentary but he understood it better than he spoke it.

Barba "Uncle" Niko was a seasoned guerilla. He was well known in the area. A few weeks earlier, he and other partisans had ambushed a twenty-seven-man patrol of Italians down in the valley in a rocky gorge. They had killed them all except for one man. With flashing eyes, he described how they had slaughtered the guard at dawn and then shot the Italian sergeant as he crawled out of his tent. When the remaining Italians gave themselves up, they were made to strip naked and they were then massacred with knives.

Fig. 7   *Barba ("Uncle") Niko Bey in Stromni*

"One of the Italian soldiers was able to escape and reach the nearest garrison. He lived long enough to report what had happened," said "Uncle" regretfully. "The Italian unit, which was dispatched for reprisals, did not even take time to dig graves for their fallen comrades. The corpses are barely covered with a bit of rubble and stink to high heaven. The stench in that gorge was overwhelming, but the village dogs were finally able to eat their fill."

The British enjoyed listening to Barba Nikos' stories when they lay around the camp fire in the evening. Dimo Karalivanos suggested that Bey would be the right man to take them north to establish contact with the andarte leader Aris. "Uncle" Bey seemed reliable enough, and in any case there was no alternative, so Myers and Woodhouse agreed to put their faith and that of their exhausted troop in him.

Barba Niko knew of a cave in the vicinity of Stromni where the men could set up their quarters. He also assured them that the villagers there would provide them with food. Bey was in good spirits when they broke up on the following day. At last he had found an important role to play in his life which had not been very successful nor fulfilling so far. He had now become father and mother to the eight Commonwealth officers and men!

The climb through the mountains with the mules was long and very tedious. Their loads caught in the branches. The path was hardly recognisable as such, strewn with rocks and boulders of all sizes. The lowering clouds brought cold, rain and the first snowfall, but they also offered safety from the Italian reconnaissance flights. The mountain trails chosen by Bey were so remote from any civilisation that the British had no need to fear a confrontation with Italian troops.

They were now in the heart of the Giona range, stumbling over scree and slippery stones, clambering up and down precipitous slopes. They spent the nights in dilapidated huts which were used by shepherds in the summer. It either rained or snowed relentlessly, they were soaked and freezing, their bones hurt and blisters on their feet made every step a misery. Edmonds and Hamson were suffering from exhaustion and fever. Only Bey seemed utterly unaffected by the long march. He knew the trails and led the British unerringly to their destination.

When they finally arrived at the cave above Stromni, Myers saw immediately that it afforded his men far better protection than any of the previous camp sites. The cave was little more than a large slit in the north face of the mountain. Its entrance was obscured by the surrounding trees. A rocky escarpment of about a hundred metres in height rose above it, unassailable. The cave was used in the summer by shepherds and their herds. It stank of sheep and dung, it was damp and no more than ten people could lie down in it.

Barba Niko lit a fire at the entrance to the cave, which nearly suffocated them as the smoke swirled in through the tall slit. But at least it permitted them to dry their wet clothes. The villagers had made blankets available to them which were dry, but smelly and full of fleas. For the first time for several nights, they slept on dry bedding. Tom Barnes and Arthur Edmonds, the two New Zealand explosives experts, built a screen out of branches to hide the fire from view from the other side of the valley. The following ten days were devoted to preparations. Their equipment was stored in the relative dryness and safety of the cave. Each Sten gun was taken apart, cleaned, oiled and re-assembled. The ammunition was checked, and stored in gun magazines. Denys Hamson inspected the dangerous Mills hand grenades and acquainted the men with their handling.

The most difficult task was preparing the dynamite. They had over a hundred and fifty kilograms of highly explosive material which was packed in cellophane sticks of a hundred and twenty-five grams. Owing to the cold, it had hardened, and they had to unwrap each stick carefully, warm it in their hands or between their legs, mould it into a soft paste to which they added vaseline, and finally repack the sticks into parcels of five kilograms.

They also had to cut wood in order to keep the fire going. Bey looked after the food supplies. The men ate twice a day. Lunch normally consisted of beans boiled in water and a piece of dry bread. Although the inhabitants of Stromni had gallantly promised to provide for the British, they themselves were effectively starving, suffering the famine sweeping the whole of Greece since the beginning of the war. In the terrible winter of 1941/42 the village mourned a number of deaths by starvation.

On alternate days, the indefatigable Niko would drive a mule up from the village, laden with bread and beans. There was no wheat, so they ate maize bread which was baked with such hard flour that it was barely edible. The men all suffered from diarrhoea and stomach cramps.

Sometimes, one of the outlying villages would donate a sheep, but it was usually so old and tough that it was difficult to chew. But there were also brighter times, when Myers took out some of the gold sovereigns, which were the unofficial currency much appreciated by the Greeks, and Niko then returned carrying a sheep or goat on his shoulders and set about preparing *Koukouretsi*. The men loved this dish which was heart, liver and lung, enveloped in an intestinal sheath and grilled over the fire on a spit. Nothing was wasted. The animal's head was cooked, and whoever had made most progress on the previous day in learning Greek according to Niko, was presented with the eye as an extra delicacy.

They continued to be ignorant of the fate of the team in the third aircraft. Although they did hear rumours that a group of parachutists had dropped in the area, these were so vague that they could not give them much credence. But this was a worry that constantly dogged Myers.

Through Niko Bey they got to know Yanni Pistolis, who lived in Lamia, the capital of the province. He was a teacher by profession, had been a sergeant in the Greek army and was prepared to do anything to eject the occupying power from his country. Pistolis knew Roumeli like the back of his hand, but above all, he had friends working in the railways. He reported that enemy traffic passed on the single track stretch by day and night. He reckoned that enormous quantities of war equipment were being rushed in an uninterrupted stream from north to south, to Piraeus. With the exception of a few sporadic passenger trains, all the transport was military. Pistolis confirmed their assumption that the long freight trains appeared every twenty minutes and that Italian troops were guarding the three bridges with three hundred men at Papadia, forty at Asopos and eighty at Gorgopotamos.

It became clear to the British that their only chance of demolishing any of these bridges was to surprise and overwhelm the Italians with a large force of Greek resistance fighters. But were the Italians not already forewarned? And where was this large force to come from? Although Myers had sent out scouts to find the elusive Aris, no contact had as yet been established.

CHAPTER THREE
The Odyssey of Baron von Falkenhausen

On 17 May, 1941, one month after the victorious Blitzkrieg against Greece, Hitler ordered in his directive 29:

Safeguarding the Greek area shall in future be the responsibility of the Italians. No German services shall therefore be involved in general questions of safety and administration of the country.

The "Führer" therefore conferred a preponderant role in Greece to his Roman partners. German troops held only Macedonia, the Northern Aegean Islands and Crete, while Bulgaria picked up Thrace. The major part of mainland Greece with the provinces of Epirus, Thessaly, Roumeli and the Peloponnese was occupied by the Italian army.

It was, however, agreed with the Italian leadership that the German army and air force would run "defence industries" in the provinces occupied by the Italians. In Roumeli, this meant mainly exploiting the bauxite mines near Domokos and Amfissa and felling timber in the mountains west of the capital of the province, Lamia. Military protection of these industries was, however, to be the responsibility of the Italian troops, according to Hitler's directive.

Friedrich, Baron von Falkenhausen, who was a major in the Air Force and had studied to be a construction engineer before the war, had been transferred in 1942 from Salonica to Platistomo Spa near Lamia in order to take charge of one of these "defence industries". He was responsible for three sawmills in the Sperchios valley, which he managed with the help of a group of twelve, soldiers and civilians who were all based at the Asklepios Hotel and farm estate at Platistomo, a small village close to the main road going from Lamia to Makrakomi and Karpenissi.

"I went to Platistomo Spa in the summer of 1942," the Baron recalls. "I felt dreadfully lonely because I could not speak a word of Greek. Our people had rented the Hotel Asklepios in a holiday resort called Loutra Platistomo. There was a hot spring there to which the Athenians used to come to bathe in peace time. The landlord was an elderly man called Haralambopoulos, with whom we got on very well. The lady of the house was Viennese, by name of Gertrud Radwein.

52

Fig. 8   *The hotel and farm estate at Platistomo Spa*

She was about forty-five years old and spoke Greek fluently. I would
never have managed without her. She interpreted for me and she
became the heart and soul of our whole group. There were about
twelve of us, civilians and German army personnel, and we were
entirely left to our own devices. The closest unit were the Italians,
over thirty kilometres away in Lamia. The Greek workers in the
sawmills and on the farm were given a decent wage and they were
glad to have work because they were indescribably poor. We did hear
of an attack by Greek partisans in September 1942 on an Italian
reconnaissance patrol, but my Greek workers reassured us again and
again that the partisans were only after the Italians.

"When I left for Athens, I told them: 'I am going to the capital and
shall be back in a few days. I am getting money and provisions. If I
return safe and sound, I shall share it out fairly. If I am shot before,
then the killer shall have it all.' That was the only way to make it
clear to them that our destinies were all intertwined.

53

"Was I afraid? Of course I was! Although a German officer is not supposed to be afraid! We were not even properly armed in that Hotel Asklepios. I once wrote a report to the General in charge and mentioned that we would be totally defenceless if the partisans were to attack us. He then called me up and said cynically: 'So you are afraid out there, are you?'

"And what was I supposed to say as a soldier, even if I was?

"'If there is an attack you cannot defend yourselves anyway. There are so few of you. And we are not in a position to protect works like yours. The area is occupied by the Italians and it is their duty to stop the underground action,' he told me tersely from the safety of his desk job. And that was that, as far as he was concerned.

"So then it happened at the end of October 1942. I had taken Trude Radwein along as my interpreter, and Lance-Corporal Schwarzenbacher, who was my constant collaborator, and we travelled to a densely forested area in the mountains of central Greece, situated off the road between Lamia and Karpenissi, in order to investigate whether we could extract timber in that new area; but then, we were captured by Greek freedom fighters."

Fig. 9   *Friedrich Baron von Falkenhausen in Platistomo*

Baron von Falkenhausen is sitting opposite me in a cafe in woodlands above Saarbrücken. He is a sprightly old man over eighty. He enjoys looking back on those times in Greece, when he was in charge of timber processing in the Sperchios valley. "I always said to my people that after the war I would stay in the country and open a sawmill somewhere." He loved Greece and enjoyed bargaining for hours with foresters and farmers in the *kafeinions* in Larissa and Lamia over the price of timber which he bought for his department in Athens, the "Luftwaffenbaubeschaffungsamt" (air force office for the procurement of building materials).

Von Falkenhausen was the first German officer in Roumeli to be taken prisoner by the Greek partisans. They freed him within four days, for he had become a burden owing to a gunshot wound. At the behest of the Commander of the 12th Army Southeast, General Alexander Löhr, he wrote a report of his adventure:

We were driving through a narrow wooded valley, when a troop of armed and uniformed men appeared, making themselves heard from about fifty to sixty metres away by shouting loudly. When they started firing wildly, there was no longer any doubt that they were Greek bandits! I took cover immediately, while they continued to shoot with machine pistols and guns. That was when a shot hit my thigh.

Meanwhile, sixty to seventy men had gathered, all armed to their teeth, bearded and awe-inspiring, and they soon made me understand that I was to surrender forthwith. I accepted the inevitable and was taken prisoner, which meant that I had to lay down my arms and they confiscated my belongings although they handed back my attache case and notebook. In the meantime they had also captured my companion further back and brought him to the group. Our fate was now very uncertain although they tried to express some sympathy for us as Germans...

Our car was set on fire after all the usable pieces, such as tyres, had been loaded onto donkeys which had been led up from a nearby house. I was lifted onto one of the animals, as I could hardly stand by this time, and the column set off. We travelled for six hours. I was suffering such pain and felt so cold, that I could hardly stay on the donkey's back. They did however give me a blanket which protected me in my summer uniform from excessive exposure...

We stopped at a dilapidated hut but at six o'clock in the morning we were told to get up and leave. Saddle-horses were now provided, but our eyes were bandaged before we were made to mount them. Apart from a few short rests, we rode uphill and downhill and it seemed that our journey would never end.

Fig. 10   *Gottfried Schwarzenbacher*

56

Towards midday we reached our destination. They lit a fire and set up camp using pine branches and blankets as best they could. So there we sat, wondering what was going to happen, staring into the flames and waiting for some happy solution, while that mob of bandits guarded us with their guns cocked.

Towards morning our eyes were bandaged again, and a doctor came and tended to my wound and dressed it in the light of the camp fire.

Fig. 11   "Archekapetanios" Aris Velougiotis

In the course of the day we had the opportunity of speaking to some of our guards who told us what the reasons and aims of their actions were. Their talk was full of idealism and passionate enthusiasm for the creation of a new Greece.

We learned that we were waiting for the return of their leader who would determine our fate. He finally turned up in the evening and came to our camp fire. In a long, official statement, he explained what they hoped to achieve by their activities and stressed that they had no wish to harm the Germans as long as they did not interfere. We would therefore be released as soon as the circumstances would permit. He said that they were committed to securing a free and better Greece and would act freely and independently of all other powers. His men had already told us this during our conversations around the camp fire. The only condition for our release was that I should take a document to the highest German authority.

Two men, with whom we had almost become friends in those long days, accompanied us for a while and then officially handed back our pistols...

Baron von Falkenhausen had, in effect, been captured by Nikiphoros. (He calls himself Dimitrios Dimitriou, nowadays.)

When he had graduated as a young officer from the Athenian military academy in 1942, he went straight into the mountains to fight against the occupying powers. His Commander, the leader and Kapetanios of all the andartes in the Central Greek province of Roumeli, was Aris Velougiotis. Aris had given Nikiphoros strict instructions not to kill von Falkenhausen and his companions when they captured them. His intention was to parade them from village to village to make an impression on the population. But when von Falkenhausen drew his revolver, one of the andartes shot him. Dimitriou, or Nikiphoros, remembers with horror that awful second when the German major aimed at him and he dared not defend himself; for he obeyed Aris blindly and would never have defied his orders.

"The Italians were responsible for the protection of our works," the Baron recalls. "So they launched extensive searches for me. It was extremely embarrassing for them having to admit that a German major had been abducted by partisans. Later, when I was in the military hospital in Lamia, I was told that the Italians had bought my freedom. They made their little deals with the Greeks when one of them was

captured. But I have no proof to support this theory. In fact, the
Italians were often mercilessly slaughtered like pigs. I saw it myself,
around the end of '42, beginning of '43. They had slit their bellies
open and left them to die. Awfully cruel."

Von Falkenhausen takes a mighty gulp from his brandy glass. He
seems to want to rinse away the past which had suddenly caught up
with him. He gazes thoughtfully at the view of Saarbrücken lying
below our cafe while he lets me read the letter which the andartes had
given him. It was addressed to the "German Army in Greece, Athens"
and started respectfully:

Sirs, we have the honour to inform you of the following:

*Since the German troops have marched in and subdued our
country, we are agonising under the most barbaric slavery. The Italian
orgies are indescribable. Murder, rape, blackmail, plunder and theft
are Italian policy in dealing with the Greek people... From the
moment slavery was introduced, we organised ourselves into a union
with the aim of making Greece free and independent...*

*The National Liberation Front (E.A.M.) and its military arm, the
National Popular Liberation Army (E.L.A.S.), are organisations to
which we belong. We are fighting for the liberation of our father
land... We harbour no hatred for the German people whom we
consider to be the most able in Europe... However, we hate their
political system... We have decided not to allow any interference by
occupying forces in Evritania. We have completely neutralised the
Italian troops. We also wish to stop the forest exploitation which is in
the hands of the Germans... We regret that, owing to excessive zeal,
the major who tried to challenge us was slightly wounded by a warning
shot that hit him in the left thigh... We do not regard the arrest of the
major and of his companions as an act of heroism. We do not consider
them to be prisoners of war and are setting them free after explaining
our views to them... The local headquarters in Lamia was ineffective
but co-operated with the cowardly Italians to send aircraft and men to
hunt us. These men who were caught would have been in a bad way,
had we not temporarily taken a passive attitude for political reasons.
We are informing you that in future we shall no longer be adopting
this attitude and shall hit hard...*

This document was signed by someone calling himself "Infantry
Major, Chief Commander of E.L.A.S. in Roumeli". The signature,

the Greek translator noted, was illegible. Without doubt it was "Major" Aris Velougiotis who had signed the letter, the self-same partisan leader whom Eddie Myers had been trying to contact for weeks.

CHAPTER FOUR
"Aera!"

Reconnaissance and Preparations

On 25 October, 1942, while Aris and Nikiphoros were "taking their three German guests on a publicity tour" through the mountains in the immediate vicinity of the British, Eddie Myers decided with mounting desperation that he, Denys Hamson and Yanni Pistolis would go and inspect the bridges. Yanni knew the terrain and the position of the bridges. Denys was selected for the mission because he spoke Greek and had previous Commando experience. He was a small, wiry man who, in Eddie's opinion, would know how to deal effectively with an adversary if an encounter became inevitable.

"Italians!" the Mayor of Stromni shouted from afar as he broke breathlessly into their hide-out just before the inspection party was to depart.

"How many?" Hamson asked gruffly. He could not stand the man and used to blame the "moron" for not providing enough food for the British.

"Hundreds," answered the Mayor. "They are on their way to the village, half an hour away."

The men quickly packed their possessions, while the Greek continued to bemoan his fate. Half an hour was a very short time but they had reckoned with an emergency departure if the Italians were to start a search. Weapons and explosives were packed in a trice. Bey gathered up his pots and pans and offered to take the British higher up into the mountains where they would be safer.

Eddie agreed to this plan. Yanni returned from the village where he had spoken to his contacts from various outlying hamlets, saying that the Italians had surrounded the entire Giona range and were sweep searching the mountain. It seemed that they supposed the British to be in the area. Apparently a whole division of well trained Alpinis were on the move but they were more probably looking for Baron von Falkenhausen rather than the British.

However, Eddie Myers had rehearsed his men for a quick get-away. Small caches for their possessions had been rigged up under pine branches. Together with the villagers they worked non-stop to bury the explosives and ammunition safely.

They set off at last and having by-passed the steep escarpment above their cave, they could look across the valley where only a few hundred metres away they could see the well-equipped Alpinis wearing green uniforms and their typical fur hats with the cock feathers. Each column was leading mules, heavily laden with machine guns, ammunition and tents.

Eddie was constantly briefed by Yanni on the movements of the Italians. They did not leave the mule tracks as expected nor, surprisingly, did they occupy Stromni that afternoon, but erected their tents on the far side of the valley. When he heard this, Myers decided to slip out that night to inspect the Papadia bridge, as his men seemed to be fairly safe from the Italians.

It had started to snow, to the delight of the men, for it quickly covered their tracks. Yanni had collected two shabby old coats from the village and Myers and Hamson put them on to hide their uniform. They pushed their trouser legs into their socks, hid their pistols and some food under their wide coats and wrapped scarves around their heads, so that even close up, they looked like poor peasants.

When Tom later saw Eddie in his get up, he thought he looked like a wandering Jew on his way to Palestine. Hamson agreed. His week-old beard curled over his chin and accentuated his long nose. With his sack of provisions under the worn coat and the long crook which he had carved for himself, he did indeed look like a prophet on a pilgrimage to the promised land.

The moonlight was bright enough for the three men to climb down the steep mountain side to the village without much difficulty. This was the first time for over a month that they had set foot in any kind of settlement, and for Denys, it was the first time for years that he had seen a typical Greek village. He had quite forgotten the appalling poverty of the peasants. Their noses were assailed by the stench and the dirt in the street. The acrid smell of oxen, goats and sheep which were kept in the houses was unbearable.

Yanni's wife greeted the men warmly. The room was lit by a lighted wick floating in a pan of oil. She cooked them each an egg on potatoes while informing Yanni about the whereabouts of the enemy. Then the men rose and went on their way. "When passing close to the

Italian camp," Myers remembers, "they sat at their camp fires and sang jolly Italian songs." Seemingly, they had not posted any guards, so that the three men pushed on into the wide valley to the west of Lamia. Here, the snow had changed to rain, making their march much easier.

Day had broken when they could hear the whistling and rattling of the trains. Myers was overlooking the Papadia viaduct with his field-glasses. It was built on two tall steel girders and spanned a wide and stony river bed. At the north end, the rails disappeared into a tunnel. "We should demolish the north pier," suggested Hamson, but he scanned the terrain sceptically, for it offered no hiding place in the low weeds and scrub. Myers could see the sentries through his field-glasses. It was immediately obvious to him that any attack would be suicide. There were too many Italians for his small group without support from the andartes to have any chance of success even with the element of surprise.

Yanni left towards evening to contact a friend who worked at the railway junction. When he came back, he confirmed Myers' assumption that the bridge was guarded by between two to three hundred Italians. They had only completed its reconstruction in the spring of 1942, after its destruction by the British during their retreat from Greece.

The three men now discussed the possibility of attacking the Asopos bridge. Yanni was not enthralled by this idea. It was at least a two days' journey away and he knew that an assault would have to be carried out down a steep slope which would be impractical for the demolition team. At this time of the year, the river was very full, so that Myers realised that the only way of blowing it up would be to send down a small, highly specialised team. They were not equipped for that sort of operation.

At dusk they left their hiding place and walked through the night to the Gorgopotamos, a turbulent river which flows into the Aegean sea south of Lamia, in order to check out the third bridge. About one kilometre up-river, there was a dam, which tamed the wild water. The water then flowed through a canal into a reservoir, and from there it was channelled through iron pipes to work the turbines at a power station installed close to the bridge.

The bridge was built in a slight curve from north to south. At the north side there were five solid masonry piers but at the south side there were two of steel. This viaduct had likewise already been destroyed during battles between British and Germans in 1941, but it had been reconstructed by the Italians. The highest pylon was about twenty-three metres high and the total length of the bridge was estimated to be just over two hundred and ten metres.

Eddie Myers was not happy about the situation as he could not get a global view of the approach area and there were too many Italian guards about the bridge. It was too dangerous to get any closer and risk being discovered. He could, however, discern that guard houses had been built nearby and soldiers patrolled the bridge regularly. As it would be impossible to blow up the stone piers he concentrated on the steel ones. He thought that he could discern their basic structure and that the legs of these piers were screwed and bolted together in an L-shape.

Just before dusk Yanni returned in a frantic state. He had been in Lianokladi, the next village on a railway junction, in order to gain further information from friends. Italian guards had stopped him, but fortunately let him go. They had discovered that he was a stranger in the district, but released him with a strict warning not to stay in the vicinity of the railway after dusk.

The shaken man insisted on returning immediately to their base camp. Although Hamson protested violently, Myers complied with his wish. They could hardly see the track in the darkness. Driven by fear that the Italians might be at their heels, they clambered up the Oiti mountain through the early night hours. Around midnight they were too tired to continue, and lit a fire so as not to freeze to death. "It was a bitterly cold night. My feet became like icicles. Whichever way I turned myself to the fire, the other half of my body almost froze," the colonel recalled.

Upon finally returning to their camp on 29 October, 1942, Eddie Myers discussed the results of his reconnaissance with Chris Woodhouse. He had come to the conclusion that the Gorgopotamos bridge should be their target, but he was anxious to obtain further information about the Italian garrison and the strength of the defences. Yanni suggested involving his nephew Costas Pistolis, who lived in Lamia and apparently had access to information concerning the defence emplacements around the viaduct. Chris and Eddie agreed to take his advice, despite the danger that Costas might well be captured by the Italians in Lamia.

But the gamble paid off handsomely. Costas Pistolis returned within a week with valuable information about the type of emplacement, guard duties and details of a barbed-wire fence surrounding the piers of the viaduct. This fitted in with what Eddie had previously discovered, so he made up his mind to attack, provided that at least fifty to sixty armed andartes could be gathered who, with the element of surprise, should be able to overcome the forty to fifty Italians.

On 2 November, 1942, the runner from Prometheus II in Athens returned with the news that the elusive Colonel Zervas was still waiting for the British. His headquarters were in the Valtos range northeast of Arta. Barba Niko estimated it at some four to six days' march away. Eddie decided at once to send Chris Woodhouse with Barba Niko as guide to establish contact with the partisan leader. They could risk making the attack on 22 November when there would be a full moon and there was, therefore, very little time to mobilise Zervas and his men.

Woodhouse and Niko Bey set off that very day, with Myers admonishing them: "You have got just sixteen days to come back with Zervas and his troops." But just three days later an exhausted Niko Bey returned in a state of collapse. He had not been able to keep up with the powerful Englishman, who had decided to continue the route march on his own to reach Zervas in the Valtos mountains.

Meanwhile, at the camp Eddie described the construction of the viaduct to his men. They had blueprints and a photograph, taken along from Egypt, of the Simplon-Orient Express crossing the bridge. Tom Barnes and Arthur Edmonds were ordered to prepare the explosive material. Six main charges were to be attached to the four legs of each steel pier: one on each leg at about one and a half metres above the ground and another two about two metres higher up. Edmonds and Barnes wanted to thus make sure that a piece of at least two metres would be blasted away from the pier, so that it could not simply be rebuilt. Tom was able to procure a saw from the village to cut wooden moulds to fit what they believed was the cross-section of the steel piers, and into these they pressed the explosives and tied them with parachute cord. Arthur Edmonds even made a model of the legs of the steel pier in order to rehearse his men in attaching the charges.

Len Wilmot had finally been able to run one of the charging machines for their wireless batteries. For the first time in more than a month, they were able to make radio contact with Cairo and more importantly to transmit. Eddie immediately requested a consignment of Sten guns with ammunition, hand grenades, bombs and provisions and gave precise directions where the containers were to be dropped. He sent the reluctant Denys Hamson out onto the windy Oiti plateau to receive the freight.

There was no confirmation from Cairo of their request, but they heard with relief that the third team under Major Cook had only been parachuted into Greece on 27 October, 1942. When Myers and Woodhouse with their teams had jumped on the night of 29 September, 1942, John Cook had again decided to return to Cairo as he was uncertain about the fire signals. This news meant, however, that Cook and his men had now been in Greece for almost three weeks. But no one knew where they were and Myers was worried that they had been captured by the Italians, and as a result the Italians kept sweep searching the mountains. The uncertainty gnawed at him.

Now that all preparations had been carried out, life in the camp slipped into a routine. The villagers of Stromni quite accepted that the British lived in a cave above their village. Food supplies were satisfactory. Myers paid well and Niko Bey transported it up by mule every day. They had plenty of brown bread and potatoes and sometimes they were given apples, nuts and honey, for the excellence of which Stromni is renowned. Meat was bought directly from the shepherds for gold. Barba Niko acted as chef and administrative officer as well. He even had mountain herbs collected out of which he always managed to cook something palatable. About a hundred metres above the cave they could draw their drinking water from a source.

Between the trees at the mouth of the cave, they rigged up some parachutes to protect themselves. The smoke from the fire was not likely to give them away as it was the practice of all shepherds to use fires to keep themselves warm. Inside the cave, beds had been made out of brushwood and bracken, and thanks to the blankets that they had bought from the villagers they had no more need to freeze. In the evenings they would gather outside around the camp fire and Niko Bey would endlessly tell stories in flowery language which Denys had to translate. They played cards, drank *chippero*, and Bey would test them on their newly-learnt Greek vocabulary.

From time to time, small partisan bands of maximum four to five men would turn up in the British camp vaguely promising support for the forthcoming operation, but they were unreliable and normally were not seen again. One day, Myers again heard the name of the elusive Aris. His *nom de guerre* was apparently Velougiotis, the name of the majestic mountain rising above Karpenissi. "He is the top leader of the andartes and his real name given at birth is Athanasios Klaras," he was told. Repeatedly, Myers begged his informers to let him meet up with Aris, but in vain. It seemed as though the guerilla leader was deliberately avoiding him.

Myers became more irritable day by day and could hardly hide his depression. It was 14 November, 1942. All their preparations were completed and apart from their daily routine, there was nothing to do, so that his men, too, began to get scratchy. Nor was there any news from Chris, but they knew it was still too early for that.

The only message to reach them in those days was bad. Yanni Pistolis reported that his nephew Costas had been arrested in Lamia together with several former officers of the Greek army. Did the enemy smell a rat? Had they been betrayed? Would Costas be made to confess? They knew that "the Italians were never averse to a little 'fun' at the expense of their prisoners," as Hamson put it grimly.

Eddie Myers gave one or two pep talks by the mouth of the cave, speaking jerkily and gazing through his men as if he saw some familiar memory behind. "We have reached our time limit," he said. "It does not look hopeful, but we will tackle it alone if it comes to it."

Five officers, two radio transmitters, six Greek volunteers from the vicinity, and six former English soldiers who had been in hiding in the mountains since the German invasion were now the total force in their camp. In seven weeks Myers had not succeeded in recruiting any more than six Greeks! Not a good score! Nevertheless, he had taken the desperate decision to attempt the attack.

Arrival of the Andartes

In the first few days of his journey, Chris Woodhouse travelled only at night for fear of running into Italian scouts. Soon, however, he decided bravely to risk continuing his route march in the daylight hours too. In a village near Agrinion, he heard from a priest that four

Englishmen were in the area who were allegedly travelling through the mountains in the company of the andarte leader Aris.

"Who is Aris?" Woodhouse asked.

"Aris is the leader of ELAS," the priest answered.

"What does ELAS mean?"

"It's the National Popular Liberation Army."

"Who is in control of this army? How big is it?"

"Aris is the military leader of two to three hundred andartes, who are organised in bands of twenty to forty men and operate in the district of Roumeli," the priest answered somewhat unwillingly. Woodhouse could not afford to check out this unsubstantiated information himself. There had been too many rumours which had turned out to be without substance, so he asked the priest to handcarry a message to Aris and those Englishmen. On a piece of paper he described the position of the cave near Stromni and ordered the British immediately to join Eddie Myers there.

Themie Marinos, who was the only Greek on Operation Harling, remembers to this day how the messenger arrived with this news from Chris Woodhouse. Marinos' relationship with John Cook was lousy. Even at their last attempt to parachute on 27 and 28 October, 1942, in the night of the full moon, Cook had opposed the jump. "I just pushed him out of the way," says the Greek, "and I leapt into the unknown. So the other three had to follow, whether they wanted to or not."

They had landed at the outskirts of the Italian garrison town of Karpenissi. "We fled into hiding in the surrounding woods, while the Italians peppered the whole area with shots during the night. Unfortunately, we lost all our goods, all the containers including photos and plans of the bridges to be blown up."

On the following day the men had been seized by Aris' adjutant, Nikiphoros, who, only a few days before, had likewise seized the Baron von Falkenhausen, Gottfried Schwarzenbacher and their interpreter, Trude Radwein.

"Aris ordered me to find an excuse to eliminate the British," Dimitrios Dimitriou (formerly called Nikiphoros) recounts. "He believed they were spies in disguise. In particular, Themie Marinos was a thorn in his side. Aris could not stand it that a Greek was not only aiding and abetting the royalist English but was also doing it in a British uniform. But I dared to contradict him: 'These are allies who wish to co-operate with us.'

"'They are representatives of capitalism,' Aris replied gruffly. 'When the war is over, they will sit on our backs, enslave us and impose their will on us, no different from the Italians and Germans at present!'"

Other andartes, however, supported Nikiphoros' opinion that the British had come to free Greece from occupation. Aris finally conceded and decided to take the four men on his "publicity tour" through Roumeli, instead of the Germans.

It was an irony of fate that the British unintentionally saved the lives of Baron von Falkenhausen and his two companions, who in captivity had actually been able to watch John Cook and his team parachute down. Baron von Falkenhausen ended his report to the Wehrmacht High Command by writing:

> *During the night before our release, English aircraft circled above the area in the bright moonlight, packed with arms and equipment which they dropped. Some containers found later confirmed this.*

At this point, the wounded German Major and his group had become a burden to Aris. He immediately saw that there was much more propaganda value to be gained by appearing with the British at his side and by informing the naïve villagers that the Allies had arrived in order to free the country of the occupying army under his leadership. Consequently, he released the Germans and continued on his way with the British.

On hearing from the priest that Chris Woodhouse was going to meet Napoleon Zervas, his rival, Aris Velougiotis decided, albeit reluctantly, that he and his men would have to join in the attack on the Gorgopotamos viaduct. People on the political right, such as the republican andartes under Zervas, were in Aris' opinion just as bad enemies as the occupying powers. He fought against them just as pitilessly. But he also knew that if the operation succeeded without him, his adversary Zervas would be in the riding seat and rapidly gain the favour of the population.

Aris finally ordered Nikiphoros to accompany the four British men to Myers. Nikiphoros, who was only twenty years old, led a shabby, motley crowd of thirty-five men. He carried a German automatic assault rifle, while his bearded comrades were equipped with guns of every kind: Bredas, Mausers, Mannlichers, Lee Enfields, and even old Turkish shotguns. Two men had Italian light automatic machine guns. Ammunition belts were slung around their bodies. Their garments were mostly in rags but some were wearing tattered military and police uniforms of Italian, German and Greek origin. Some had goatskin shoes, others Italian army boots and many walked barefoot on scree and snow. "Our greatest wish is to kill an Italian soldier in order to get hold of his boots," they later admitted to Edmonds in front of the cave at Stromni. But almost all wore a little cap, on the front of which were embroidered the four Greek letters E.L.A.S.

A day after John Cook and his team had finally turned up at the cave above Stromni, Chris Woodhouse also got back. Myers had gone to sleep when he lightly tapped his shoulder. "I've got back, Colonel. I have carried out your instructions. Half a day behind me is Zervas, with a force of over fifty andartes, and following him on the same route is Aris with more than that number. By tomorrow night both bands expect to reach the village of Mavrolithari, only two hours away from here. I have come on ahead with only Zervas' adjutant, Captain Michalli Myriadis, so as not to be late."

Myers got up. Slightly dazed with sleep, he could hardly believe how much more promising the situation had suddenly become thanks to Chris' extraordinary route march. Both men shook Myers' hand. Michalli, a tall dark Cretan stood rigidly at attention while Chris reported on his journey. Eddie looked at his watch. It was a quarter of an hour after midnight. Chris had been on the move for fourteen days; he had travelled over the mountains right across central Greece and back again, and there he was — a quarter of an hour late!

"I am not late," joked Woodhouse with proverbial British understatement. "By Greenwich time, I have three quarters of an hour in hand!"

Woodhouse had reason to be cheerful. Two days after sending messages to Cook and Aris through the priest, he had been met by Michalli in a ramshackle old house. On 10 November, 1942, he met Zervas himself in Argyrion, a hamlet consisting only of a few poor huts. Napoleon Zervas received Woodhouse in a khaki tunic devoid of all insignia; he was about fifty-five years of age, rotund and seemingly jovial beneath his heavy, slightly greying beard which seemed to be the hallmark of the partisans. A pistol was supported by a leather belt around his ample waist and a short dagger was tucked in on the other side. Zervas had greeted Chris most warmly. He had embraced him and, in Greek fashion, had kissed him on both cheeks. "Evangelos! Evangelos!" he had cried out. "You are the saviour. Evangelos will be your name in the Greek mountains." Understanding the necessity for haste, he immediatedly ordered the departure of a hundred and fifty andartes on the next day.

As a Republican, Napoleon Zervas had not been allowed to serve in the battle against the Italians on the Albanian front while the Greek dictator Metaxas had been in power. When the German army had subsequently overrun Greece, most Greek officers in the regular army felt that it was pointless to conduct guerilla warfare in the mountains as it would only give rise to reprisals against innocent villagers.

However, one of the few personalities who thought differently was Napoleon Zervas, previously better known as a playboy and gambler. Against all odds, in 1942, he went back to his home province of Epirus to take up the struggle against the Italians. He grew a heavy black beard which covered his round chin. He was pro-British and he soon involved his freedom fighters in skirmishes with the Italian troops.

At the end of August 1942 he received his first package dropped by a British airplane and hoped at last to equip his EDES andartes (Greek Democratic National Army) with some urgently needed materials. This first package however only contained some old Italian shotguns, shells without mortars and the left foot of twenty-two army boots!

When Chris Woodhouse suddenly appeared in those wild and rugged Valtos mountains, he seemed like an apparition of a prophet. General Napoleon Zervas could wish for nothing better than to face the enemy in co-operation with an organised and disciplined British unit.

Many of Zervas' men were Cretans who had joined him in Epirus province after the collapse. They were all strictly anti-Communist. Their enthusiasm made up for their primitive equipment. Woodhouse noted their extreme poverty as they marched along the narrow mountain tracks. Hardly anyone was wearing a uniform, much less reasonable foot-wear. They walked on strips of rubber tyres which were pulled together with wire or they had goatskin shoes. Their weapons consisted of light Italian machine guns which they had looted, and old Mannlicher repeating rifles which dated back to before the First World War.

Zervas was always cheerful; he spoke softly but decisively. He convinced Woodhouse, who was at first sceptical, that his men could fight. The rotund man was not fit enough for the very long march, so that the rest periods became longer and more frequent. To avoid being a hindrance, he finally rode a mule which also carried his daily log books. On their journey they halted for a night in a village called Viniani, where they learnt that Aris was in an adjoining village. Here was the first chance for Woodhouse to test his diplomacy and he was indeed successful, after an exchange of letters, in bringing the two rival leaders together.

Aris had fourteen Italian prisoners in tow who did not have long to live. They were only of value to Aris to bolster his image with the village population. The two bands of andartes met awkwardly in the market square while Woodhouse held discussions with their leaders. Aris was small in stature but he probably had the mightiest and most impressive beard of any andarte and, like Zervas, he wore a khaki uniform without insignia. Bandoliers of ammunition were slung around his chest and a long dagger dangled at his left hip. He had a rough voice made hoarse by his many speeches in the villages. His nose was small and crooked and he examined his new acquaintances with mistrustful, dark brown eyes. He swung a short riding crop from his right wrist.

Aris always spoke rapidly and focused on the core of any problem. Coming straight to the point, he agreed to take part in the operation. Woodhouse soon realised that Aris ran a tight ship and that his men were "disciplined and battle-tried". The three men thought it likely that the Italian garrison in Karpenissi would get wind of the concentration of guerillas which had by now swollen to two hundred men and therefore decided to leave about fifty EDES andartes in the area of Viniani.

They spent a night in the mountain village of Kolokythia where Aris had set up his headquarters. Here, Woodhouse had to make his first decision over the life or death of another human being. A young man was brought before him, Zervas and Aris.

He devotes a few lines in his autobiography *Something Ventured* to this event:

72

He was a gipsy and carried an Italian pass signed by an Italian officer in Karpenissi. The charge was undeniable, since he had been caught in a neighbouring village asking questions about the guerillas. Zervas, Aris and I formed an immediate court martial. The outcome was inevitable. We could not afford the manpower to guard a prisoner; we could not risk his escape. He was hanged in the village square.

Zervas commented with military brevity on the youth's arrest:

Monday, 16th November 1942. Komninos arrested the traitor Kalambouras, and took him along with him. At Kolokythia we hanged Kalambouras at eleven-thirty.

"Nikos Kalambouras was my best friend. He was no gipsy," laments on the other hand Yannis Karageorgos, a tailor in Athens who grew up in Kolokythia and who was only sixteen years old when Kalambouras was hanged. "The spying charge was totally unfounded. Nikos was scarcely older than me. They tortured him, they beat him, they castrated him and then they hanged him in front of the church." The tailor cries while he relates the event although almost fifty years have passed.

Did Chris Woodhouse feel that in acquiescing in this way he was making his mark on his new associates who were the absolute rulers over the life and death of their underlings?

Chris Woodhouse reckons that in three weeks he had travelled over three hundred and fifty kilometres through the mountain terrain. A truly outstanding achievement, particularly because he had to circumvent many villages by day and found it preferable to do a part of his journey by night. Being entirely on his own, he had to live with the constant fear of discovery or betrayal, for again and again he needed to take complete strangers into his confidence in order to find the way to Zervas.

He had, in fact, succeeded in achieving the impossible: not only had he found the two antagonists, Aris and Zervas, and convinced them to join forces to combat the enemy in the interest of Greece, but he had also made contact with Cook and his group, thus reuniting the complete Harling team in a cave in central Greece seven weeks after leaving Egypt.

Fig. 12   *Christopher Montague Woodhouse: "We could not afford the manpower to guard a prisoner"*

The "Archekapetanios" and the "Strategos"

Many members of the German military were openly of the opinion that their lightning victory over the Greek army had been given away to the Italians. They mocked the Italians' defeat in Albania. German officers ridiculed their allies by having the forbidden song "Koroido Mussolini" played in restaurants.

A large part of the Greek population was openly in favour of the Germans. Germany, in contrast to the original aggressor Italy, was not hated. There was some understanding for the German military action as, after all, one could not desert a friend. That would be dishonourable. There was also some gratitude that after the German campaign their prisoners of war, Greek officers and soldiers were released to go home and not interned. The German army abstained from "cleansing" the hinterland of scattered British and Greek units and from "pacifying" the area.

This relationship between Germans and Greeks was, however, subjected to its first test when the Italians were permitted to enter Athens in triumph. Then Hitler decided to hand over the major part of the Greek mainland and the peninsula of Peleponnese to the defeated "fratelli" as their zone of occupation. Finally, the friendly relationship suffered lasting damage when two students pulled the swastika down from its flagpole on the Acropolis in Athens in the night of 31 May, 1941.

Greece had always been dependent on imports of food and now found herself cut off from the outside world through the allied blockade. Furthermore, the occupying army had to be supplied. While 472,000 tons of grain were imported in 1938, imports fell in 1940 to 273,000 tons and down to 50,000 tons in the first half of 1941. In addition, Bulgaria stopped agricultural supplies to the south out of Thrace which had been annexed.

Starvation struck particularly in the areas around Athens.

While the foreign soldiers enjoyed the mild spring sunshine and snapped tourist photos on the Acropolis, the population was dying like flies. Emaciated figures dragged themselves through Athens' streets. Corpses lay on the pavements. 300,000 Greeks are estimated to have died. In that black winter of 1941 and 1942 alone, nine out of every ten newly-born children did not survive.

In this desperate situation it was not surprising that the outlawed Communist Party of Greece, the KKE, which had gone underground in 1936 when the dictator Metaxas was in power, now began to surface again. When Stalin made his famous radio speech on 3 July, 1941, and called on all oppressed countries to create bands of partisans and to fight the enemy with subversive action, his message was spread through the Greek underground movement and was well received. Young people, members of all social strata and former soldiers and officers were immediately keen to take up the struggle against the hated Italians.

On 27 September, 1941, the Central Committee of the Communist Party (KKE) formed EAM (National Liberation Front) as a political organisation and ELAS (National Popular Liberation Army) as its military wing.

The abbreviation ELAS was well chosen as it sounds so much like Hellas. At top level, a triumvirate was entrusted with making decisions. It consisted of the "Stratiotikos", the military leader, the "Politikos", who was responsible for publicity and instruction and who was to inform the population about the aim and purpose of EAM, and finally the "Kapetanios", who was in charge of the "physical and spiritual wellbeing" of his unit. This three-man system of shared leadership was adopted right down to the smallest unit: three men with equal rights were always to make the decisions and at least two of them had to be members of KKE.

Yioryios Siantos became general secretary of the KKE after Nikos Zakhariadhis was sent to a concentration camp in Germany. Andreas Tzimas, who was the youngest deputy in the Greek parliament before the Metaxas dictatorship, was elected to the central committee and he recommended that Athanasios Klaras should be instructed to go to the mountains to sound out the chances of forming a guerilla movement there.

Tzimas knew Klaras from the time that they had both been arrested and imprisoned during the Metaxas dictatorship and he was convinced that Klaras was ideal for this task in Roumeli as he knew the area well. So Klaras returned in April 1942 to his home town Lamia, the largest in Roumeli, in order to build up the first ELAS unit. He was born there in 1905, the son of well respected parents. He became a teacher, but was soon banned from the profession "for homosexual offences". He joined the KKE but during the Metaxas regime he was persecuted and arrested and he spent over two years in jail.

There is some speculation as to why he finally capitulated to Metaxas and signed a declaration of repentance; some say that it was to gain his release for purely opportunistic reasons, while his supporters say it was in order to be free to serve his party better. Whatever the truth was, the taint of capitulation clung to him.

Fig. 13   *Aris Velougiotis with his 15-year-old friend*

Klaras formed his first andarte group on 22 May, 1942, in Sperhias, a mountain hamlet near Makrakomi. He adopted the undercover name of Aris Velougiotis. Others followed his example and thereafter all andartes were only to be known by their pseudonyms. This diminished the danger of betraying other family members in case of capture. This first group of freedom fighters remained small. Why would the mountain peasants want to join those foolhardy guerillas? They had hardly seen any Germans or Italians, who were concentrated in the bigger towns and maintained garrisons in smaller towns such as Lamia and Karpenissi. Insurrection against the occupying power led to reprisals which could mean hostages being shot and villages being burned, as well as confiscation of their vitally important foodstuffs.

But Aris was charismatic and wily. He knew the mountain villages from his youth. The Italian troops did not dare venture there for fear of ambush. So the Kapetanios had a free hand. He entered the villages flying the Greek flag, he kowtowed to the priest and the village elder and made eloquent speeches to the inhabitants: ELAS was the saviour of Greece, it would free the people from Italian oppression, just as the Klephts had thrown off the Turkish domination in the past! He explained the EAM strategy, the priest rang the church bells, and the speech generally ended with a rousing rendition of the national anthem.

The Kapetanios of all Kapetanios, the "Archekapetanios" Aris Velougiotis, turned up at a cracking pace — one day in Gardiki, the next in Roumeli miles away from Gardiki. Enthusiastic young men joined him. Local EAM units started up everywhere. His name was on everyone's lips and the Italians hunted him with unusually large units. Without success, however, for his group vanished nimbly into the mountains at the slightest hint of a confrontation.

Aris ably proceeded to attract the lethargic village inhabitants to his cause. From time to time he showed captured German and Italian soldiers like Major Baron von Falkenhausen, Gertrud Radwein and Gottfried Schwarzenbacher, to the people of several villages in order to enhance his prestige. Roaming cattle thieves and gangs who blackmailed the peasants with mafia methods were given summary trials and then executed or whipped on the village square. Some lucky ones were not eliminated but permitted to join the andartes.

78

Fig. 14   *Nikiphoros: "I would never dare to contradict Aris"*

These acts immensely enhanced his reputation. Even ultra-right circles in Athens commended his deeds. A myth was created.

When Napoleon Zervas turned up in the British camp in Stromni, he made a good impression on everyone with his relaxed appearance and cheerful manner. He laughed a lot, making his whole body vibrate. Everyone responded to his scintillating personality and respected his authority although he did not look particularly impressive. He wore his old khaki uniform, a shapeless civilian cap, worn-out riding boots and, in addition to an automatic revolver, he had attached a bejewelled dagger to his belt to celebrate the occasion.

Myers instructed his men to show respect to the charismatic andarte leader and so they all assembled and saluted in military style. Zervas appreciated the honour paid to him by the British. Eddie Myers who was thankful for his arrival, offered him the princely sum of a thousand gold sovereigns to ease him into his new job. Then the Englishman made a tactically clever move: he requested Zervas who was called Strategos — or General — by all his men to take command of the operation while Myers would be happy to regard himself as Chief of Staff. Zervas accepted graciously.

The "Strategos" was impressed by his own importance. Much later he wrote:

The colonel frankly told me that if I had not arrived by twelve o'clock on 18 November, he would have committed suicide.

While Zervas and the British were confident about the success of the planned attack, Aris saw the situation more realistically. If it failed, "it would be the end of the guerilla movement". Aris knew that his men would never be persuaded to take part in a second assault. He was convinced that they would run away and scatter to the four winds. Moreover, he warned his new associates that at any time he might receive instructions from his superiors in Athens not to co-operate in the attack. So far he had always followed the standing instructions not to attack formed bodies of the enemy in open combat. "My decision to assist you can be revoked by Athens at any time," he warned Zervas and Myers. But this was never an option considered by the EAM leadership in Athens. They knew just as well as the "Archekapetanios" that if the Gorgopotamos bridge was successfully blown up without ELAS involvement, their organisation's image would suffer irreparable damage.

Myers explained his plan to Aris and Zervas on 21 November, 1942, pointing out the advantage of attacking during one of the next

80

Fig. 15   *"Strategos" Napoleon Zervas*

few nights when there would be an almost full moon. Because of the
deep   gorge   which   separated   the   two   extremities   of   the

two-hundred-and-eleven-metre-long viaduct, it was necessary to make up two entirely independent groups to attack and overcome the Italian guards stationed at either end of the viaduct. A stronger group would be required at the southern end because it would also need to attack some barrack huts where the Italians slept. Finally, third and fourth units would be required to cut the railway line north and south of the bridge, to delay reinforcements from neighbouring garrisons.

The demolition party under Tom Barnes would go in after the sentries had been overcome to blow up the two steel piers and the three bridge spans supported by them. Myers estimated that at least two demolitions, separated by an hour or more, would be necessary to complete the destruction. Allowing two hours to prepare for each explosion, a total of four hours would have to be reckoned with for the whole operation. As Italian reinforcements could come from Lamia by train to the bridge in about two hours, further action to delay the enemy north of the bridge would have to be taken into account in the time estimate.

"What do you think, Aris?" asked Zervas. "How long will it take to overcome the Italian guard units?"

"Half an hour, three quarters of an hour at most," he replied. "If the Italians fight longer than that, then I am pessimistic, because then we shall lose."

When Zervas and Myers countered that in that case a second attack would then have to be attempted on the following night, Aris flatly opposed them. "Not with my men," he said. "If we don't make it the first time, my men will be so demotivated that they will not attack again on the following night nor on any other night."

It was snowing up in the mountains and sleeting down by the bridge and a cold wind was blowing. The attackers felt optimistic. Their reconnaissance parties all confirmed that the Italian guards were not very alert and that there were no soldiers posted in outlying positions. The men were casually going about their business around the barracks. They were evidently not expecting an attack.

During the night of 23 November, 1942, the final preparations were made. The assault was to take place on the night of 25–26 November, 1942. As Aris and Zervas were both keen to see the bridge and the terrain for themselves before the attack, Myers and Woodhouse decided to accompany them in a small advance party to carry out a final reconnaissance.

This group of leaders spent the night of 24 November in a shepherd's hut on Mount Oiti. They intended to make use of the dawn to creep down to within a kilometre of the viaduct. From there they would gain a bird's-eye view. Woodhouse recalls how "Aris and Zervas, lying side by side in a straw hut, with their legs sticking out, were exchanging anecdotes in an ebullient mood, but they were deadly serious in their intentions".

The weather continued to be dreadful. The sky was totally obscured with clouds. At times, a few snowflakes mixed in with the driving rain. But when they awoke on the morning of 25 November, 1942, the weather was ideal for the attack. It had cleared a little, sufficiently to give them an excellent view of the bridge. They crawled on hands and knees over the stones and took cover in the bushes as they approached. There was no sign of any Italian early-warning positions. But through the swirling clouds they caught some clear glimpses of the viaduct lying far below. It looked like a toy bridge made out of a meccano set.

"After a good hour we agreed that Myers' plan should be executed the following night," Woodhouse relates. "We crawled back to the hut on all fours and climbed Mount Oiti towards midday to meet up with our units in the evening."

"Aera!"

A further scout party confirmed on the afternoon of 23 November, 1942, that the enemy seemed utterly unsuspecting, so all parties set off on the following morning.

It was snowing as on the previous day, and although most of the andartes shivered with cold in their ragged clothes, there was no complaint about the wretched weather as the low clouds sheltered them from Italian air reconnaissance. There were about a hundred and fifty men moving in a long drawn-out line. Twenty mules were laden with heavy equipment. Unnecessary noise was avoided. Only the crunch of the snow could be heard under the boots of the British. They knew that they had a five-hour climb up Mount Oiti in front of them.

Late in the afternoon they reached a deserted sawmill above a narrow gorge where they set up their night camp. While the officers were able to sleep in wooden sheds, the freezing andartes had to make do with finding refuge outside between the stacked planks. They lit great fires in protected nooks and did not worry about being discovered as the falling snow did not allow visibility over a hundred and fifty metres. The partisans had brought along maize bread and half a dozen sheep which were butchered and roasted over the open fires. Niko Bey was in his element.

In the early hours of the morning the British were woken by loud screams coming from outside their sheds. They rushed out. Some careless guerillas had lit their fire too close to the stacks of planks and one of these had gone up in flames. Swearing furiously, they tried to control the fire with snow and pine branches. The blaze was mirrored in the grey clouds and shone right into the valley. But they were lucky. They were able to check the fire and no one down in the valley seemed to notice what was going on up in the mountains.

They broke up very early the next morning. Spread out at intervals, the units marched for a good three hours until they reached the timber line below the summit. Here they hid in the trees to wait for their leaders Aris, Zervas, Myers and Woodhouse.

Edmonds was feeling great. The weather was ideal for the operation. "We could hardly see, but I could hear the whistling of the trains very clearly," the New Zealander recalled. No fires were lit now. No unnecessary risks were to be taken at the last moment. So everyone sat around, whiling away the afternoon by playing cards and waiting for nightfall. Edmonds felt like a boxer waiting in the dressing room to be called into the ring to fight an unknown adversary. Time dragged, the men tried to hide their apprehension with earthy comments. They had been waiting for over two months for this day. What would the night bring? Would they ever come out of this remote area alive?

Low clouds enveloped them as darkness fell. Wisps of fog created an eerie atmosphere. Myers checked nervously that no noise was made unnecessarily and that no fires were lit in spite of the increasing cold. Tom Barnes, Denys Hamson and Arthur Edmonds again verified their routine for attaching the explosive packages to the bridge.

Four mules were available to carry the prepared packages. According to Denys' estimate they were about fifteen hundred metres away from the bridge as the crow flies. They would lead the mules about half an hour downhill to a point below the Gorgopotamos waterfall. The noise from the waterfall would mask their approach. There the animals would be left with the muleteers while the three

British and nine andartes would carry the explosives up under the viaduct. Yanni Pistolis would lead them in the dark. Each man would be carrying ten to fifteen kilograms of explosive material.

Eddie went with Chris as his interpreter to each partisan unit to repeat all the orders in detail one last time. Nikiphoros was to lead the reserve party which would be deployed in an emergency. They were all gathered on the north side of the viaduct, so that two parties would have to cross the river to launch their attack from the south.

Fig. 16   *Napoleon Zervas: "The explosives were transported by mules. It was indescribably arduous. We were trudging through a metre of snow"*

Watches were synchronised, and at the last minute Aris, Zervas and Myers agreed to accept Aris' proposal to open fire exactly at midnight on the north and south sides of the bridge simultaneously. At 23.00 the men should be in their appointed places. Allowing four hours for the attack and demolition, they should be able to get away between three and four o'clock in the morning and retreat to the mountain forest under cover of darkness.

Fig. 17   *Greek women carrying war material for their andartes*

At 18.00 the first parties left. They literally faded away. They made no sound, their movement could only be sensed. Eddie followed with the demolition unit. Questions were buzzing in his head. Had everything been foreseen, adequately planned, had everyone understood?

He was never able to speak to Zervas and Aris directly. He had to rely on his interpreters and sometimes he would ask trick questions to check that they had actually translated what he had said. Now he called his key men by name and was relieved when each one immediately confirmed his readiness. "It was amazing how the mules found their way in the dark, hardly making a sound and putting their hind hooves with unerring accuracy in the exact place where their front hooves had been set down," Eddie recalled.

He again called Cook and Barker over to him before they set off with the explosives strapped to their backs by parachute cords, reminding them at the last minute to cut the telephone cables that ran alongside the rails.

Themie Marinos followed behind them with the young agile andarte Lambros. They were to blow up the northern part of the track. For the umpteenth time Myers repeated that they should first cut the telephone wires and only then attach the explosives. Marinos was not to demolish the track until reinforcements were on their way to the scene.

Marinos and Lambros were followed by a unit of about forty men, a mixed ELAS and EDES unit. Among these, there was Karalivanos, the first andarte whom the British had met. Myers had threatened him with death if he did not fight bravely. The colonel could not help remembering that this weird individual had callously deserted him and his men when they had really needed his assistance. Although Aris said he did not disagree with eliminating Karalivanos, he pointed out that Karalivanos had shown a certain amount of integrity when he first met the British. "He could have killed you for your gold, but he did not do that. That counts in his favour and you should take that into consideration," he said, attempting to appease Myers.

It was now 22.30. In the darkness Edmonds could just make out the outline of the reservoir from which the water shot straight down into huge tubes to drive the turbines of the small power plant situated fifty metres below. The men unloaded the explosives from the backs of the mules below the dam. Although the full moon was obscured by clouds, there was enough light to see the immediate vicinity. It was getting late and they scrambled down the last escarpment without quite knowing how they managed to reach the bottom. Names were quietly called out and Tom checked that everyone had arrived unhurt. Hamson had to reassure his Greek porters who were afraid that they would not have enough time to get out of the valley before the explosion. He promised to dismiss them in time.

Fear gripped the men now that there was no more to do until the attack. They crouched in earth holes, hid behind boulders and waited for Myers' signal. The moon suddenly shone out from behind flying shreds of cloud and lit up a ghostly landscape. They heard a train approach from the south and cross the viaduct.

"That was the last one for a long time, friends," said Hamson.

Tom chided him for challenging fate. It could bring bad luck.

Aris, Zervas, Myers and Woodhouse had meanwhile crawled forward to the edge of the steep slope where they could see the viaduct through the slight mist below. It looked huge. Nothing stirred. It was a few minutes to midnight. They waited a quarter of an hour, lying on their stomachs. Just as they began to think something had gone wrong, gunfire rang out from the north side of the bridge and pandemonium shattered the calm of the night. Rifle and automatic fire cracked away. They saw the flash of exploding hand-grenades. Myers could hear three or four light machine guns. He knew that the attacking party had only two such guns. They were up against a strong opponent. Bullets were flying over their heads and Woodhouse hardly dared lift his head above the rocks sheltering him.

After about twenty minutes of this intense gunfire Zervas became worried and restless. "At this rate of fire, our people will soon run out of ammunition," he barked at Chris nervously.

Before Woodhouse could answer, their attention was drawn to the south side of the bridge where fighting had also suddenly broken out. They distinctly heard the shrill voice of a platoon leader. "Aera!" shouted the andartes. Aera, the old war cry which once Leonidas had uttered in this very Thermopylai Pass when he urged his Spartans to fight to the death against the Persians.

But suddenly the fire on the northern end died down and an excited messenger reported that the group attacking at the north had been beaten back by the Italians. Aris' and Zervas' insistence on staying at the north end with the reserve unit now proved its worth. Nikiphoros with his men was immediately put into action in an attempt to re-establish the situation.

After another twenty-five minutes of sporadic shooting, Zervas became even more anxious and was convinced that the attack should be aborted. "If the north side is not captured within the next quarter of an hour, I shall fire the green Very light for the general withdrawal," he cautioned his three co-commanders and demanded ultimately,

88

"Where is the Very pistol?" No one had it, as his aide had taken it forward in the general excitement!

Quick-wittedly Myers seized the opportunity to take command.

"Go forward and get the pistol," he instructed Woodhouse. "But don't give it to Zervas when you come back. Follow only my orders. Is that clear? The green Very light must not be fired except under my orders."

Chris returned ten minutes later with the pistol and the good news that Nikiphoros at the north end of the bridge was gaining control, and exceptionally loud cheering at the south end followed by a white signal indicated that the andartes had taken overall control.

The demolition party under Tom Barnes, Denys Hamson, Arthur Edmonds and Inder Gill was lying flat on the ground when Eddie Myers ran down to an elevation where he could look straight across to the opposite side of the valley. He flashed his torch and shouted at the top of his voice, "Go in, Tom! The south end of the bridge is in our hands. Go in!"

Edmonds could see Lamia lying in the valley below. Car lights leaving the town flashed. No doubt the Italians had realised that there was fighting at the bridge. He felt something sharp tear his trousers but he didn't care. Now lights were coming on in the power plant too. Denys sent an andarte to the frightened workmen to reassure them that they would not be hurt as long as they kept quiet.

The demolition party had trouble keeping up with Tom Barnes who led them along the muddy path to the viaduct. The rubber soles of their flimsy shoes would not grip and it was difficult for them to keep their balance with the heavy equipment on their backs. About fifty metres before the bridge they passed a heap of rocks. Hamson decided that this would give ideal protection once the fuses were lit. Yanni led Tom to the barbed wire surrounding the pylons. His wire cutters severed it without difficulty, then Tom scrambled valiantly through the wire fence. He seemed to have a total disregard for danger and ran straight to the first large steel pier. His men followed.

Arthur Edmonds was alarmed when he saw the first metal pier before him. The four legs were sunk in a square block of concrete which, to his mind, would have been large enough to hold a hundred men. Doubt assailed him when he tried to imagine how they could possibly break up those girders with only centimetre-wide struts. An icy shudder shot through him when they found that the cross-section of the four legs was not L-shaped but U-shaped. All their preparatory work during seven weeks in camp was in vain as the carefully prepared pieces of timber with the bars of explosives could not be attached to the legs. Barnes did not hesitate; he ordered his party completely to dismantle the prepared charges and to repack them by hand into the vertical U-shaped girders.

Hamson ordered the porters to deposit their load at each of the four legs of the pier, while Arthur Edmonds, Tom, Inder and Denys redistributed the charges. The porters were posted around the pier and Denys instructed them to shoot only when they were absolutely sure that the enemy was near. Nevertheless, they jerked their triggers nervously whenever there was any movement. Edmonds used his torch to work faster, but this attracted a salvo from the opposite slope. Hamson heard screams from above on the bridge, and suddenly an Italian was thrown over the railing and landed somewhere in the bushes behind him.

Fighting had meanwhile resumed on the north end of the bridge. Bullets were whizzing over the heads of the demolition team and they could hear the high ping of shots hitting the metal construction. Tom and his men worked like fury in the moonlight, which was muted but bright enough for their purpose. They were bathed in sweat with fear and exertion.

Hamson went calmly from man to man distributing explosives and fuses. The repacking of the charges would cost them a considerable delay. Tom estimated at least an hour.

Chris suddenly appeared out of the darkness and asked worriedly how much longer it would take. He indicated that Zervas was becoming more concerned by the minute and was constantly advocating a withdrawal as he was convinced that the andartes were running out of ammunition.

"Another ten minutes," Tom shouted back. "Give us a few minutes more, we're almost ready." Simultaneously he asked Hamson to get the andartes under cover.

"They scampered off like frightened rabbits," Denys recalled. "None of them had ever witnessed a demolition before and they had no idea how big the explosion would be."

Having satisfied himself that all was ready, Tom pulled out his whistle to give the agreed signal. He glanced at his watch. It was almost exactly two minutes to two on the morning of 26 November,

1942. Almost simultaneously the white Very light went up at the north side of the bridge indicating that the partisans had captured it. Three sharp bursts from Tom's whistle warned that the explosion would occur in two minutes.

Chris Woodhouse was back with Aris and Zervas when he heard Tom's treble whistle. They all knew that they only had minutes to take cover, but the tension was so great that they stood wordless, silently counting the seconds. Woodhouse noted the strain on Zervas' face as he stared down at the bridge.

Hamson, Tom, Arthur and Inder crouched behind a heap of rocks after lighting the fuses. Time stood still. Tom counted, "Two minutes — two and a half minutes — two minutes forty-five seconds — three minutes." Hamson peered nervously over the rocks. Three minutes and fifteen seconds had ticked away when suddenly the night was shattered by an almighty flash. The noise seemed to burst his ear drums. The highly explosive charge blew sky high. The deafening sound hung for a moment in the air and then reverberated back from all sides as echo followed echo, and two of the heavy bridge spans lifted about a metre into the air and then crashed into the gorge below. Suddenly all the lights in Lamia went out.

Relief flooded over the men. They could hear shouts of joy on all sides and they clasped each others' hands spontaneously and danced a little jig, a macabre dance over the bodies of men who had just been killed. "We sang triumphantly as we danced the klephtic ballad of the *Three Lads of Volos*," Woodhouse related later.

Myers had thrown himself behind a clump of earth when he heard Tom's last whistle. He watched as part of the bridge superstructure crashed into the valley below and immediately made his way down, intending to join Tom Barnes to check on the blasting and give instructions for the demolition of the second steel pier. But when he reached the Gorgopotamos river, he found a raging torrent. He shouted to Tom who could only have been about fifty metres away on the other side but he could not make himself heard. So he hurried back up again through the tall grass and the barbed wire to the end of the viaduct, where he got onto the top of it and followed the railing to the first stone pier from where he could clearly discern the two spans, complete with railway tracks that had been broken off. Below him, he could see Tom Barnes, so he again shouted above the roar of the river at the top of his voice, "How long to bring down the other steel pier?" Barnes answered that they needed another forty-five minutes at least.

At that moment there was a loud explosion from the north followed by heavy machine-gun fire. It sounded like Themie Marinos had blown up the track and was now engaged in fighting off enemy reinforcements approaching from Lamia. Myers shouted to Barnes to be as quick as they could with the next blast as they now had insufficient ammunition to hold off any fresh Italian force for long. Back on the hill he heard Chris Woodhouse's shout that Zervas had conceded another ten minutes but insisted that the green withdrawal signal then had to be fired.

"On no account will you allow that until you hear the next explosion from the bridge," Myers barked at Woodhouse.

"All right," Chris shouted back, "but for heaven's sake don't make it more than twenty minutes. I can't hold Zervas any longer!"

Themie Marinos and his party had meanwhile reached a point about one kilometre north of the bridge where the track curved slightly. The banks on either side were higher than the railway track. Themie posted Lambros with his band of andartes with one machine gun on the side of the track. After the massive explosion a locomotive with three carriages, travelling at walking pace, promptly clattered up. The train could be seen clearly because, incredibly, the second carriage was fully lit — an ideal target for the andartes with their machine gun.

Marinos had learnt to handle explosives in Egypt. He kept his head and lit the fuse at the very last minute before the locomotive arrived. Eerily, the lights still shone in the second coach and when the charge blew up just in front of the engine he could hear the Greek driver scream desperately, "The andartes are attacking and will kill us all!"

The track and the engine were lifted into the air but settled again and the train rolled on as the charge had been too small. Startled Italian soldiers jumped out of the lit compartments and clambered up the banks. "But just then the bursts of machine-gun fire from the andartes stopped, precisely when the men spilling out of the coaches would have been sitting ducks and facing certain death," recalled Themie Marinos. "I ran up to our machine gun and found it unmanned. The andartes had simply run away."

He found Lambros on the other side of the slope and dragged him to the machine gun. Meanwhile, the Italians had taken cover but did

92

not fire as they were not being shot at. Everyone seemed to be satisfied with the undeclared truce. The scared engine driver, however, had in the meantime succeeded in putting the train in reverse and was slowly returning to Lamia.

Fig. 18   *Inder Gill* (left) *and Themie Marinos. "They all just ran away, andartes and Italians"*

Colonel Myers contends that "heavy" casualties were inflicted by the andartes on the enemy in the railway coaches before they succeeded in withdrawing to cover behind the railway embankment.

The truth would seem closer to Marinos' description of events that "they all just ran away, andartes and Italians".

Barnes' initial impression when the bridge was blown up was that the steel pier was still standing. He soon realised, however, that the blast had lifted it high and crashed it back bent onto the foundation. At least two metres of steelwork had been blown away from each leg. While one of the bridge spans had dropped right down into the gorge, the other one was hanging down at a sharp angle. He had no words to express his pride in the outcome of his demolition work. Men were yelling, hugging each other and hoots of joy resounded everywhere. Edmonds heard Woodhouse shout, "Hurray! Hurray!" from above.

Fig. 19   *Chris Woodhouse: "We sang the Greek ballad of the 'Three Lads of Volos' in triumph"*

Contrary to Eddie's instructions to blow up the second bridge pier, Tom decided to attach the remaining explosives to the two fallen spans and make it impossible for these ever to be used again. He succeeded in attaching the remaining explosives to the twisted bridge spans within fifteen minutes whereupon he again pulled out his whistle and signalled the second blast which successfully transformed the pier and two spans into a useless distorted steel mesh.

A second later Woodhouse shot the green Very signal up into the air. From his cover, Myers decided it would be foolhardy to go on the bridge again to inspect the damage. An Italian sniper could be waiting to pick out a man standing in the moon light on the bridge. Instead, the colonel went over the terrain "counting the Italian dead" and was the last to leave the area of destruction and join the departing andartes.

The euphoric Supreme Commander Napoleon Zervas later wrote to his friends in Athens:

All the British looked on me with tears in their eyes and embraced me, and some kissed my hands. The colonel wept as he told me that I had rendered a colossal service both to himself and to Britain. And now they attribute their objective entirely to me. They regard the demolition as their first effort for our country. Today they promise me everything, absolutely everything, and they tell me that I shall receive immediate congratulations and medals from their Government. For myself, though, the action was child's play.

Giovanni

Eddie Myers followed his bodyguard through the thicket, picking up the pathway which they had slithered down a few hours before. Here, in front and behind him, he could see weary andartes climbing up the hill. Dawn was breaking but the clouds hung low. He noted with satisfaction that snow was beginning to fall and would soon cover their tracks and protect them from air attack.

The colonel was so exhausted that he eventually accepted a ride on a mule. Not having eaten since the afternoon of the previous day he found his emergency ration in his pocket, a piece of chocolate cake, which he munched hungrily.

Arthur Edmonds felt it was unbearably difficult to trudge up the mountain. A leaden fatigue overcame them all in an anticlimax after the tension of the operation.

Napoleon Zervas later described their laborious climb back to his friends in Athens:

*The major handicap was the snow, which was heavy and
continuous; I went on foot, without food and in up to a metre of snow,
with mud up to the waist; the hills up and down to the bridge were
beyond description. Eleven hours on the road. We climbed up Mount
Oiti and came down again, in addition to the exhausting march from
Arta, where I started, as far as Lamia, where I ended up. You
understand, my brothers, that I am speaking for my men, not for
myself. I am now used to it; my stomach has vanished. I have lost
thirty-two kilos, and I am fit. And the worst of it was that more than
half my men were completely without boots, and the rest almost
unshod. They had to use skins for shoes, and they wore coats
belonging to their ancestors.*

In the moonlight a group of ELAS-andartes could be seen shoving
a miserable-looking man in front of them. He was a small, unshaven
Italian wearing dark green trousers and a grey vest. He had no shoes
and no cap. Someone walking behind Edmonds called him a pig —
kerata — and the Greeks prodded him like a piece of cattle and
proudly showed their prize off to the British: "Look what we have
here!"

The Italian looked beseechingly at Denys Hamson. "Please, I am
wounded," he said.

"*Dove?* Where?" asked Hamson, who spoke Italian. Following up
this challenge eagerly, the Italian opened his shirt and showed him a
scratch rather than a wound which had probably been caused by a
ricochet splinter. Hamson asked him his name.

"I am called Giovanni, from Lecce, Southern Italy."

"Bull" Hamson commented years later. "He was a typical southern
Italian, swarthy and brutish." On instructions from Myers, he started
questioning him while the Greeks proudly showed the booty they had
taken off the Italian.

"He is a dog. He was throwing grenades at us to the last."

"Look, I wear his boots."

"And I his tunic," said another.

"And I his cap," said the fourth.

"Why the devil did you take this one prisoner?" Hamson asked. "It
was made perfectly clear that no prisoners were to be taken."

"Ah," they said, "the others were killed. We finished them off one
by one. But this one we thought we would keep, at least for a while,

for sport." They laughed and grinned. Neither Aris nor Zervas intervened, and less still Woodhouse or Myers.

While the Greeks prodded their prisoner up the hill, the others exchanged information on the operation. The four commanders were gratified to learn that not one of their men had been killed. Four andartes had been wounded.

They reached the sawmill in the late afternoon, where the faithful Niko Bey was already waiting. He danced with joy, hugged his friends effusively and served them a meal of roast mutton.

The sky was still overcast on the following morning, so there was no risk of being found by enemy aircraft. Zervas wanted to leave to return to his headquarters in Valtos. Aris wished to visit villages in the area, presumably to hold court over cattle thieves and to recruit young andartes. The British were in excellent mood. They had fulfilled their mission perfectly without injury or loss of life. A particularly important enemy supply route had been effectively cut for several weeks. War equipment from the Axis powers would pile up north of Lamia and Salonica and only reach the North African battle ground after a considerable delay. Tom reckoned that it would take up to two months to repair the bridge.

The next step was to inform Prometheus II in Athens of the good news by runner as their wireless was again not working. Everyone was thinking of the march to the West coast of Greece to rendezvous with the submarine which was to evacuate them to Egypt. Only Chris Woodhouse and Themie Marinos would be staying on as liaison officers with Zervas, as had been originally arranged back in Egypt.

Aris had no intention of following Myers' suggestion and join forces with Zervas to fight the enemy. Myers was too naïve and untrained in political matters to understand at this stage that the republican Zervas and the communist Aris were pursuing diametrically opposed aims. Myers also made a major error in not acceding to Aris' request likewise to be given a liaison officer. Myers lacked the decisiveness to act on the spot. Still today former andarte leaders of ELAS complain that they lost face when Myers did not grant them a British liaison officer while Chris accompanied Zervas. They felt they had been treated like second-class citizens.

However, on Zervas' recommendation, Myers graciously conceded to pay Aris three hundred gold sovereigns as consolation, "although they are Communists". He promised the two guerilla leaders that he was recommending them for British decorations. Zervas immediately refused, saying he would sooner have the next plane drop him a case of whisky, whilst Aris preferred to request a load of boots for his andartes. Myers promised to follow up these wishes.

It was time for farewell. Barba Niko cried when he left to return to his family. Without him, the British would not have fared anything like as well. Hamson gave him his dagger as a goodbye present. Dimo Karalivanos and his small group were now praised by Myers as "they had fought like lions". He asked Aris to refrain from punishing Karalivanos for his past conduct.

But one man stood apart from all this activity. Giovanni was still the butt of the andartes' "sport". He had been given some food but during the continued march he stumbled more than he walked, staying near to Hamson, the only person he could speak to. He had no shoes, he wore only a shirt, he was half frozen and knew he was almost certainly going to die. No one cared about him, and no one was likely to take his part.

Hamson warned him to keep going otherwise "they would give him short shrift". The andartes prodded, pushed and beat him forwards. When Myers realised that it was becoming more and more impossible for Giovanni to keep up with the andartes, he called Hamson over. Chris, Marinos and Aris discussed Giovanni's fate.

Marinos complained to Aris: "You cannot let the prisoner go on screaming. He is getting on our nerves. We can't stand the racket he is making. All his noise could give us away."

Aris seemed to have expected these remarks. He jumped up, stepped over to Myers and told Marinos to translate, "We have to get rid of him."

Myers refused wearily. Woodhouse sided with Myers. It could not be right to execute the prisoner. But Aris insisted. Myers protested, but rather half-heartedly.

Today, Marinos excuses his colonel. "The two day march tired Myers out to such an extent that he did not have the strength to oppose Aris. Zervas was not even informed."

But Marinos' statement does not correspond to the facts. Zervas wrote: *We have with us an Italian prisoner. He is hampering progress; he cannot go further. They ask permission to execute him. I don't want this to be done, but stern necessity imposes it.*

98

Fig. 20   *The Harling Team on the return march (left to right)*
           Back row: *Capt. Th. Marinos, Major D. Hamson,*
           Capt. N. Barker, Major C.M. Woodhouse, Lieut. I.
           Gill, Brig. E. Myers, Capt. J. Cooke, Capt. A.
           Edmonds, Capt. C. E. Barnes First Row: *Sergeants*
           L. Wilmot, M. Chittis, D. Philips

Woodhouse and Marinos did not voice any further protest either.
On the contrary, Woodhouse instructed Hamson, "Denys, get all the
information you can out of the Italian prisoner. The Greeks are going
to kill him. He is an encumbrance and a liability, I'm afraid, and
there's nothing we can do about it. It's just one of the rules of this
bloody kind of fighting."

Hamson nodded and went back to Giovanni who was lying curled
up in the snow. Aris followed with some andartes. Denys tried to
interrogate the Italian but he was "listless and stupid", as he later
wrote in describing the state of mind of a man who was living in fear

of death. Giovanni volunteered the name of his lieutenant and confirmed that there were about eighty men guarding the bridge but that "many simply ran away in the first few minutes of the attack".

The Briton could not prise much more out of the Italian who was chilled to the bone and shook with fear and cold. The stubble of his beard looked remarkably black on his wide chin. His eyes were sunk in. Hamson stared at him. "Giovanni, I'm afraid you're going to die. It is the law here. Do you want me to do something for you?"

Woodhouse, Myers and the others kept their distance, not wanting to have anything to do with the horrid business.

Aris' men had meanwhile started arguing about who should be the executioner. An older andarte suddenly pushed a baby-faced youth of sixteen forward who obviously did not want to be singled out.

A number of voices shouted, "Yes, let the youngster kill him. With the knife. He is unblooded yet. Let him do it."

Fig. 21   *Napoleon Zervas* (left) *and Eddie Meyers after their successful attack*

One man came forward and gave the boy a short sword, a curving twelve-inch blade with an old-fashioned handle. They all laughed coarsely and made ribald jokes at the boy who grinned bashfully back at them. Gingerly, he took the sword from its owner who roared at him, "Handle it like a man, don't be afraid of it. A fine boy you are. Let us see if you can cut throat as well as you can hedge!"

Giovanni was led out farther into the snow and stripped of his remaining clothes — vest, pants and trousers. Naked, he knelt in the snow, half bowed forward. The Greeks exhorted the boy, "Strike now, strike true, at one blow." The sword rose and fell. There was a groan, echoed by the Greeks with laughter. "Bungled, boy! Once again, and again."

Themie Marinos recalls that the youth stabbed him four times before Giovanni collapsed. "The inexperienced boy slaughtered him like a pig. Blood gurgled from his throat. His limbs jerked. He was dead."

The boy was relieved and ashamed. At that moment the laughter and the ribald jokes worried him more than the fact that he had just murdered a defenceless human being. Giovanni's clothes were shared out and his corpse was left lying in the snow in a puddle of blood.

When questioned today about these events, Myers and Woodhouse remember every detail of the demolition of the viaduct but have only a vague recollection of Giovanni's murder. Only Marinos speaks freely about it. Myers and Woodhouse push the killing onto Aris. "The Italian was killed by Aris. We had given strict orders not to take any prisoners," Woodhouse explains crossly. "Why didn't the Greeks follow instructions?"

Woodhouse justifies Giovanni's murder with the same kind of order as that notoriously issued by Hitler, which decreed that any person involved in a Commando operation was to be handed over to the Security Service "Sicherheitsdienst" (the SD). This meant certain death. But it seems hardly possible that the British in Greece already knew at the end of November 1942 about Hitler's order which he drew up on 18 October, 1942, in a fury over Commando operations:

> Members of so-called Commandos commit particularly brutal and cunning acts, and it appears that many of them are recruited from criminal circles in enemy countries. Instructions we have intercepted show that these Commandos are ordered to tie up and summarily kill defenceless prisoners as soon as they believe that the prisoners constitute an encumbrance or a hindrance to achieving their objectives.

From now on, all enemy Commandos in Europe or in Africa shall be massacred to the last man, even if they look like soldiers in uniform or demolition troops with or without weapons, and whether they are in battle or in flight. It makes no difference whether these men are in the act of being landed for action by ship or aircraft or parachute. Even if they surrender, no pardon shall be granted. A detailed report of each incident shall be sent to the OKW (Supreme command of the Wehrmacht) for publication in the Wehrmacht report. If police in countries occupied by us hand over Commandos, agents or saboteurs, these men must immediately be sent to the SD (Security Service). It is strictly forbidden to keep any of these people in military care or in prisoner of war camps, even as a temporary measure.

CHAPTER FIVE
Changing of the Guard

Generaloberst Alexander Löhr

Alexander Löhr, Austrian Senior General and Commander of the 12th Army Southeast, was in his office in Salonica early in the morning of 26 November, 1942, when he was informed by Transport Headquarters in Athens that the Gorgopotamos bridge had been blown up.

Löhr immediately recognised the wide-ranging implications of this report and decided that, although the Italians were nominally in charge of repairing this part of the vital rail link, he would instruct the German 117th Company of Rail Engineers (EBK) stationed in northern Greece to undertake the reconstruction. He personally drafted a telegram headed "SECRET COMMAND MESSAGE" which was received by the Wehrmacht High Command (OKW) at 12.00:

NIGHT 25/26.11. GORGOPOTAMOS BRIDGE SOUTH OF LIANOKLADI DESTROYED BY 200 MAN BAND WHO OVERCAME ITALIAN GUARDS AND ADDITIONAL REINFORCEMENTS. ONE PYLON BLOWN UP, TWO SPANS BROKEN OFF. MARCHING ORDERS SENT TO GERMAN 117TH COMPANY OF RAIL ENGINEERS, LOCATED PRESENTLY AT GOUMENISSA BRIDGE (60 KM NORTH OF SALONICA) TO REPAIR DAMAGE.

RECONSTRUCTION TO BE COMPLETED EARLIEST IN A WEEK.

TRANSSHIPMENT VIA STYLIS, CHALKIS.

I URGE YOU MAKE SERIOUS REPRESENTATIONS TO COMANDO SUPREMO TO ACHIEVE STRONGEST POSSIBLE SECURITY ALONG VITAL RAIL TRACK.

"Supergrecia", the Italian High Command in Greece, had simultaneously reported the rebel attack to their "Comando Supremo" in Rome: "Seven men killed, three wounded and two declared missing." General Geloso followed up on the next day reporting that "the German commander has decided to have the reconstruction carried out by the Germans". Geloso estimated that the repairs would take two months.

Even if all available ships were immediately deployed to carry the cargo from the ports of Stylis and Chalkis to Crete and Piraeus, the logistics of keeping supplies flowing to the North African troops would grow steadily worse. It was therefore a matter of urgency to reconstruct the bridge quickly and to ensure that further similar assaults should be foiled. The demolition of the bridge only confirmed the general opinion among the German occupying troops "that the Italians were useless and incapable of keeping law and order in the country".

Alexander Löhr, a small and dynamic man with a fuzzy, Hitler-style moustache, had already seen battle as an Austrian infantry officer in the First World War and was considered to be the founder of the Austrian Air Force. He participated in the campaigns in Poland and in the Balkans as Oberleutnant of the flying squads and he was engaged in fighting against the Soviet Union until the end of June 1942. His Headquarters were located in two elegant villas in Arsakli, which is today the little town of Panorama, with a fabulous view of the gulf of Salonica and the snow-clad Olympus behind.

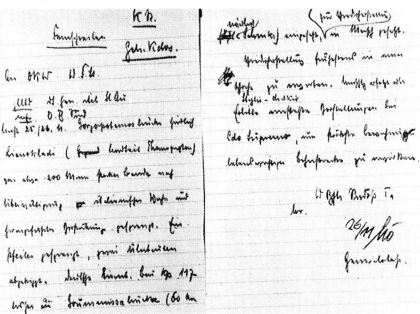

Fig. 22   *The draft of the telegram written in General Alexander Löhr's own hand, and sent to the OKW on 26 November, 1942, in which he reported the destruction of the Gorgopotamos bridge and ordered the 117th EBK into action.*

104

Löhr made a lasting impression on all who came into contact with him, among whom there was a certain Oberleutnant Waldheim. Another man, who was a captain from Salzburg, still today talks glowingly of him. "You won't find another general like him. He was always kindly to his inferiors and always did his best to limit human loss. He was never radical or extreme, he was just an agreeable person." And a lawyer in Vienna, who once was a replacement for Löhr's adjutant, goes so far as to say, "He was simply the most noble and refined man I have ever met." He described him as being infinitely kind, calm and considerate. If he did have a flaw, it was "in his acceptance of what was ordered from above".

Fig. 23   *The Senior General Alexander Löhr*

Having taken up his duties in south eastern Europe, the general was determined to define clearly the relationships between the German and Italian occupying powers. He used the destruction of the Gorgopotamos bridge as a pretext to take over guard duties of the single-track railway from the "spineless fratelli". Just three weeks earlier, on 2 November, 1942, the "Führer" had appointed him Commander of the Wehrmacht in the South East to create "clear and coherent command structures" and had also put him in charge of the 12th Army. Now he had to justify his promotion and the trust it implied.

Hitler's "Commando Order" did not go far enough for him. On 28 October, 1942, just one month before the destruction of the bridge, this "most noble and refined man" issued his addendum to his Führer's order, which shows the brutality, inhumanity and single-mindedness with which this man unquestioningly pursued the German war aims.

The Führer's order, with all its implications, applies to the whole area under the South East Army command. In the South East region, the war ended last year with the defeat of the Yugoslav and Greek armies. Whoever is now still found carrying a weapon shows that he intends secretly to continue the struggle to harm the occupying powers, destroy their supply bases and other essential military sites, to interrupt important lines of supply and to create disorder. This is, in effect, the same war strategy as that used in remote areas in the East by partisans and English or American saboteur commandos. This action is in flagrant contravention of the international Geneva convention. It follows that the perpetrators of this fight — no matter which faction they belong to — cannot be regarded as members of an armed power. Conclusions must be drawn accordingly. This affects not only any person found with a weapon, but equally anyone proved to be actively supporting this struggle. Voluntary surrender changes nothing. Every enemy group, in all circumstances, shall be shot to the last man. Only when every rebel knows that he has no chance of getting away with his life, can the army be expected to subdue insurrection. Success must be total. There are no half measures. Notions of "the heroism of a freedom-loving nation" etc. are misplaced. Most precious German blood is at stake here. I expect every officer to be personally involved in ensuring that this order is carried out by his troops without any exceptions and with brutal harshness. Any failure to do so will be investigated and I shall relentlessly call those responsible to account.

These written orders handed out to the Battalions are to be collected up by the Divisions and then destroyed. Compliance is to be reported to the Commander South East through the usual channels.

To save "most precious German blood," every rebel was to be put to death "with brutal harshness", regardless of whether he surrendered or was captured in battle. This was the basic philosophy in the fight against partisans and this self-same philosophy led to the other inhuman orders called "Atonement Operations" (Sühnemaßnahmen).

As early as in March 1942 the Commander of the South East Army had already issued the following directive concerning "the fight against rebels":

The overall situation demands that in this region law and order must prevail under all circumstances. Any measure may be taken to ensure success. Captured revolutionaries must be hanged or shot. The slightest criticism, opposition or violation of the law against carrying weapons shall immediately be dealt with by the most severe deterrent punishment. All troops must be trained to apply unconditional harshness. The more stringent and severe the atonement operations are, right from the beginning, the less they will need to be used later. No false sentimentality! It is better to eliminate fifty suspects than to lose a single German soldier. If ambushes, destruction, explosions or other sabotage acts have been carried out in the vicinity of villages strongly suspected of having given assistance to the rebels, these villages shall be destroyed. A transfer of the population to concentration camps may also be effective. Villages with communist administrations shall be destroyed and men taken as hostages. If it is not possible to apprehend or capture those participating in the rebellion, general reprisals may be made by, for instance, shooting the male inhabitants of the surrounding villages.

The ratio indicated was 1:100, meaning that a hundred Greeks were made to expiate the death of one German. One German wounded was worth fifty Greek deaths!

Löhr's request to his superiors in Berlin to "make very serious representations to the Comando Supremo in Rome" caused Mussolini's staff to demand an explanation from "Supergrecia" as to why the calamity had happened. A lame excuse was cabled by the Italian Commander, Captain Geloso, on 29 November, 1942:

FOR MONTHS, WE HAVE DONE OUR BEST TO INCREASE RAILROAD SECURITY, BUT STOCKS OF BARBED WIRE WERE TOO LOW TO ENABLE US TO POLICE THE SECTION ADEQUATELY.

However, Geloso seized the opportunity to demand three additional battalions and more barbed wire to "guarantee the protection of the railway line between Athens and Salonica" and he reported that orders had already been given to station further reserve units along all railways.

Thus, the British had not only successfully destroyed the Gorgopotamos viaduct but had also achieved their second aim of tying up additional Axis troops in Greece.

When communication lines between Lamia and Lianokladi were finally re-established, the true extent of the damage to the bridge could be assessed. The Germans now also estimated six weeks for reconstruction and the number of casualties were reported to Berlin: "Seven men were killed and five severely wounded in the blast." The report further stated that the explosives were of British origin, but British involvement was not inferred. Rather, "it was the work of well-trained Greek partisans".

Hitler now took charge personally of the matter. A memo of a meeting held on 30th November, 1942, states:

Revolts in the area occupied by the Italians have not subsided. Bands of guerillas have made surprise attacks and these bands have succeeded in putting one of the Thermopylai bridges out of operation for some time. Temporary repairs to the damaged bridge are being carried out by us. Reconstruction is estimated to take at least six weeks.

In addition, several reports were received in Berlin concerning enemy flights over central Greece, confirming that "in the area of Lamia, drops of weapons, equipment and parachutists to assist small revolutionary groups are suspected".

Alexander Löhr urged Hitler to act to stop things getting out of hand. The Germans needed unity with Mussolini to nip partisan action in Greece in the bud. Löhr had already determined that the 117th Company of Rail Engineers should repair the bridge damaged through Italian incompetence but, as a countermove, he demanded more authority in protecting the railways in Italian occupied territory.

A product of his time

Captain Christ, who was in charge of the 117th Company of Rail Engineers, received Löhr's direct order in the morning of 26 November 1942. His company was in service at Goumenissa on the Axios river north of Salonica, where they were repairing a damaged bridge and equipping it with heavy ice-breakers.

Just over a year earlier, in summer 1941, the Pioneer Battalion was stationed in France, but with the German invasion of the Balkans, this unit was drawn successively further south. Far from the actual battle ground, in "pacified" countries, the men built bridges, rail tracks, watch towers and security installations along the railway lines leading from northern Europe to the south-eastern area.

Senior Paymaster Hermann Meyer was responsible for provisions, clothes, pay and the general administration of 117th Company of Rail Engineers (EBK). He had turned thirty-nine on 7 September, 1942, so he was too old for the fighting troops but not too old for "active service for his fatherland". He was born in 1903 in Ülzen, a small town with a population of just 8,600, situated at the edge of the Lüneburg heath. It was known to travellers as the railway crossing for trains from Berlin and Stendal to Hanover and from Hamburg to the south.

His father was a brakeman and travelled continually on draughty trains up and down the country while his mother brought up young Hermann, and his half-sister Käthe, a child from her first marriage, inculcating them both with strict, protestant, Prussian values of patriotism. The aggressive war aims of the Kaiser in the "Great War" were supported without reservation by the family. His father could never understand, nor come to terms with, the sudden defeat in 1918. Those to blame for the calamity were the so-called "November criminals", and the lower middle class family Meyer was quick to decry them.

Hermann Meyer went to primary school in 1910 and gained entry to the high school in 1913 — an unusual step for the son of a working man — from which he graduated successfully to take up a place in autumn 1922 at the evangelical teacher training college in Ülzen. In September 1925 he completed his training as a State school teacher.

Like so many of his compatriots, the newly-qualified twenty-three-year-old had no chance of obtaining state employment as a teacher. The new Weimar Republic was hardly able to offer its young people good prospects for their future. He continued to live with his parents, depending for money partly on his father's wallet and partly on doing odd jobs on the rail track. In the autumn of 1925, like every able-bodied man in the Ilmenau Basin, he was hired to harvest the swede crop. Then in that winter of famine he was lucky to find employment with an auctioneer in a slaughter house.

In his spare time, the young man collected pictures of war heroes. He read the biographies of legendary war heroes such as Baron von Richthofens "Der rote Kampfflieger" and he admired the fortitude of the Baron's father, who had not only lost both sons in the "Great War" but who had then himself died a "heroic death". He venerated the "heroic courage" of the 12,000 young Germans ("our *élite*") who had thrown themselves into round after round of machine-gun fire near Langemark in the first year of the war. He dreamt of avenging the death of millions who had sacrificed their lives in vain.

His albums contain photos of Kaiser Wilhelm II ("I will lead you into glorious times") and of Ludendorff and Hindenburg, the two military dictators towards the end of the First World War. The young man devoured their books on German victories at Tannenberg and in the Masurian Lakeland and he idolised Ludendorff who, as early as 1923, was already hand in glove with Hitler in Munich. Not surprisingly, it was only a small step for young Hermann later to become an avid Hitler supporter.

As a trainee teacher, he felt that the Treaty of Versailles in 1919 and the ensuing unemployment and impoverishment of a large part of the German population, had caused a severe disruption in his life. Runaway inflation in 1923 led his lower middle class family in Ülzen to lose practically all its savings so that, despite being a graduate, he had no option but to hump pig carcasses for auction to make some kind of a living.

While preparing for his second teachers exam, he wrote:

In terms of teaching practice, the last three years were of no value. Their only value was to give me insight into the social poverty of the working class. You have to live in such poverty to truly understand it.

But then, finally, in 1929 he was hired from May to September as youth leader and sports teacher in the Lensterhof children's home in Cismar in Holstein.

A wonderful, hot summer followed the cold winter, so I started my new job in a happy frame of mind. I had about thirty youths in my care who at first caused me some difficulty. In the midst of so many little children, these older boys behaved like little lords and defied house rules. My predecessors, who had no teacher training, were much to blame for using a quite unsuitable, heavy-handed, military tone. I took a completely different approach and instead of being an instructor I tried to become their friend. I soon overcame their initial distrust. I let the boys choose their own leaders with reponsibility for peace and quiet and for putting suggestions to me. One of these leaders had been the worst kind of lout, but once he was given responsibility he showed a different side of himself. Soon, I was able to assert my own wishes...

The young people came from widely differing social backgrounds and thus held very contrasting political views which needed to be reconciled. In a small circle, in the evening, there were often debates on political matters, particularly when a group of final-year students from the Ruhr area joined us at the height of the summer. Tempers sometimes ran high, but again, calm, objective and friendly discussion led to a moderation of many of those differences.

The management of the children's home praised Meyer's "excellent pedagogical sensitivity" and his ability "to instill, in a non-authoritarian way, enthusiasm for a common goal among boys from widely differing backgrounds".

He then managed to find a job at the municipal high school for girls in Ülzen in 1930. Two years before Hitler came to power he wrote about a Jewish pupil:

K. tends to be an outsider and is often depressed. This is not helped by her very unfavourable family circumstances. Eight younger brothers and sisters have to be cared for. K. has to get up at five forty-five a.m. as she has a long walk to school. She does not take part in classes on religion because her father belongs to another religious community. At first, this non-participation was treated disparagingly by her class-mates. I immediately sought to remedy the matter as soon as I heard of it and explained to the children that their behaviour was bitterly unjust.

The educationalist Gaudig was Meyer's ideal. He was inspired to teach according to his progressive philosophy. Meyer's many enthusiastic statements in favour of Gaudig's ideas for "free intellectual school work" in every-day teaching run like a red ribbon through his short pedagogical career.

According to Gaudig, teaching should aim in equal measure to impart knowledge and to build character according to the individual's talents. Not only should reasoning and memory be developed but also mind and spirit as a whole. The teacher should free the intellect of his pupils and not seek their dependence. Gaudig's most important goal was to try to humanise instruction, to democratise education and to abolish authoritarian, "misguided schooling".

Hermann read Sigmund Freud with intense interest. He attended study groups in Ülzen to further his education. A lecture on psycho-analysis inspired him to discuss Wexberg's and Freud's theories about the psychology of the individual.

Apart from trying to give himself a solid foundation as a teacher in the nineteen twenties and job hunting in his profession, he spent time travelling and hiking. In the summer holidays when he was only sixteen or seventeen, he had been on extended hiking trips in the surrounding countryside, to the Harz mountains, the Weser highlands and the chalk cliffs in Rügen. He had joined the "Wandervögel" in 1921, a national hiking club, and had ventured further afield in 1925 and 1926 to Frankfurt, Heidelberg and the Rhine, visiting its historic German fortresses and castles and the Blücher memorial in Kaub.

Later, while at teacher training college, he travelled with friends to Königssee, to the Salzkammergut in Austria, to Switzerland and Northern Italy, taking in the Duomo in Milan, Genova and its harbour and old streets, Pisa and the leaning tower, and from there on to Venice, that romantic city of waterways. His next long tour in summer 1930 took him via Strasbourg to the French Riviera and thence on to Barcelona, Seville, Cordoba and Granada, down to Morocco. He returned via Paris and Verdun, visiting the battlefields where so many of his heroes had lost their lives.

He carefully stuck his travel photos in albums with captions painstakingly written in white ink. A postcard of the Gallery of Mirrors in Versailles bearing the English text "Table on which was signed the Peace Treaty 28th June, 1919," is revealingly translated using the Nazi terminology which called the peace treaty the "Treaty of Shame".

Thus, Hermann Meyer, the well travelled patriot and candidate teacher, began to turn to the burgeoning national socialism movement.

112

For years he had sought in vain to work in his profession. Even when in 1931 he passed his second teaching exam with good results, he could not fulfil his wish to have a class of his own. All he could do was to stand in for colleagues around Ülzen and from time to time, give a few lessons at the Lyzeum, the girls' high school.

After another replacement intermezzo at Hanstedt and Bennemühlen, he finally obtained a full-time teaching job which became vacant on 1 November 1933 in Mellendorf, a little village north of Hanover, surrounded by woods, heath and moors. Employment as a state school teacher went hand in hand with membership in the NSDAP (German national socialist labour party). He became member number 1562737.

Was it opportunism? Perhaps. But it was more likely to have been the consequence of a typical, German evolvement in those times. When the German national party nominated the reactionary Ersatz-Kaiser Hindenburg in 1925, Meyer and most other students, teachers and professors of the twenties voted for him, because their leanings were anti-republican, still pro-monarchic and above all nationalistic and revanchist. And when the economic crisis of 1929 engulfed the world and led to six million German unemployed by 1932, he too put his cross against the NSDAP on the voting slip with the slogan "Hitler, our last hope".

His bookcase was now full of national socialist works. Besides the obligatory copy of Hitler's *Mein Kampf*, there was also Houston Stewart Chamberlain's *The foundations of the 19th century*. This notorious anti-Semite was born an Englishman but lived in Vienna for twenty years, as did Hitler. He considered that the dual monarchy of Vienna was being racially swamped by the influx of too many foreigners. Just one sentence out of this bible of racism:

An easy talent, often a strange beauty that the French call 'un charme troublant' is frequently an attribute of bastards; in cities, such as Vienna, where many diverse populations converge, this can be observed every day; but at the same time there is a strange instability, a low resistance and a lack of character, in short, a moral inferiority about these people.

Chamberlain regarded the Germanic race to be "standing at the edge of a racial abyss, involved in a silent battle of life and death". We know that Hitler and his followers adopted this "philosophy" and spoke of "Eastern rubbish" and considered that Jews were "the most depraved filthy trash that should be smashed up".

Hermann Meyer, teacher of religious education, who still in 1931 had vehemently defended the rights of a Jewish girl and who had passionately wanted to teach according to the progressive, liberal methods of Gaudig, was now contemplating whether to leave the protestant Lutheran church. Without doubt, he was expected to adopt a new creed which was formulated by the Reichsleiter Dr Robert Ley in a letter issued to all schools on 10 February, 1937:

Adolf Hitler! We render homage to you alone! On this day, we wish to repeat our oath: On this earth we believe in Adolf Hitler alone. We believe that national socialism is the only faith leading to salvation for our nation. We believe that there is a God in heaven who created us, guides us, leads us and visibly blesses us. And we believe that this great God has sent us Adolf Hitler so that Germany may provide a foundation for ever and ever.

As a new party member, he was frequently scrutinised by their controllers. Time and again, as a State employee, he had to repeat his oath in many variations and fill in forms confirming that he was indeed of "Arian origin". The Nazis were adamant that the educators of "Germany's youth and future" should comply with the ideals of their movement and they repeatedly made him sign that "none of my parents nor grand parents have ever belonged to the Jewish religion".

In June 1934 he had to fill in this questionnaire:

- *Were you ever a member of the Communist Party?*   No

- *Were you ever a member of the SPD, the Reichsbanner, The Republican Union of Teachers, or of the Rote Falken etc?*   No

- *Do you come from non-Arian, in particular Jewish, parents or grand parents?*   No

And then again in August 1934:

I swear: I shall be faithful and obedient to the Führer of the German Reich and nation, I shall abide by the laws and conscientiously fulfil my official duties, so help me God.

In August 1935:

I herewith declare under oath, that I have not belonged to any Free Masons Lodge in the postwar period, and that since 1933 I belong to the NSDAP.

In 1937 Hermann met Erika Glüh, a twenty-seven-year-old kindergarten teacher who was herself the daughter of a teacher. She was likewise a national socialist although not a party member "because the membership fee was too high". They both attended the Nuremberg party conference ("that unforgettable experience we had together") and married later that same year.

Hermann was appointed district head of the national socialist welfare association (NSV) and head of the local cultural branch. He became particularly involved with the plight of the Germans fleeing the Sudetenland. The youth hostel in Mellendorf was requisitioned by the NSV and made ready to house their German "national comrades". Erika organised collections for the destitute refugees: "We started by borrowing hand-drawn carts from the farmers, then we put our own winter coats in them and went from door to door, asking people to do the same."

Erika and a friend once went to Hanover where Hitler was to address an assembly. She remembers that as soon as she saw him, she jumped spontaneously onto a table and screamed "Heil!" as though possessed. "Those were mad times. We lived intensively and believed unswervingly that we were building a better Germany. To us, Hitler was our true saviour."

In January 1939 Helga was born. The last few peaceful months slipped by. But after Poland had been invaded in September 1939 and France and Britain refused Hitler's peace terms, Hermann told his wife soon after his thirty-sixth birthday that he had volunteered for military service. "When the new Germany is brought into existence, how will I be able to explain to my children that I stood aside instead of offering my help?" He took this decision freely and with military conciseness he informed the education board in Burgdorf that he was relinquishing his teaching duties. "I have been called up for service in the army. Heil Hitler. Hermann Meyer. Teacher."

He was first sent to Bad Nenndorf, Hanover and Celle for training as an inspector of war administration. His superiors wished to keep him in the academy in Hanover because of his "excellent teaching qualities", but he opted for service in the occupied territories.

Instead of his back pack, sleeping bag and walking boots, he now set off on his travels in a smart uniform and polished army boots. In June 1941 he took a train via Aix-la-Chapelle and Eupen ("What a rich and fertile land retrieved by the Führer") and Paris to his station in fashionable Biarritz.

He continued to be an enthusiastic sightseer. Having purchased a new camera, he snapped beautiful landscape pictures, elegant villas and parks in Biarritz and again and again he photographed the Atlantic surf breaking on the golden beaches. His albums look very much like the souvenirs of his pre-war travels.

From Biarritz he was sent to Nevers on the Loire and then on to Amiens on the Somme in April 1942. Following the Balkan campaign, his company was moved to Serbia and Goumenissa, Greece. It was here that General Löhr's order was received on 26 November 1942, commanding the unit of railway builders to move immediately to repair the rail viaduct south of Lianokladi.

The next morning Hermann Meyer, Captain Christ and their comrades stood on the slope above the Gorgopotamos bridge to assess and photograph the damage. They all agreed. The partisans had done a first-class job. It would take several weeks to reconstruct the viaduct.

Fig. 24   *Hermann Meyer noted on the back of this photo: "Gorgopotamos bridge with a view of the Thermopylai"*

116

Reconstruction

The 117th Company of Rail Engineers (EBK) consisted of about two hundred and sixty men, almost all of whom were former railway employees or officials. Captain Christ was aided by six officers, a doctor and a paymaster. As a civilian, Christ had been a senior inspector of the state railway, his six lieutenants had been inspectors and the thirty-five non-commissioned officers foremen. It was exceptional that Hermann Meyer, the senior paymaster, was not drawn from the railway too.

The company was capable of amazing mobility. With years of training and experience, it could pack up and move on without delay. Thus, on 26 November, 1942, when Löhr's order was received, they departed immediately, leaving only a small rearguard in Goumenissa to follow on.

Originally, the unit was set up to build new railway lines but as the war ground on the engineers found themselves almost exclusively reconstructing sabotaged bridges. The equipment required was transported in their thirty railway carriages.

Fig. 25   *Hermann Meyer* (left) *in the rail trolley on the way to the work site*

These carriages lodged not only the two hundred and sixty men, but also afforded separate compartments for the officers. Benches had been torn out of several carriages so as to install offices, a kitchen, a sick bay and a tool wagon with a fully equipped workshop. Even motor vehicles, rail trolleys and the former state railway's five-ton trucks were carried along.

Since many soldiers stationed in Greece had contracted malaria, the windows of the living quarters had been covered with wire mesh against mosquitoes. A metre-high cement wall had been built in the dormitory carriages since they had been attacked by partisans in Yugoslavia. However, their main fear would not have been of an attack, as they were travelling to Lianokladi in an almost unassailable armoured train, but rather of scorpions and snakes and the dreaded malaria at their work site.

Fig. 26   *"Voluntary" child helpers with their German foreman*

The company was divided into three platoons, each run by an officer who was a qualified civil engineer or mechanical engineer in civilian life. Each platoon leader headed about sixty men who were again sub-divided into three groups, each led by a non-commissioned officer. Although the men were trained to use arms, to fire machine guns and throw hand grenades, the army command was careful not to involve this highly specialised unit in battle. An infantry company could be "topped up with new people", but the rail engineers were not easily replaced. They were regarded more as "an armed building firm" rather than as soldiers.

It was impossible to shunt their construction train right up to the Gorgopotamos bridge — the terrain was too steep — so they laid a track in the fields between Lianokladi and Lamia and parked there. Tents and barracks for Greek "voluntary helpers", whom they had picked up after the fall of Salonica lodged there. These were mostly Greek ex-soldiers who earned a pittance in this way.

Captain Christ decided to build an auxiliary bridge to start with. Two wooden trusses were to be hoisted to replace the steel columns which had been blown up. A request for bridge supports had been made to OKH (Army High Command) and these were being manufactured by the Peine steel works in Lower Saxony. But where was the timber to come from for the two wooden trusses? The German Commander in Lamia referred Captain Christ to the sawmill in Makrakomi which was run under the authority of the Luftwaffenbaubeschaffungsamt (Air Force building material procurement office) in Athens. As Major Baron Friedrich von Falkenhausen was recuperating from his gun shot wound in the military hospital in Lamia, Konrad Lehmkuhl was contacted, who was now in charge of the farm estate and Hotel Asklepios in Platistomo Spa.

In the next few weeks Hermann Meyer dealt mainly with Konrad Lehmkuhl and the two civilian administrators Franz Meier and Erwin Kaufmann. He went to and fro between Platistomo and Lianokladi organising the timber deliveries and the provisions for the two hundred and sixty men and their Greek "voluntary helpers".

Franz Meier, in particular, was responsible for the punctual delivery of the logs. The 117th EBK wrote him a letter of thanks which he kept for use as a recommendation for later employment:

Your assistance to the company in its task of reconstructing the Gorgopotamos bridge after its damage by bandits is very much appreciated. Your help and input contributed considerably to the fact that the bridge was repaired and re-opened to traffic ten days before time.

As Tom Barnes had surmised, it was necessary to completely destroy the 24-metre high steel pylon to which one of the two demolished bridge spans was still attached. Only when the twisted remains had been cleared away could work start on erecting the wooden trusses. The lower part of the trusses was set on concrete foundations and clad in steel plates. Then each log was screwed to the next to form a web, thus guaranteeing absolute strength and carrying power.

They worked in two shifts right around the clock. The work site was a hive of activity night and day. At times, there were more than five hundred Germans and Greeks at work.

Fig. 27   *"On 6th January, 1943, the Gorgopotamos bridge was again open to traffic"*

Meanwhile, the problems caused by supplies piling up north of Lianokladi were difficult if not impossible to solve. A small proportion of vital military equipment could be carried overland by mules through the Thermopylai Pass, but most had to be off-loaded at the ports of Chalkis and Stylis and these were not equipped to deal with the colossal task. The German Admiralty was so overstretched by the new situation that the Admiral responsible for the Aegean made the desperate suggestion that a "rail track should be laid, bypassing Thermopylai". This was a preposterous suggestion which would have cost the earth. The Commander for the South-east wrote back: *"Not possible at present. Suggestion being considered."* But he never reverted back as the developments were to shatter all long range plans.

Meanwhile, work was progressing rapidly, and already on 5 January, 1943, the Chief of the 117th EBK was able to report that the provisional repair to the bridge was completed and that it was open again for use. General Geloso proudly cabled his Comando Supremo in Rome on the same day:

Today we carried out satisfactory tests on the bridge over the Gorgopotamos which was blown up by sabotage on 26 November.

And on 6 January, 1943, the Comandante del Settore di Lamia, General Di Giudice, reported in his daily log, that "regular train traffic over the Gorgopotamos bridge" was functioning again.

The first freight trains were driven over the viaduct. The stock pile of equipment slowly dispersed. But the 117th EBK still had a task to fulfil. A marshalling yard at Lianokladi and several small bridges over the Sperchios were to be built and protection for the Gorgopotamos bridge needed to be strengthened. Although a part of the company was sent off to Katharini in the north to build defence installations, the rest of the company including Hermann Meyer and its Commander stayed provisionally in Lianokladi.

Hotel Asklepios

Reconstruction work on the bridge continued even at Christmas time. But whenever they had any free time, the men from the 117th EBK enjoyed a few care-free hours at the farm hotel Asklepios. Hermann Meyer turned up regularly at Platistomo Spa as he was in charge of the supplies of timber and foodstuff for his company and during the absence of the major, Baron von Falkenhausen, he soon became a welcome guest for the ten men to talk to in their remote outpost. The Greek farm hands also took to him, the "Uffzier" who would "look after us if the Italian soldiers robbed us".

There was a large open fire in the hotel where they would rest, cracking nuts and chatting. They talked about home, their family, the war. They complained about the huge inflation in Greece, about their inadequate pay, which was handed out in drachmas and was therefore without much value. In the evenings they would sit at the table together and listen to the news at eight and the "Lily Marlene" broadcast from Belgrade. The men felt safe — only the younger ones sometimes worried that they might be sent to the eastern front. They had their work, which they did as well as they could. The war seemed remote and they were glad to be doing their military service in this "pacified country". Although they repeatedly heard of trouble with bands of partisans, they were happy to leave the matter in the hands of the "fratelli", who were, after all, responsible for law and order in the district!

Franz Meier, who was one of the civilians employed in Platistomo spa, could hardly believe his luck in being sent to such a heavenly, beautiful place. The scattered farm and hotel buildings lay in the midst of cedar groves, eucalyptus trees, colourful meadows and pine forests. The drive up from the village wound along under wonderful old plane trees. In the summer, oleander, bougainvillaea, wisteria and various lush types of broom were in flower. Slightly below the hotel the spa lay partly hidden by high grasses and reeds and old olive trees. Not far away on the church tower and castle of Kastri, storks had built their nests and would fly to the marshy area between the spa and the Sperchios river to fish.

Franz Meier wrote to his mother and his young wife Berta on 18 October, 1942:

I live well here. We are secluded from the world. No newspapers and the radio only comes on for the army report and news between eight and eleven p.m. That is good for one's nerves. This hotel where we are housed used to be a convalescent home run by the Greek state. I have an office on the ground floor and a room on the first floor. Excellent bed, good wardrobe, a marble-topped table and two rattan chairs, a dressing table and carpet and even running water.

From my window I have a marvellous view of the nearby mountains. They are about two to three thousand metres high and already have snow on their peaks. It looks wonderful at sunset and sunrise. We are in central Greece, in Makrakomi. On the map 39 degrees of longitude and 22.2 degrees of latitude. You can have someone look it up on the map for you, dear Berta. We are west of Lamia, about forty kilometres away from the railway. So far, things are not at all bad, and I am so glad to be shot of that horrid smelly place, Athens. I hated it there. Poverty and famine are rife in the city. There are 30,000 destitute children. They walk around in filth and ragged clothes. It is so terribly sad to see. Last winter about 20,000 people died of hunger. They simply lay down in the streets and the bodies were driven away. This year some arrangements are being made for soup kitchens and other distributions. But it still looks very bad. When you see mothers with starving children you really feel upset, and then you think with pride and love of our beloved home country where everything works so well. If only the people here would realise what our Führer has achieved. Our children — even the poorest — are protected from such a terrible fate. People just lie in the streets at night or in their wooden carts. I am so glad to get away and was so lucky to have been chosen to come here...

You must not worry about me although we are in a very lonely spot, but God will not abandon us Germans, and Providence has always been with our Führer and we hope that it will continue to do so...

Franz Meier's letter does not mention that the former first-class hotel Asklepios was initially thoroughly looted and plundered by the first wave of Italian and German troops. Froso, the grand-daughter of Haralambopoulos who was then the manager, complains that when the hotel was requisitioned, "four chests with my mother's dowry, consisting of silver cutlery, precious china, vases, paintings, musical instruments and Persian carpets were carted off north."

Nevertheless, Grandfather Haralambopoulos made a deal with Baron von Falkenhausen and his group. He preferred the "correct" Germans to the leftist partisans. He was sixty-three, an aristocratic type, rich and had a reputation as a ladies' man. "He was the first Greek to own a Rolls Royce, and as well as various houses and apartments in Lamia and Athens, he also owned a lot of land in the Sperchios valley which was farmed from the Asklepios estate", his granddaughter Froso says proudly. "He loved and admired Trude Radwein who had already left her husband and come to Platistomo to him in the nineteen thirties." Since then "Madame", as she was called respectfully by the employees, had become the manageress of the hotel and estate. Everyone, whether German or Greek, loved the "good soul", who was ever helpful and always available to solve their problems or translate for them.

Trude Radwein and Gottfried Schwarzenbacher, both Austrians, became deeply bonded together, partly as a result of the trauma of being taken prisoner with von Falkenhausen and not knowing for four days whether their lives were to be spared. The lance-corporal was thirty-five years old, a married man from Graz, and he found himself in love with the striking, dark blonde, grey-eyed Viennese. Her former lover Haralambopoulos did not seem at all tortured by jealousy. On the contrary, he offered them the use of his flat in Athens for a weekend in February 1943 and warned Trude "to stay in Athens as partisan activities around Platistomo were making it dangerous". But she could not leave her compatriots and her darling Friedl so she returned with him to Hotel Asklepios.

The ten hotel "guests" were all older. Some of them had been wounded at the beginning of the war and had therefore been sent to a "safe" posting.

Fig. 28 (left) *The Viennese Gertrud Radwein with her cat in front of Stavros Haralambopoulos' house in Athens*

Fig. 29 (right) *Gottfried "Friedl" Schwarzenbacher*

The two youngest men were single. These were twenty-three-year-old Corporal Martin Winter and twenty-six-year-old Lance-Corporal Albert Fritzenwanger. Lance-Corporal Karl Gross (thirty-three) and Erwin Kaufmann (thirty-eight), a civilian employee, were not married either. All the others were married men with families at home. These were: Georg Lehmkuhl from Oldenburg, deputising for the wounded major, Franz Meier from Regensburg, Karl Hässler from Burg near Magdeburg, August Pruchhorst from Klein Mentau, Gottfried Schwarzenbacher from Graz and Herbert Fritsche from Berlin.

This was a close-knit little community. It had few outside influences apart from the evening news and the soldiers' newspaper "Wacht im Osten", printed in Salonica. They were almost all party members, no one doubted the final victory and they believed blindly in the leadership of their country; every man was convinced that he was making a historic contribution to the creation of a new Europe and a better future.

Fig. 30   (left) *Albert Fritzenwanger*
Fig. 31   (right) *August Pruchhorst*

Franz Meier expresses this view convincingly to his family in his Christmas letter of 1942:

Our Führer will no doubt again spend Christmas at the front with his soldiers. One of our comrades here personally experienced more than once that the Führer would suddenly turn up in the middle of the night to visit his troops close to the eastern front and then drive several hundred kilometres on the following day to visit his soldiers somewhere else. He said that many comrades cried for joy when the Führer showed up so close to the front lines. Well, I believe that the Führer is a shining example to us all, and that what he manages to achieve has no parallel, and in comparison, our small sacrifice of being separated from our loved ones at home counts for nothing at all and is hardly worth mentioning. We do our duty and help in our small way to reach the final victory. Next year will hopefully bring us peace and until then we shall be steadfast, come what may. We must not falter but always believe in our beloved Adolf, who has always done things right until now and will continue to do what is best for his people...

Fig. 32   *Martin Winter*

126

Changing of the Guard

For the German military command, it was incomprehensible that their Italian allies had been so negligent in protecting the Gorgopotamos bridge, particularly because only a few hours before the attack on 25 November, 1942, an Italian train transporting troops and ammunition had hit some buffers close to the Gorgopotamos river. The resulting explosion demolished six carriages. Fifteen men were killed and another fifteen were seriously wounded. The news transmitter "Anna" reported the incident to the OKW on 26 November, 1942, and assumed it to be sabotage. Nevertheless, railway security was not stepped up instantly.

Already at the beginning of November 1942 the occupying powers had heard of parachute jumps and drops by the British. Franz Meier's letter dated 4 November, 1942, to his wife Berta would seem to allude to John Cook, Themie Marinos and their two comrades who had parachuted almost over the Italian barracks in Karpenissi on that last night of full moon in October 1942.

About seventy kilometres away from here, there is a band called "freedom fighters". They only fight against the Italians, and they are always getting killed over there. They don't do anything to the Germans. They seem to be afraid of us. And they will not come down to us here because they hide themselves away in the mountains. During the last full moon there were also a few English planes which flew over that area. They threw down ammunition, arms and medicines attached to parachutes. The last time, the Italians found twelve parachutes with various goods including a radio transmitter and many weapons. Four spies parachuted down, one was caught but the others got away. A big clean up is now taking place and the Italians have taken sixty prisoners. Hopefully, they will shoot them immediately. Nothing is likely to happen to us here, at least that is what we all hope because we are really quite far away and on flat land, and they do not venture out of the mountains.

Of course, it is not true that the Italians captured one of the parachutists. But, if even the relatively unimportant civilian Franz Meier, secluded in Platistomo Spa, was informed about the existence of four parachutist "spies", then it was indeed grave negligence on the part of the Italian leadership to disregard this widespread information and not to take the necessary measures to strengthen security around the bridge, particularly as "all the plans, photos and blue prints of the three bridges were packed in the lost containers", according to Themie Marinos. And Chris Woodhouse tells with a grin of the two Greek brothers (who today run the Hotel Gorgopotamos below the bridge), whose grandmother ordered them to move their sheep herds up into the mountains on the evening of 25 November, 1942, "because the bridge is going to be blown up during the night by the andartes". In spite of all the efforts made by Myers and Woodhouse to ensure secrecy, everyone in Roumeli seemed to know of Operation Harling — except the Italians.

These examples only serve to underline a naïve and foolhardy failure to read the signals indicating a significant and imminent attack. Little wonder that the Germans were enraged and bitter when the news hit the telegraph network. Those "incompetent" Italians could no longer be left in charge of protecting the railway; there was full agreement between Löhr and his staff on this point and pressure was accordingly exerted on the OKW.

From the point of view of the Germans, it was also high time to take drastic steps against the rebels because the success of this attack would no doubt influence the Greeks. Young men immediately joined the andartes to play their part in the fight for freedom. The underground news bulletins in Athens reported the event, the BBC included it in the world news. Songs were composed to honour the heroes who had successfully destroyed such an important target. Other andarte groups were encouraged to attack German and Italian sites of strategic military importance. Hardly one week after the Gorgopotamos operation, Berlin was informed of an attack on the Goumenissa bridge where the 117th EBK had just completed its work.

During the night of 3 and 4 December Greek bands attacked the important Goumenissa bridge. Their action was thwarted by the prompt arrival of the train with reinforcements from Salonica. Some losses: one soldier killed, one wounded. Four suspect Greeks, among them one officer captured. Will be shot after questioning.

The dispute began to get more brutal. Death sentences were already decided before suspects were even questioned.

While Löhr took personal and direct responsibility for rail protection in his territory after the fiasco of the Gorgopotamos bridge, Hitler approached Mussolini on the subject. A secret German/Italian commission met in Lamia on 6 December, 1942, to negotiate on future guard duties. General Geloso, Senior Commander of the Italian 11th Army, "was not in principle opposed to line security being taken over by the German Commander Southeast".

General Geloso had already reported on 4 December, 1942, that he had spoken to Löhr about guarding the line:

General Löhr has suggested that German troops should be in charge of surveillance. I agree with this suggestion that guard duties should be under a single authority.

Geloso was empowered, by return of post, to negotiate along these lines. "Italian and German troops who have so far been guarding this railway line will in future take their orders from a special German staff under the control of Army High Command 12."

The subject was likewise discussed on 7 December with the "Führer" in Germany:

Attacks on railway bridges. Lessons should be learnt and we should be prepared for all eventualities. The Chief points out that as a priority those targets should be protected which the enemy can destroy without much preparation. The destruction of bridges in Greece resulted in an order to discuss line security with the Italian AOK 11. Accordingly, the senior commander of the 11th Army, General Geloso, was consulted. It was decided that we should guard the northern part and the Italians the southern part of track in Greece. We shall employ protective tactics, i.e. discourage enemy approach. As in Serbia, we shall use watch towers and draw up a tactical plan for rail security. How much this may affect Italian sovereignty is not foreseeable at present. We must create an information and spy network, with agents working in the Italian area too. Top mobility for guards, use of trolley-cars on the rail track, fast patrols. Also take hostages. Anti-aircraft guns. Two auxiliary trains from Serbia. One battalion of gunners (Landesschützenbatallion) from Serbia to take over guarding the Thermopylai block and one regiment of gunners from Athens (Landesschützenregiment).

Consequently, Löhr issued his orders on that same day:

With a widening of hostilities in general within the Mediterranean area, the enemy will attempt, by stirring up and encouraging revolutionary movements, to create the conditions for a new front line in Europe. More than ever, we must do our utmost to prevent this. Every incipient move to form bands must be strangled at birth and every enemy group discovered must be smashed and wiped out. If we fail to do this by the spring, then we shall not have fulfilled the task given us by the Führer.

However, before the Italian leadership was prepared to hand over to the Germans, they wanted revenge for their dead and for the destruction of the bridge. The relevant order had already been issued by Supergrecia on 26 November, 1942. Now it was time to act on it. At dawn on 10 December, 1942, fourteen Greek men were marched out of the prison in Lamia to the bottom of the bridge and shot in the presence of a large number of Italian soldiers. There was no trial. Most of the men came from the neighbouring village of Ypati. General Rossi of the III Army Corps has signatory responsibility. His message to Supergrecia on 10 December, 1942, says curtly:

This morning at seven a.m., fourteen Greeks shot as a reprisal. List enclosed. General Rossi.

Fig. 33   *10 December 1942. Fourteen Greek hostages were shot below the Gorgopotamos bridge as a reprisal.*

General Geloso also commanded on 2 December, 1942, that all Greek officers should be arrested and sent to Italy, reasoning:

All these officers were formerly freed by Hitler's order, on condition that they would not concern themselves with political matters etc. They have not kept their word.

Geloso suggested to his "brothers in arms" to proceed to "arrest all Greek officers who are still free in German territory. Arrests are to take place simultaneously".

When this wave of arrests swept through Lamia, the fate of courageous Costas Pistolis was sealed. "Civilians who approach the railway after dusk are to be shot", read Geloso's further ruling. The brave Greek who had served the British so well in scouting out the rail installations was murdered in Lamia prison in December 1942.

However, these acts of revenge hardly seemed to daunt the Greek underground movement. The High Command Southeast was informed by its political section on 11 December, 1942, that "following the destruction of the Gorgopotamos bridge, propaganda leaflets have proliferated, walls and roads are being painted with slogans and a new communist association ELAS — National Popular Liberation Army — has been discovered". They made a mistake, however, when they dubbed the anti-communist Napoleon Zervas as being the Chief of ELAS.

The republican "Strategos" was praised by the BBC as the hero of the Gorgopotamos operation while the ELAS Kapetanios Aris Velougiotis was given no mention by the British propaganda. It was not even known that his *nom de guerre* was Velougiotis. Supergrecia received this curious message on 30 December, 1942, that:

a band of unknown size under a Major Aris and his Lieutenant Velougiotis was at the village of Paleokatuna on 26 December, 1942. They beheaded two Greeks who opposed the movement.

The takeover of responsibility for the railway guard duties by the German troops as mentioned by Hitler on 7 December, 1942, was agreed in writing on the following day in Lamia between Generalmajor Hermann and Il Comandante Superiore of the 11th Italian Army, General Brigata:

Recognising the importance of the section of the line between Salonica and Athens, and as a result of the increasing activities of bands, the High Command of the Wehrmacht and the Comando Supremo have agreed to strengthen security by extending certain sites into military bases and by bringing in German troops.

In each case, a commanding officer shall be appointed to be in charge of extension and protection. Close co-operation shall be ensured through an Italian liaison officer.

Surveillance of the section, from Salonica up to and including Gravia station, was put into the hands of the German troops, while the Italians controlled only the line from Gravia to Athens.

An intervention unit would be held in constant reserve ("Eingreifreserve") in case of further sabotage acts in the German sector, i.e. a motorised company strengthened with heavy weaponry stationed in Lamia and Lianokladi. Supergrecia likewise transferred two reserve units to Lamia.

Löhr had rules drawn up on 12 December, 1942, "governing the operation and extension of line security" and also demanded an "enquiry into the demolition of the Gorgopotamos bridge".

1. *Sequence of events:*

On 25 November, 1942, towards 24.00, an attack by a band of about two to three hundred men took place on the Gorgopotamos bridge which is two hundred and eleven metres long and spans a rugged valley south of Lamia. It was a three-pronged approach made down from the mountain. The two flanks occupied undetected the outcrops overlooking the railway and the bridge on both sides. From there they directed their fire concentrically at the Italian held bridgeheads where there were immediately losses in the sleeping quarters which were not bulletproof. The two groups on the flanks also cut off the track to the right and left of the bridge with mines and by blowing them up, so that it was impossible to bring reinforcements up by rail...

The explosives were of English origin and carefully prepared. The hand of an experienced explosives expert can be detected in the method of execution; assistant staff was well trained but without personal experience. The explosive charges were made ready for use by attaching them to pieces of wood with prepared cord or magnetic clips.

132

2. *Deductions:*

a) *Guard troops must be strategically deployed so as to prevent any enemy approach to a possible target*

b) *Targets must be converted into military bases and given adequate security and provisions. Crews must have bulletproof quarters.*

c) *Guard troops assigned to the railways must also join with well-armed scout patrols to comb through areas surrounding the tracks to sniff out the bandits from their hide-outs...*

d) *Include the population to serve short term to patrol and protect sections of the track. If mines explode, tracks are disrupted, etc., the last civilian patrol shall be made responsible, possibly shot. In the event of an attack the villages in the neighbourhood of the attack shall be punished. Demand hostages! Imprison strangers to the area!*

e) *Large-scale and ruthless inclusion of the civilian population in the construction work and conversion of positions.*

This process of escalation outlined in the above "deductions" culminated in Hitler's order (Führerbefehl) "concerning combatting bands" signed by Keitel on 16 December, 1942.

The Führer has ordered:

1) *The enemy collects fanatic, communist-trained combatants in bands who ruthlessly commit any act of violence. More than ever before the question is to be or not to be. This combat now has no relevance to a soldier's chivalry or the agreements of the Geneva convention.*

If we do not face these bands in the East as well as in the Balkans with the utmost ferocity, we will not have the means in the near future to rid ourselves of this plague.

The troop is therefore empowered and obliged to take any steps without any limitations, even against women and children, as long as they lead to success.

To show consideration of any kind is a crime against the German people and the soldiers at the front who have to bear the consequences of attacks by bands and can have no sympathy for them nor their accomplices.

2. *No German deployed to combat the bands may be brought to account by disciplinary action or court martial for his behaviour in combatting the bands and their accomplices.*

The commanders of troops deployed to combat bands are responsible urgently to inform all officers of units under their control about this order; they are to ensure that their legal advisors are cognisant of this order and that no sentences are passed contravening this order...

Thus, within the space of only two weeks, an escalation of hostilities was conducted in "pacified" Greece, such that the Greeks' determination to fight back was destined to be significantly fired up, and now definitely directed against the German occupier. The destruction of the Gorgopotamos bridge was not only a rallying cry for the Greek resistance movement; it also brought the German occupation and its command into the area of Roumeli which was difficult terrain to control. The new staff in charge of rail security under Löhr's direct command arrived in Lamia from Larissa on 17 December, 1942.

Forgotten now were the days of German and Greek co-existence. Forgotten were the days when the Greeks met the Germans with respect and saw the Italians as the real enemy. Forgotten too were those little vignettes, when for instance the Greek workmen loaded logs onto German trucks and sang patriotic, partisan songs, much to the delight of the German soldiers accompanying them on the drive through Lamia.

CHAPTER SIX
S.O.E. makes a U-turn

The drastic measures taking place in Roumeli did not directly affect the British nor the andartes who had been participating in Operation Harling. Myers decided to march with Zervas to his headquarters at Megalohari in Valtos. In all the villages they passed they were greeted with enthusiasm and hospitality. Most villagers in the western part of Roumeli did not know Zervas as this area was under Aris Velougiotis' control. The political organisation, EAM, was, however, well established and Myers was impressed that most youths belonged to ELAS. Obviously, Aris had done a good job of recruiting.

Upon arriving in these villages, Zervas would deliver a speech, relating in florid style the success of the Gorgopotamos operation. With each successive speech, the number of Italians they fought and the heroism of the partisans tended to increase. Chris Woodhouse would then address the amazed villagers on behalf of the British. The national anthem was sung, bells were rung and the villagers were then expected to share their meagre provisions and simple lodgings with their heroes.

In Mavrolithari Myers sent a messenger to Athens to inform Cairo that they would expect the submarine to pick them up between 22 and 23 December, 1942, on the west coast, approximately eight kilometres south of Parga. Woodhouse and Marinos were staying on in Greece and were now joined by Wilmot and Phillips too, who still hoped to repair their radio transmitters.

The rest of the British and New Zealanders set off on the long arduous trek to the coast. It was 11 December, 1942. Hamson was sceptical as to whether it was feasible to reach the far side of Greece in less than two weeks. He was sufficiently experienced to know that ten kilometres on the map could easily be a day's march over Greek terrain. And who knew whether the submarine would turn up in some God-forsaken bay? In fact, he had taken a bet with Themie Marinos that the submarine would not materialise.

Hamson and Myers did not get on well with each other. Hamson criticised most of Myers' decisions and thought it was too stupid being

made to swear not to breathe a word to anyone, including Zervas, of
their plan to be evacuated from the coast. Again, they marched
relentlessly through deserted country, arid and treeless valleys. There
was nothing but stones and scree and no protection from possible
Italian scout parties. Avoiding the roads they took to the endless mule
tracks in the hills, marching up to sixteen hours a day, to then seek
refuge in the evening in some one-eyed hamlet where the villagers
were so poor that they had little or no food to share with the British. If
it seemed that the peasants were reluctant rather than unable to share,
Hamson was usually the one brutal enough to force them to produce
some food. They ate anything they could lay hands on but hunger
gnawed at them. Only the prospect of evacuation by submarine
spurred them on.

Finally, on 20 December, 1942, they glimpsed the Adriatic in the
distance across the Akheron delta. Under cover of dusk, they slipped
down the final slope, stole past a village nestling by the river and hid
in thick shrubbery on a cliff over the sea. From here it was at most
two hours on foot to the bay where the submarine should be waiting.
They spent the day getting ever more edgy and worried. No one could
quite believe that suddenly a submarine would emerge from the
unruffled turquoise sea and carry them off. They dozed, stared at the
infinite blue sea or spoke of food, dreaming of milk-shakes, bacon and
eggs, rum, real bread and butter and other such delicacies that might
be served up on the submarine.

In the evening they set up their accumulator connected to a torch,
flashing their signals out to sea every two minutes in spite of the risk
of discovery by the Italians occupying a nearby village. Edmonds
recalled that during his shift, "I had the distinct impression that a
submarine was rising out of the sea, but it was a hallucination. Before
dawn I packed up and returned to our hide-out in the reeds and shrubs.
There were, after all, four more nights to hope on."

Two nights went by. Anxiety mounted. Had Cairo ever received
their message? Would the submarine actually find the right cove? The
situation was becoming desperate. What else was there to do but to
stare out to sea with hunger twisting their bellies and depression
gripping their souls? Far off, they could make out the island of Paxos,
and when the light was favourable they could see the southern tip of
Corfu. Twice they spied enemy vessels close to shore and once they

saw a sea-plane that "was probably on a submarine hunt". It had, of course, to be "their" submarine!

Having only eaten dry maize bread and drunk brackish water over the last few days, on Christmas Eve Myers handed out a generous sum to his guide to buy some food from the neighbouring villages. The man returned with a bowl of pork stew. He had been able to "convince" some peasants to slaughter a pig and to cook it. The meat was terribly fatty but the men devoured it greedily, and suffered from stomach ache and diarrhoea the next day.

Eddie Myers felt ill, bleak and exhausted. He had never imagined such hunger pangs. For three days now, they had been hiding out in damp reeds and scrub. If the submarine did not turn up, there was no alternative but to march back to Valtos. Their provisions were exhausted, and the villagers could not feed them for love or money, as they were starving themselves.

But before they left for their final night's vigil, a Greek stranger was brought to them. He was a runner from Chris Woodhouse. Myers' heart sank as he unfolded the well-worn piece of paper, recognising Chris' handwriting:

Last night I was dropped a new wireless set. I have also received a message from Cairo saying that they will not be sending a submarine for you. Fresh instructions are being sent to you by safe hand by one, Captain Bill Jordan, who is due to be dropped within the next two days.

For a moment Myers thought he might faint. He could not believe that Commander-in-Chief Alexander would go back on his word. He struggled to keep himself in control.

His men clamoured to hear the news but became extremely dejected and bitter when they did. Hamson, in particular, railed against this U-turn by Keble and the S.O.E leadership. They had carried out their task and now neither the Navy, the Air Force, nor the Army was able or prepared to evacuate them. Myers had great difficulty in trying to motivate his disappointed men to tackle the arduous return trek. But they had no alternative. He felt weak and sick. Hamson was a constant irritation because he found fault with every decision and tried to get the others on his side. Even today, Myers remembers Hamson with bitterness and, making an expressive gesture, he growls, "I almost had him shot on the way back."

The animosity between the two men probably had a deeper cause. "Hamson never disguised his anti-Semitism," Marinos said. "He enjoyed making remarks about Myers' Jewish looks and hooked nose."

The men were tired in body and soul. They had gone to war full of idealism to fight those "Macaronis, Huns and Jew-murderers", but when it came down to the nitty gritty, Hamson, at least, let his anti-Semitic feelings rip. And none of the other men condemned his racist remarks. On the contrary, some supported his attacks on Myers, which bordered on mutiny.

Finally, the dejected men packed up their belongings and left on their return journey. Night after night, they struggled on, up and down steep and stony goat tracks until they reached Megalohari on 3 January, 1943.

Themie Marinos and Bill Jordan, who had arrived only two nights before, gave their comrades a cheerful welcome and handed their totally exhausted colonel a bulky envelope with new instructions from Cairo.

The excuse given by S.O.E. for failing to keep the rendezvous on the west coast of Greece was simple: a submarine was lost only a few days previously in a similar operation and S.O.E. could not risk losing another one.

But the real reason for this U-turn was different. Cairo had been informed by Prometheus II that former Greek Army officers had formed a resistance group in Athens, wanting to organise and direct all partisan movements in the mountains. Keble thought he would put Myers and his men in charge of instructing and supporting this group. Cairo suggested that Woodhouse should move to Athens as liaison officer to Myers, who would be regarded as the senior commander of the BMM (British Military Mission) in Greece to co-ordinate the activities of all the andarte bands. S.O.E. was particularly keen that Myers should conduct a multitude of sabotage acts to tie up as many German and Italian troops in Greece as possible and to deflect attention from the planned landing of Allied troops in Sicily.

Myers informed his men of these new instructions on 4 January, 1943. Main targets for sabotage were nickel and chromium mines, the railroad tracks and any other vital industry connected with the German war effort. No one, however, except John Cook and Nat Barker, volunteered to stay on in Greece. All the other members of the Harling team insisted that the original promise to evacuate them as soon as possible should be honoured. "We volunteered to come initially, we have completed our mission, and now we consider it only our due that this promise is kept." But Keble could not be persuaded, and insisted that his new instructions had to be carried out.

Myers now had to communicate this message of doom to Woodhouse who was travelling with Zervas. Soon after the Gorgopotamos operation, Aris and his band of andartes had crossed the Acheloos river into Zervas' territory. Aris had heard that a British aircraft had dropped materials and weapons and he wanted to claim his share. Chris succeeded in bringing about a meeting between the two leaders on neutral ground to work out a common goal, but he had to realise that "they agreed not to fight each other, but they disagreed on practically every other point".

This was not surprising, given that so far Aris and his ELAS movement had not benefited at all from the association. They had provided the lion's share of manpower for the Gorgopotamos operation, but the BBC and the British press had only given praise to Zervas! Aris and the KKE leadership in Athens felt they had been duped. But in the absence of a royalist resistance movement, the British foreign ministry had decided to back the Republican Zervas and his EDES group instead.

Myers estimated that at the end of 1942, EDES numbered about five hundred partisans while Aris in Roumeli had about four hundred ELAS-andartes under his command. Thanks, however, to the active EAM/ELAS organisation in the villages it seemed likely that in a few weeks it would easily outnumber EDES. He guessed that in March, 1943, Aris would already have more than 4,000 guerillas under his command in Roumeli. Given this situation and the S.O.E. instructions, Myers dispatched his deputy to Athens to make contact with the former Greek officers.

So, Chris Woodhouse, with his usual verve, set off on his mission on 12 January, 1943. Myers was, however, laid low by a fever which developed into a serious case of pneumonia. Fortunately, radio contact was now re-established with Cairo so that medicines could be dropped on one of the next nights which probably saved him from death.

Even from his sick bed, the colonel tried repeatedly to make Cairo evacuate his officers. Keble refused until Myers finally caved in and proposed that if they stayed in Greece they should all become British Liaison Officers (BLOs) "in order to instruct the andartes in guerilla warfare, to pass on their requests for arms and equipment and to co-ordinate the resulting drops".

Keble agreed at once, in particular because in the meantime Myers had been visited by a former Greek General, Stephanos Sarafis, who intended to establish a guerilla unit in the Pindus mountains and was asking Zervas and Myers for support. With hindsight, Myers later wrote that when he first met the General he "should have paid more attention to his rather weak chin and evasive, watery blue eyes than to his aquiline features, military moustache and straight, short-cropped, dark but slightly greying hair, which gave him superficially quite a determined appearance". At the time, however, he had a good impression of the man, who after all was a general, not a communist and apparently a "good soldier".

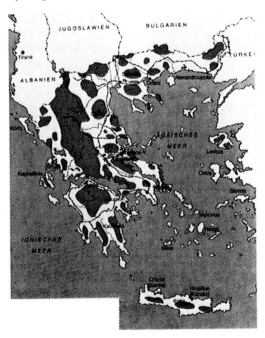

Fig. 34   Map of the areas freed by 1943. Many parts of Greece had already been withdrawn from German influence by 1943

Stefanos Sarafis had indeed good credentials. He had been military attaché in the Greek Embassy in Paris before the war. He had only recently left Athens to co-operate with his friend, Major Kostopoulos, to set up a resistance organisation in the Pindus Mountains. Sharing Zervas' opinion that EAM/ELAS was ultimately run by the communist party, he discussed with Myers his idea to create a "National Bands" movement which would unify all the resistance groups under one non-political umbrella.

Discussions between Sarafis and Myers included Zervas and a certain Psarros. It was agreed among them that three central Resistance Movements should be established: one under Zervas' command in the Epirus, the second under Sarafis in Thessaly and the third under Psarros in Roumeli. The British would arrange for each to receive immediate drops of three hundred rifles, machine guns, ammunition, clothes and equipment. These three organisations would receive their orders from "Middle East Headquarters" through Myers. In effect, Myers would thus become senior commander in Greece.

How they were to make Aris and ELAS accept that Psarros was to run their resistance movement in Roumeli they preferred not to address at the moment. This was rather short-sighted if not naïve, as no EAM/ELAS leader or member had any intention of being controlled by Myers or any of his underlings.

However, Myers was struck by the idea of forming a unified National Bands movement and he was excited to have found a trained and disciplined military officer to discuss plans with. They parted with Sarafis promising to suggest a suitable terrain for parachuting the first supplies.

As a next step, Myers decided to divide the mountains into four areas for his officers to carry out their training and liaison duties. Tom Barnes was allotted Epirus, Arthur Edmonds was responsible for Roumeli where he would relieve Nat Barker, whom Myers sent on to North Thessaly with Hamson. Sheppard and Nick Hammond, who had only recently parachuted in to Greece, were put in charge of the area of Olympus and Macedonia. Chris Woodhouse, promoted to Myers' official deputy, was replaced by Themie Marinos as liaison officer with Zervas.

Thus, in the shortest time, the colonel had effectively set up an organisation to support the guerilla groups. Cairo confirmed to Myers, who harboured some doubts, that they would supply equipment to

Greece by making regular Liberator sorties: eight in March; sixteen in April and increasing thereafter to an average of twenty-four per month by late autumn. This would indeed change the situation as compared to October 1942, when the British first set eyes on the andartes then armed with nineteenth century weaponry!

Chris returned from his mission on 20 February, 1943. He had been extremely lucky to extricate himself from the Gestapo because, while he was in Athens, Prometheus II was uncovered by German radio surveillance and the brave radio operator was killed. In desperation, Woodhouse had to turn to the EAM Communists for help to hide and to return to the mountains. Although Chris had succeeded in meeting up with former Greek officers, he found that they had little conception of guerilla life nor any inclination to take charge of the resistance movements in the mountains. It soon became apparent to him that they had little more than hot air to offer the freedom movement and he was amazed to find that he was far better informed about Greek realities than the Greek Officers Corps.

On the same day that Prometheus II was attacked, he had talks with the leaders of the Communist Party. Yioryios Siantos, the Secretary General of the KKE, and Andreas Tzimas, a member of the Central Committee, proposed that the young workman Hatzipanayiotou, who had given himself the *nom de guerre* of Kapetan Thomá, should protect Chris and escort him back to the mountains. Woodhouse acquiesced only reluctantly because, being an anti-communist, he was loath to be beholden to them.

The Captured General

Denys Hamson was actually relieved to find himself given a task, although he continued to remind Myers repeatedly of his promise to evacuate him from Greece. Eddie had made him a BLO with Major Vlakhos who called himself a royalist and was forming a band of resistance fighters with the help of twelve young officers south of the Pindus mountains.

General Sarafis and his officer Kostopoulos, however, had been surprised and disarmed in a night attack by a group of ELAS-andartes. This shocking news came through on 11 March, 1943, just as Hamson set off, and led Vlakos and his officers to conclude that ELAS had become so predominant that it was mortally dangerous to continue trying to establish a royalist guerilla movement.

Vlakhos informed his BLO Hamson in black and white terms of his position. "Mr Captain, you'd better go back to your H.Q. and tell the colonel what has happened. I am sorry, but we have no job for you here. I have received a message from the ELAS leadership, that my life is at stake if we do not stop our so-called separatist activities."

Vlakhos withdrew that same evening to the mountains and gave up the idea of creating his own resistance organisation.

Earlier, in Thessaly, Kostopoulos, General Sarafis' deputy, had successfully recruited some fifty former ELAS-followers to his republican cause. The ELAS leadership was very worried by this development and considered it to be treason, for it jeopardised their long term aim to take over political power in the country at the end of the war. ELAS was also still smarting from the fact that, after the destruction of the Gorgopotamos bridge, one of their officers, Major Kostorizos, and twenty-five andartes had "deserted" to Zervas.

The ELAS leadership decided to act. Kapetan Koziakas, in charge of western Thessaly, sent Kostopoulos a note, suggesting a meeting to thrash out common plans to attack the enemy. Sarafis, Kostorizos and Kostopoulos agreed and took a hundred and thirty andartes to meet Koziakas. On their way there, they heard that Major Andonopoulos, a friend of Kostopoulos, had been taken prisoner by ELAS-andartes, but they continued their march "in order to negotiate Andonopoulos' release", as the general explained at a later stage.

Instead of releasing Andonopoulos, however, they were taken by surprise in their sleep by ELAS units and, without a single shot being fired, they were disarmed and captured. With their hands tied behind their back, they were led into the unknown. General Sarafis, who had been foolish enough to be so easily ambushed, frankly admitted to his guards that he was impressed by ELAS discipline and requested them, humiliated as he was, to bring him to the responsible EAM/ELAS leaders to "sort out everything".

Although he was handcuffed, Sarafis praised the leadership and discipline of the ELAS movement, whilst his comrades Andonopoulos and Kostorizos feared for their lives. Being former ELAS fighters, they knew the rules: desertion, even to another guerilla organisation, meant certain death.

Guarded by hundreds of ELAS soldiers under the leadership of Kapetan Pericles, the andartes stayed in the fields close to Platistomo Spa, without paying any heed to the Germans in Hotel Asklepios, much less fearing them as there was no sign of protection by Italian units.

In fact, already as early as November 1942, Konrad Lehmkuhl, deputising for the wounded Major von Falkenhausen, had noted in his report:

In the villages surrounding Makrakomi there are often armed and uniformed bands of five to six hundred men. In the long run, we will not be able to continue to work the plant at Makrakomi unless a stronger military force is provided to protect it.

The Italian army has cleared out of the entire area west of Lamia, so that apart from the small service post at Platistomo, there is no military unit within a distance of forty kilometres.

Thus, Kapetan Pericles with his andartes and prominent prisoners walked unchallenged on the Lamia–Karpenissi road, marched through Makrakomi and on to Sperhias where he was awaited by the young andarte leader, Tasos Lefterias.

Lefterias, born in Crete, was twenty-three years old when he experienced the German invasion. Marked by that traumatic experience, he passionately hated the occupying power and became one of the most brutal and ruthless protagonists of the Greek freedom fight. As a member of the illegal KKE, he was smuggled out of Crete and then operated in Athens under Siantos' control.

In the beginning of February 1943, Tasos Lefterias was informed that Aris had had fourteen so-called collaborators shot in the market square at Gardiki and that he was terrorising the peasants. In the name of the Central Committee, Lefterias was sent into the mountains to inform Aris that he was sacked. The KKE considered Aris to be too autocratic, fearing to lose its supporters in the mountains. This news stung Aris to tears and he felt that his only chance of redeeming himself was to present his case personally to the Central Committee in Athens.

BLO Nat Barker described the drama he witnessed at Gardiki during his stay with Aris. Eight men and six women had been charged with having betrayed hidden arms to the Italians. They were taken to the square where the villagers had been gathered. Aris demanded that they confess their guilt. The accused all declared they were innocent so Aris and his men brought their whips into action and, one by one, beat them into a state of semi-consciousness when they either confessed or collapsed and were shot. One man, who was tougher than the rest, stood up to his scourging and continued to defy Aris. But the Kapetanios was equal to the occasion; he drew his knife, made incisions on the man's back and poured boiling olive oil over them. The man died soon after.

With the men disposed of, Aris turned his attention to the women. They were taken to the school, stripped of their clothing and beaten. Three of them died from the beating — the remainder were taken outside and shot. The fourteen bodies were left by one of the paths on the outskirts of the village and orders were given that they were to be left unburied for three days so that all could see the punishment ELAS meted out to traitors.

Only after the villagers' murder did Barker ask Aris if it was not possible that these people were innocent since confessions extracted by such methods could hardly be taken as proof. "I'd rather kill ten innocent people than allow one traitor to escape," Aris replied, according to Nat Barker.

Having been humbled by being sacked by Lefterias, Aris now prepared to travel to Athens, disguised as a priest. He shaved his mighty, bushy andarte-beard and even had his gold tooth extracted to avoid recognition at any of the control posts. He knew that some members of the Central Committee had very little respect for him, because during the Metaxas dictatorship he had put expediency before principle and blithely renounced communism and the Party in order to be released from prison. Nevertheless, he was determined to use every defence and guile to continue to be the "Archekapetanios" in Roumeli. Indeed, who would take his place? Nobody, including Lefterias, had his intimate knowledge of the mountains, nobody had his capacity to inspire followers, nobody commanded respect like he did. But would he succeed in convincing those men in Athens who had no knowledge of guerilla warfare in the mountains?

He managed to slip into the capital unchallenged by controls. Siantos and Andreas Tzimas, both Central Committee members, reproached him gravely for killing people without proof of guilt.

Fig. 35   *Aris Velougiotis: "I'd rather kill ten innocent people than allow one traitor to escape"*

Tzimas, in particular, argued that the native population should be convinced, not beaten, into political adherence, and that instead the struggle against the occupying powers should be stepped up.

Aris was clever in describing how different life in the mountains was from any analysis of conditions conducted in the capital and he pointed out that it was thanks to him that EAM and ELAS had received a great deal of publicity after the Gorgopotamos operation and that their numbers had consequently swelled. He reminded Siantos and Tzimas of the thousands of young people who had joined up and been equipped in his fiefdom of Roumeli. Even the most remote villages had formed a local EAM group which was attracting new recruits. Indeed, towards the end of February, the youth organisation EPON, a subsidiary of EAM, had been introduced into every village and was producing an unequalled supply of future ELAS soldiers.

He admitted that there had been mistakes, but he insisted that the population was solidly behind the movement. "By the end of March 1943, there will be over five thousand armed andartes, although the British support is negligible in comparison to that given to the much smaller EDES movement under Zervas," the andartes leader underlined.

Aris Velougiotis played his cards well. He succeeded in convincing the Central Committee to leave him in charge of military command at the Roumeli headquarters and continue to function as the "Archekapetanios" of all andartes. He did have to accept, however, that Andreas Tzimas would accompany him to the mountains and be his equal as the Politikos.

This arrangement suited Siantos extremely well. Aris had been taken down a peg and was now forced to deal with the KKE through Tzimas. At the same time, Siantos, the old fox, had thus ensured that the young and extraordinarily bright Tzimas had been ousted from a position where he might have threatened Siantos within the Central Committee. Away from the power centre, Tzimas would have to at least prove himself in his new role.

Although Andreas Tzimas was only thirty-three years of age, he had white hair, having been imprisoned by the Metaxas regime for being a communist member of parliament. But he was freed after the German invasion because he declared himself to be a Yugoslav Macedonian. According to Woodhouse, "he was the most capable man and the clearest thinker of his Party". Myers considered that "he was the only one you could have a logical, unemotional discussion with and who understood contradictory positions. He was always sensitive, diplomatic and courteous and disliked showing the extent of his powers". He was one of the few truly well-educated men in the EAM; he spoke French and German and could quote Faust fluently.

No news of the capture of General Sarafis and his officers had as yet reached the Central Committee when the Politikos Tzimas and the re-instated Kapetanios Aris set off on 9 March, 1943, to their mountain headquarters in Kolokythia. Meanwhile, Tasos Lefterias, deputising for Aris, met up with the ELAS prisoners in Gardiki.

Sarafis attempted to pacify Lefterias, and, in an impassioned speech, declared that his only goal was to create an andarte army strong enough to free Greece.

"That is truthfully the only reason why I went to the mountains," he explained. And he flattered Lefterias: "In the last few weeks I discovered that such an andarte army does already exist under ELAS command."

Thus, already in that first encounter, the republican, "the man with a rather weak chin and evasive blue eyes", told Lefterias, who had power over his life at that moment, that he would gladly join ELAS. Lefterias immediately understood the advantage of gaining such a well-known and respected high-ranking officer to their cause. He promised in return to let him live. But there was no further discussion about the fate of Kostorizos and his comrades who had abandoned ELAS because of its communist tendency. Sarafis dropped them; Lefterias should do what he wanted with them. The main thing was that his own life had been saved!

While the general enjoyed his new-found freedom, Lefterias invited the newly-assigned liaison officer, Arthur Edmonds, to sit in judgement over the "deserters".

"Lefterias was a tall, athletically-built man about twenty-six years of age," Edmonds describes him. "He had pleasant features and judging by the size of his beard he had been in the mountains for about two months. He wore a khaki jacket and riding breeches without puttees, and an old pair of boots which usually had their laces trailing untidily on the ground. He carried the usual knife in his belt and bandoliers across his chest. As he walked along with us he carried his rifle across his shoulders with his arms spread across it. He had a casual manner but would suddenly become terrier-like when angered."

"What was your pre-war occupation?" Edmonds asked, trying to make conversation with the Cretan.

"A sort of student," Lefterias answered unwillingly. His mind was on more important things as they walked to Sperhias to hold court martial over the ELAS deserters. He was intent on giving them an "orderly" trial and not to fall upon his compatriots in an uncontrolled fashion like Aris.

The trial was to take place in the Sperhias theatre and it was already full of andartes and curious villagers when they arrived. The New Zealander had to push through the crowd to approach the stage, where the "judges" and the "accused" were sitting opposite each other. Andartes, with semi-automatic machine guns, stood threateningly behind the prisoners. The court consisted of three people, chaired by Tasos Lefterias who had studied law for two semesters. He called on various "witnesses" and asked for their statements.

"They took no oath as apparently the fact that they were members of EAM or ELAS was proof of their word," Edmonds reports. One of the witnesses was Kapetan Pericles, who had guarded Sarafis from the mountains to Sperhias. This gross, self-important man who had arrogantly assumed the name of the most outstanding statesman of ancient Athens, stood in the middle of the stage with legs wide apart, hands on hips, and a whip dangling from his right wrist; he looked at the audience instead of the judges and accused Kostorizos of repeatedly claiming that the EAM was an organisation infiltrated by communists.

"I don't know what this had to do with the charge of desertion but it appeared to me that the audience would be well convinced that this political commissar with the black whip on his wrist didn't like people to say that EAM was a communist organisation," Edmonds says, shaking his head.

How did "judge" Tasos Lefterias react to Pericles' accusation? He was, after all, a member of the communist party himself. The whole trial was farcical but it was also deadly serious. Arthur Edmonds, who had since been promoted to major in the allied army, did not for one moment consider intervening to stop this show trial or at least to point out that the accusations were untenable. On the contrary, he was an interested spectator. "I knew from the start that it looked bad for the

149

accused. Other witnesses stated that they knew of the accuseds'
misdeeds which varied from drunkenness to attempted rape. Then
Tasos Lefterias took the floor and gave a speech on the evils of drink.
Pericles, now seated at the back of the stage at the end of a row of
chairs, apparently was not affected by the speech as he and another
andarte thought it amusing to hide their heads from the audience — by
pulling a curtain before them — in order to take frequent pulls at a
bottle of 'chippero'."

Kapetan Pericles' real name is George Houljaras. Nowadays, he
lives near Lamia. When asked about the "trial" and his malicious
statements which led to death sentences for the seven accused, he says
he cannot remember anything anymore. He still looks as gross as
when Edmonds met him. He still adulates Aris and indulges with
relish in reminiscences of the heroic deeds of ELAS, but he cannot
remember anything about those murders in Sperhias. "Don't you
regret that act?" I ask curiously.

Fig. 36   (left) *Tasos Lefterias as a young soldier at the
Albanian Front*
(right) *Arthur Edmonds as BLO to ELAS in the
mountains of Roumeli*

In disbelief, Houljaras looks at me with his squinting eyes. "I regret nothing, nothing at all!" he snarls and abruptly ends the conversation by storming out of the room.

"Tasos' speech was not really evidence against the accused," Edmonds noted, "but it went to show the large audience that the accused, if condemned to death, were sentenced by an organisation which championed virtue and moderation."

"Kostorizos and his officers were tortured, spat upon, and humiliated and, after a Mickey Mouse trial under Lefterias, they were shot like dogs," rants Dimitrios Dimitriou, alias Nikiphoros, bitterly. "Kostorizos was a brave flying officer during the war in Albania against the Italians, and later, in the Gorgopotamos operation, he had distinguished himself again. One of his officers who was also accused, and whose *nom de guerre* was Nikitaras, had a wonderful voice. He had been a student at the theological seminary in Constantinople where he had singing lessons. He was known in all the villages, where people loved to come to listen to him. When he was condemned to death, he begged Lefterias, 'I came to Greece to fight the enemy and I don't want to die by a Greek bullet. Give me the chance to fight the enemy, upright and free, and let an enemy bullet kill me.' But Lefterias had no vision and he did not have the generosity of spirit to be merciful."

Tied together by their wrists, the seven men were led out to face their execution squad. "The first volley missed Kostorizos," Edmonds remembers. "He looked striking and dignified with his long beard and R.H.A.F. uniform and cap.

"'Come on boys — you've forgotten me,' he called, standing with a dying companion handcuffed to each wrist.

"The next volley ended his life."

Stephanos Sarafis did not waste any sympathetic words over the murder of his comrades in his memoirs. All he wrote about his stay in Sperhias was:

Flight-Sergeant Kostorizos and three of his guerillas who were accused of desertion and attempted poisoning were kept separately from the rest of us. Sperhias was a very pleasant small town, full of

life. The people looked after us marvellously: ouzo, wine, very good
food. We were served by girl-members of EPON.

The Greek National Day

Although the protection of the railways in Roumeli was now the
duty of German troops under the direct responsibility of their
commander, there were reasons to complain. In February 1943 Löhr
reported:

The activity of the bands is concentrated on Greek police stations
close to the demarcation line between Germans and Italians. As a
consequence, gendarmerie posts and field watchmen are disarmed,
foodstuffs are seized, archives are burned, rail track and bridges are
sabotaged, and mines are attacked and destroyed.

The bands generally consist of forty to four hundred men who are
well-equipped and often armed with heavy weapons; they are well
organised and have good communication lines. All we have to combat
these bands are small rifle commandos, with limited amounts of heavy
weapons so that their deployment against the bands has very little
chance of success. Almost all our regular troops are required to guard
the railways.

The swift equipment of resistance fighters with British arms and
ammunition and their training by the BLOs was obviously beginning to
bear fruit. In spite of the heightened presence of German troops in
Roumeli in March 1943, General-Secretary Siantos was satisfied that
ELAS had more than kept up with this escalation and that it was now
strong enough not only to deal with political dissidents and Italian
troops, but also to attack the German occupier himself.

Prior to his departure from Athens to the mountains, KKE-Chief
Tasos Lefterias had instigated a three-phased plan to increase andarte
activities. First, Roumeli was to be cleansed of collaborators and
policemen appointed by the enemy. Second, attacks on Italian
strongholds were to be intensified. Third, when sufficient experience
had been gained, attacks on German targets should start.

As the local Greek police had been either eliminated or recruited,
and the Italian occupying troops were so intimidated by ELAS
andartes that they hardly ventured out of their barracks, Lefterias
could already proceed to phase three of his plan by March 1943.

This escalation did not spare the police in Platistomo Spa. Baron von Falkenhausen, still convalescing in Lamia, worried about "his people" and asked Franz Meier to report on the situtation. He replied on 22 March 1943:

The bandits took our four policemen away and occupied the village of Platistomo on 17 March. They detained two German vehicles from seven-thirty a.m. till ten a.m. and conversed with our soldiers, assuring them that they would not bother us. They took one of the vehicles on a short drive. In fact, they have generally become very audacious, walking about openly in the villages, as it is too cold for them up in the mountains. They must have a force of something between a thousand and twelve hundred men by now.

On 25 March, 1943, the Greek National Day, which marks the anniversary of the Greek struggle for freedom in 1820 against the Turks who had occupied the country for four hundred years, ELAS dared to hold a parade in the liberated town of Siatista. An Italian major had surrendered to the partisans there. The entire district of Grevena was now freed from foreign occupation and Archbishop Gerassimos was able to celebrate mass safely in the cathedral in honour of the freedom fighters. Siatista was the first liberated town in occupied Europe!

And in Athens, EAM organised a demonstration on Syntagma Square, which was reported by the Commander South:

It took place against a background of nationalism. No red flags, only Greek. Communist associations were not evident. Walls daubed with blue slogans, no longer red. Patriotism is the buzz word. Outwardly, since 25 March '43, the situation is entirely calm. No strikes.

But this report fails to mention that EAM was conducting a massive propaganda offensive by distributing pamphlets in Athens and its environs, and EPON, which had only just been formed in February, exhorted the youth of Greece to unite. Even Churchill had pamphlets dropped, albeit a day late, making this appeal:

To the Greek people! Your servitude shall end! Today the King and his government are in Cairo to prepare for the day which shall bring freedom back to Greece, for which the Greek people have never ceased to fight. When the time comes, and you shall

*be given advance warning of that time, you must all rise up as
one man, and then the Greeks shall ban the tyrant from Greek
soil. Greece, united in her victory as in her sorrow, shall take
her proud place among the free countries of the world. Victory
is certain!*

Tasos Lefterias ably chose this day to make his dramatic appeal to
all andarte leaders of Roumeli to fight the German occupation. A
meeting of Kapetanios was called in the schoolhouse of Marmara, a
village lying between Sperhias and his headquarters at Kolokythia.
Guerilla leaders from the districts of Evrytania, Fthiotida, Domokos
and Dorida packed the small room.

In Aris' absence, this was Lefterias' first opportunity to make a
mark for himself as a leader. The andartes respected him already for
making short work of Kostorizos and the other "deserters" and they
admired his courage in taking Stephanos Sarafis prisoner who was,
after all, a general known beyond the Greek frontiers. His daring
decisions confirmed their conviction that, since the Gorgopotamos
operation, EAM/ELAS had developed into a powerful resistance
movement to be seriously reckoned with.

Lefterias' cold, light eyes roamed across the shabby room and
studied the andarte leaders as he proclaimed that the time had come to
attack the Germans directly and to chase them out of Roumeli. "So
far, we have not bothered the Germans and concentrated only on the
Italians. But the Germans are as much our enemies as the Italians.
Today, I can report to you with satisfaction that there are no more
Greek policemen working in the service of the enemy in any of the
villages in Roumeli. They have either joined our cause or they have
been eliminated. Our ELAS has become strong and powerful. But the
Huns still exploit our land and control our railway stations in order to
export our mineral resources to their armaments industries. They
requisition our harvests to feed their troops. They fell the trees in our
forests in order to reconstruct those very bridges and rail tracks that
our brave resistance fighters have risked and given their lives to
demolish. So far we only fought the Italians, but it is now time to fight
the Germans!

"We must target the mines and farm estates and those railway
junctions which are strategically important for the transshipment of
cargo. If we can do this, then we may say with pride that we have
freed Roumeli from the enemy."

Lefterias spoke of attacks in the next few days on the mines in Kaniani and Topolia, on the railway station at Aghie where minerals from the mine at Domokos were loaded up, on the small German unit guarding the train tunnel near Nezeros and on the sawmill at Makrakomi. Arthur Edmonds would be in charge of strategic planning while local EAM/ELAS representatives would carry out these attacks. He issued instructions that any Germans or Italians taken prisoner should be brought to headquarters at Kolokythia. "We will then decide what to do with them. We might be able to exchange them for our andartes who are imprisoned in Lamia."

Fig. 37   *ELAS-Kapetan Belis, in charge of the area around Domokos*

Huge numbers of volunteers had joined the andartes in the last few weeks. But ELAS continued to have problems equipping the recruits, feeding them and, even worse, training them and giving them qualified officers to lead them. Eddie Myers alone had the power to help. Lefterias knew that he had to prove to him and Edmonds that ELAS was now willing to seriously confront the enemy and was not only up to engaging in the elimination of dissident partisan groups. Destruction of railway stations and German-run works would appeal to Myers and possibly appease his fury about the recent attacks on Sarafis, Vlakhos, as well as Zervas and the murder of the "deserters". Lefterias was conscious that only concrete deeds would induce Eddie Myers to distribute further arms supplies from the Middle East to his ELAS soldiers.

Following Lefterias' speech, on that same day, ELAS-leaders firmed up their plans and discussed the targets with Arthur Edmonds. The sawmill in Makrakomi and Hotel Asklepios in Platistomo Spa should be taken by local andartes, led by a young Crete, Niko Venetico Psiloritis, and an Evritanian, Odisseus. Kurnovon would be attacked on the way to Platistomo. The two Kapetanios Thanos and Ermis planned to destroy the marshalling yard of Aghie near Kajitsa. Lambros, Fotis Parnassiotis and Alekos Milonas, a cousin of Aris Velougiotis, planned to blow up the bauxite mines near Topolia in the Parnassus mountains. And a further commando under Karagounis was formed to destroy the Apostolia mines near Kato Kaniani.

Following the Marmara conference, Arthur Edmonds familiarised Lambros, who had already gathered some personal experience when he assisted Themis Marinos in blowing up the northern track of the Gorgopotamos bridge, in the use of explosives. He then left Marmara with Tasos Lefterias and Kapetan Belis in order to explore the feasibility of blowing up the mines in the area around Domokos.

Search for Sarafis

On 12 March, 1943, Myers cabled impatiently to Cairo, anxiously requesting an air drop of supplies for Sarafis. As yet, he had no idea that Sarafis had been captured by ELAS and that the general had offered his services to the communists.

Myers was getting progressively more worried about the actions of ELAS and informed Cairo that ELAS/EAM had to be handled very carefully because "they use British arms primarily to fight other resistance groups to pursue their aim of gaining control over Greece, instead of combatting the real enemy".

Zervas, on the other hand, continued to enjoy Eddie's full support. At Woodhouse's suggestion, Zervas, that sworn Republican, denied his own principles in order to be supplied by the British and had sent his congratulations to the Greek King, who was in exile in London, expressing his loyalty. But Zervas had no other choice for he had received an ultimatum from the ELAS leader Koziakas calling on him to release Vlakhos and his officers, who had "deserted" ELAS and were being sheltered by Zervas. "Otherwise," Koziakas threatened, "ELAS would attack Zervas and his EDES and push them into the sea."

Myers and Woodhouse felt they had to intervene in order to prevent the threat of civil war. In another attempt to unite all the resistance movements under one authority, they drafted their "National Bands Agreement", a military treaty between Greek resistance groups and Middle East Headquarters. Although subsequently amended in minor respects, its full text reads as follows:

1. *All andarte bands are to be known for military purposes as 'National Bands'.*
2. *Greece is to be divided into areas. A competent leader, recognised by mutual agreement of Brigadier Eddie as representative of GHQ, Middle East, and of the Greeks, will be appointed military commander of each area. Each commander will be solely responsible for all military decisions in his area. All 'National Bands' in the same area will co-operate fully under the military commander's orders.*
3. *The 'National Bands' of one area will not enter another area except by mutual agreement of respective military commanders.*
4. *The 'National Bands' of one area will give maximum assistance to those of another area on request by the other area commander concerned, or by GHQ, Middle East, through their liaison officers.*
5. *No member of any 'National Band' is ever to mention politics in public. Every member is free to have his own political views.*
6. *There must be no barbarism against anyone by any member of 'National Bands'. No one must be executed without fair trial*

and without the nearest British liaison officer being made fully aware of the facts.

7. *Any Greek andarte who, up to the date of the signature of this Agreement by his own recognised leaders, has transferred his allegiance to another 'National Band', will be given complete amnesty.*

8. *All Greeks enlisted in the future will be free to choose which 'National Band' they will join.*

9. *If, in the opinion of the British Liaison Staff, there is any failure to carry out the above Agreement, GHQ, Middle East will immediately order the cessation of war material until the failure is rectified.*

10. *These terms are to be given publication in the Press of the Resistance Movements, to be read to all andartes, and will be recognised by GHQ, Middle East.*

Myers was adamant: any partisan movement wanting to qualify for material support by the Allies had to sign the agreement. Copies were made; Chris obtained Zervas' signature and Myers set out to find leaders of all bands and get them to sign it.

After days of hard marching, Myers found Koziakas, who had captured Sarafis and threatened to drive Zervas into the sea. The ELAS leader not only refused to sign the document, thus referring him to Aris, but also told him about Sarafis' fate and that he had sent him and his officers under escort to Roumeli where they were going to be tried as collaborators.

Myers was dumbfounded. He was told that Sarafis had been taken to Kolokythia, which was "enemy-free" and a few hours' march from Sperhias or Gardiki. The trial would take place as soon as high-ranking officials from Athens could turn up who would produce irrefutable evidence. It was very likely that Sarafis would be condemned to death.

The colonel immediately decided to rush to Kolokythia to forestall the trial and obtain Sarafis' release. On 26 March, 1943, he set out across the rolling, fir-covered hills of Thessaly to the valley of the River Sperchios. Two days later he reached Gardiki meeting up with Nat Barker and Arthur Edmonds who informed him, much to his relief, that Sarafis was in no immediate danger but was being held no more than a day's march away.

Having learnt that Sarafis' trial would not take place for several days, Myers decided to await the arrival of Tasos Lefterias who was reportedly due to pass through Gardiki. He prepared to express his indignation regarding attacks on other partisan units and the treatment of his protégé Sarafis.

CHAPTER SEVEN
The Attacks

The "Battle" of Platistomo Spa

The glorious blue sky in the morning of 28 March, 1943, heralded the start of a splendid spring day. It was Sunday. Everyone at Hotel Asklepios was feeling buoyant. The Germans had had a quiet night. Albert Fritzenwanger, who came back from the sawmill at Makrakomi early in the morning, informed Georg Lehmkuhl that all was calm and that the andartes had seemingly left the area.

Lehmkuhl wrote his weekly letter to his "dear Martha" on that Sunday morning, relating that he had sent her figs, tobacco and tea. Inflation had rocketed to such an extent that one Reichsmark was now exchanged for six hundred instead of sixty drachmas. Lehmkuhl had requested that his salary be paid in advance in order to make immediate purchases, "as later on we shall only receive half for our money". Seemingly, he felt better after a rotten bout of malaria: "I was quivering all over with the fever." He wrote:

We don't go to any of the surrounding villages at the moment. Last week our two German lorries, which were on their way from the service station to the works, were stopped by bandits and, as a result, arrived two hours late at the works. But nothing actually happened. The village was occupied by about eight hundred bandits. I am here only temporarily until this section is disbanded and I shall then probably be transferred to Salonica.

As a civilian, Lehmkuhl was a master builder from Oldenburg, and although he was deputising for Baron von Falkenhausen, he had very little liking for the military. The other Germans and the Greek workers enjoyed teasing him about being a pacifist and for carrying a fake wooden pistol which he wore on his belt, and on which he had carved: "THOU SHALT NOT KILL."

Gottfried (Friedl) Schwarzenbacher, who was in charge of their fleet of vehicles, also knew full well that they would have no chance of defending themselves if the hotel was attacked by partisans. He was formerly the headmaster of a technical college in Graz and got on extremely well with his Greek drivers. Friedl was always ready to help whenever necessary. "He always involved himself wholeheartedly, nothing was ever too much for him, and he was always in good humour," says his former boss von Falkenhausen. Often, in the evenings, he would visit workmen whom he had befriended at the sawmill or on the farm. "We don't mind you Germans," his friend Tasos Apostolio in Makrakomi and the foreman Vasilis Platias told him frequently. Tasos worked in the sawmill and Friedl regularly visited him and his wife. She even embroidered a little cushion for his wife Maria which he was going to bring home on his next leave. They laughingly nicknamed him "Kokinos" because of his chubby red cheeks and were highly amused by his embarrassment.

Fig. 38   *Georg Lehmkuhl, the deputy with the wooden pistol on which he had carved: "Thou shalt not kill"*

Many Greeks from the surrounding villages of Makri, Makrakomi and Platistomo would freely come and go in the hotel, mixing with the Germans there. The teacher from Platistomo, Athanasias Skouroyiannis, was one of the popular guests. Another was Mantheos Iannacopoulos from Makri who worked at times at the sawmill. His wife Georgia was a nurse tending Baron von Falkenhausen under Dr

Tsagaris in the hospital at Lamia and it was through the Baron's recommendation that Friedl had hired Mantheos.

But in the last two weeks the position of the Germans at Hotel Asklepios rapidly deteriorated. Lieutenant Haydn from Lamia wrote on 19 April, 1943:

The bandits are becoming more and more pushy. On a number of occasions, bands occupied the sawmill at Makrakomi and disrupted work for days. In addition, workmen on the farm and in the sawmill have been repeatedly prevented from going to work. The almost constant presence of bandits in the area around Platistomo and Makrakomi and the resulting contact with members of the small German unit there made them assume, quite falsely, that the bandits had no quarrel with the Platistomo section.

Indeed, towards the middle of March, bandits frequently stayed openly in the village of Platistomo and were encamped for days in the fields neighbouring the Spa.

Ten to twelve Germans were regularly stationed at Hotel Asklepios in Platistomo Spa. Although the partisans were becoming constantly more intrusive, they had no option but to put up with them.

It was Kapetan Pericles who was camping fearlessly on the Germans' threshold with his andartes and prominent prisoner Stephanos Sarafis. The Germans had no power but to watch them and inform Lamia of the bands' presence. Just as Franz Meier had described the situation to Baron von Falkenhausen, so too did Gottfried Schwarzenbacher when he sent a message to Major Sitzenstock, the most senior officer in Lamia, reporting that "German lorries have been halted but were then allowed to proceed". And again, on 26 March, 1943, one day after the andarte conference in Marmara, he signalled headquarters in Lamia that lorries had again been stopped and that on that day "eight hundred to a thousand bandits were in Platistomo".

On Saturday, 27 March, 1943, NCO Hässler notified Lamia local headquarters:

One of our lorries was due to travel to Lamia and the hotel owner Haralambopoulos wanted it to transport a bale of leather there, for which he had a permit from the Italian "Comando Presidio". However, the lorry was halted at the entrance of the village of Platistomo by three armed civilians; at first it stopped but when the men became threatening, the driver drove through to the sawmill.

According to Haralambopoulos, two of the highwaymen were peasants from Platistomo.

When the lorry arrived at the sawmill, the soldiers accompanying it were told that it was useless to carry on as their presence had been signalled ahead and that they were likely to be attacked at Makrakomi which is on the way to Lamia. The soldiers telephoned the deputy head of the section in Platistomo Spa who directed them to turn around and bring back the leather. Meanwhile, the three original bandits had turned up at the building and demanded that the leather be deposited there. They also made it clear that if this incident was reported to Lamia they would kill the total work unit in Platistomo.

Once the leather was returned, the lorry was allowed to travel to Lamia without any further interference.

Hässler also confirmed that "a thousand to fifteen hundred bandits were in Makrakomi and outlying areas" and requested military support which was, however, not granted by local headquarters in Lamia. He was simply recommended to "pass this message on to your unit in Athens and put in a request for your transfer".

As he was not allowed to use the telephone, for reasons of secrecy, and feeling quite desperate, for he knew "that things would soon turn bad", he wrote the letter that same day. It took ten days for his request to reach his unit in Athens.

In spite of the lorry incident, Lance-Corporal Baldowsky was allowed to ride on a lorry going down to Lamia late on Saturday afternoon, to go to the cinema. Lehmkuhl authorised his leave. He knew that it was pointless and suicidal to attempt any defence of the works against hundreds of andartes. In the absence of any help from Lamia, Lehmkuhl simply followed von Falkenhausen's strategy of "creating a good relationship with the villagers and workers", although all German military had been instructed in August 1942 that "contact with the Greek population was not desirable".

The hotelier Stravros Haralambopoulos and his family left for Lamia early on Saturday morning. "He knew that there was going to be a major row in Platistomo Spa so he got out," says his grand-daughter Froso. "He had his informants among the andartes."

"So why didn't he warn his German friends?"

"He did warn the Germans. Every conversation centred on that horrid possibility that they could be attacked. But the Germans were soldiers, they couldn't just get out. They themselves advised my grandfather to go to Lamia or Athens. Trude could have gone along because she was his employee, but she didn't go. Firstly, because she loved Friedl, and secondly because she knew that without her as an interpreter, the Germans wouldn't even be able to communicate and would have no chance at all."

On the Friday evening Franz Meier had been on the telephone to Hermann Meyer asking him to come on Tuesday, 30 March, 1943, to arrange the transport of vegetable supplies for the railway engineers in Lianokladi. He, Franz Meier, was about to go on leave and wished to hand over to his comrade Erwin Kaufmann who had just come back from home.

Lance-Corporal Baldowski was expected back from his overnight outing to Lamia around midday on Sunday. When he had not turned up in the afternoon, nobody worried seriously about him. Haydn chronicled a week later:

In reality, Baldowsky tried to telephone the hotel. He was supposed to get a ride on a lorry on Sunday morning back to Platistomo Spa. When the lorry did not turn up, he tried a number of times to make contact during the morning, but without success. Apparently the partisans had already cut the telephone wires to Platistomo Spa by then. Having no other option, the lance-corporal stayed in Lamia.

Athanasios Skouroyiannis, the head of the private school "Nea Elvetia" in Athens, drew up a report in the nineteen sixties describing the "battle of Platistomo Spa".

The legendary rebel troops of ELAS only attacked the Italians up until February 1943 and did the Germans no harm. But after February 1943 they decided to attack German garrisons too, and in particular those that were situated where they were likely to inhibit the freedom of action of ELAS.

One of these was a unit of fourteen people stationed at Platistomo Spa. Their task was to gather information about the force and movements of the Greek rebel troops of ELAS and EAM.

On 27 March, 1943, a group of twelve ELAS-rebels were ordered, under the brave leadership of the Cretan Psiloritis and Kapetan Stratos, to attack the garrison and we were asked to help them.

The rebels were armed with one old machine gun, three automatic rifles and six shotguns. Two of the men had no guns at all. Their only weapons were their batons.

A meeting was called. Psiloritis, Kapetan Stratos, Athanasios Skouroyiannis, who was the Secretary of the local Party, Georgios Efthimiou, Mamo and Nakos Panopoulos were present. It was decided not to attempt a frontal attack on the Germans who were so well equipped, while the rebels were so badly armed.

We were well advised in our efforts by Vasilis Platias who worked as a foreman for the Germans and who eventually led the ELAS-rebels into the Germans' dining room.

The idea for this plan originated from the Platistomo-organisation. Accordingly, Athanasios Skouroyiannis and Georgios Efthimiou left the village of Platistomo shortly before sundown on 28 March and went to the Germans at the Spa. It must be added here that the Germans knew Athanasios Skouroyiannis.

As dinner was being prepared, the German superior invited Athanasios Skouroyiannis and Georgios Efthimiou to join in the meal. We declined but accepted a drink. Our plan was to keep them together and occupied until late evening.

We left the building at the agreed time. We said good-bye and walked out. Within a hundred metres we met Psiloritis and his ELAS troops from Platistomo and Neas Giannitsou. We reported that the Germans were sitting all together and eating their dinner.

Led by Vasilis Platias, the ELAS troops stormed the dining-room where the Germans were held under armed threat. They were all arrested. Athanasios Skouroyiannis insisted that they should be roped together, and late in the night they were abducted to the village of Kolokythia where the headquarters were located. The German lady, Madame Gertrud, Stavros Haralambopoulos' manageress, also went with them.

Two former hotel maids, Niki and Sophia, now live in Athens. While the two old ladies cannot forget that dramatic evening in the hotel, they make events sound much less heroic than Skouroyiannis.

"I was in the kitchen with Nikos Gouvras, the cook, when someone suddenly stuck a pistol in my back and yelled, 'Don't scream!'" Niki relates. "It was Skouroyiannis from Nea Giannitsou, my own village, and he had only just been spending the afternoon with the Germans. It was about eight o'clock in the evening. The Germans were either in their rooms or in the dining-room. They were wearing light indoor clothes; some were writing home to their families. Skouroyiannis grabbed my neck with his left hand and continued to bore the pistol into my back with his right. 'Where is Madame?' he asked. 'In her room,' I answered. He pushed me out of the kitchen, we crossed the court yard and walked up the wide steps to the hotel."

Fig. 39   *German soldiers captured by partisans in the Balkans*

"I was with Madame Trude in her room when I saw Niki come in," Sophia takes up the story. "I would have screamed but Trude reassured me by saying, 'The men have only come back to talk again.' But meanwhile the whole hotel had been occupied by the andartes. They ordered Trude and the Germans to get ready to leave while reassuring them that they would not be harmed if they followed instructions."

"The leaders were all men from Giannitsou and Platistomo," Niki laments. "They were friendly with the Germans, whose families were being supported by them. They used to invite them even to family celebrations. One of the Greek workers once scalded his chest with boiling water. Gottfried immediately sent for a German nurse from Lamia who arrived that same night and she saved his life."

"They assembled all the Germans in the dining-room. The andartes told Niki and me to get their clothes from their rooms," Sophia continues. "They would not allow them back into their rooms for fear that they had weapons there."

"Madame Trude told the andartes, 'You can take us away, but let the two girls go free. I am responsible for them, please let them go home. They are innocent.' She was wearing a green striped summer dress and summer sandals. I was at least able to fetch her dark brown fur coat from her room. Then they were led away."

"Most of the German men were quite dazed when the andartes broke in. I can remember the look of surprise and disbelief on their faces. Most were silent. But I recall that they could hardly believe that they had been so betrayed by Greek friends with whom they had just spent a pleasant afternoon. When they were tied together, none of them had more than light clothing on. Nobody had boots and only one or two even wore a jacket. The andartes had taken everything away from them already," commented Niki.

In 1985 the "battle" against the Germans in Platistomo Spa was again described in detail in the ELAS journal "Ethniki Antistatis":

The Nazis did not start their dinner during the farmers' visit, who prolonged their stay for about an hour. Meanwhile, with darkness falling, the andartes crept down from the surrounding mountain slopes.

The Germans and Gertrud then began their meal which they enjoyed, having taken the waters in the spa earlier on. Some of the andartes reached the outside of the building and disarmed the guard whom they took by surprise. Psiloritis, Odisseus and others then ran into the building, pointed their machine guns at the Germans and ordered them not to stir from their seats. The Germans were surprised and stated repeatedly, "Mr Haralambopoulos is not here."

A few days after the assault, Lieutenant Haydn noted:

The service building in Platistomo has been totally looted. Whatever fixtures and fittings as may still be there are smashed, doors and windows including the frames are broken. Documents are torn and scattered over the premises and some have been found in the surrounding villages. There was no sign of any personal belongings any more. All the provisions, cattle and farm implements have likewise disappeared. The two lorries, the passenger vehicle and motor-cycle have gone, including petrol supplies of about a thousand litres. The Greek night guard at the sawmill, who had been tied up and left in his room by the bandits, said that all night long the lorries roared through Makrakomi, presumably carrying off the loot from the service building. Various other Greeks corroborated this.

Some of the left-over fixtures were probably stolen by inhabitants from the surrounding areas, as various finds show. A number of statements confirm that the stolen German vehicles have since been used by the bandits. According to the Italian "Comando Presidio", they have been employed to good effect in assaults on other targets. The lorry drivers are former Russian prisoners of war who recently escaped from the camp at Stylis.

Baldowsky and the Greek forester from Lamia have inspected the sawmill which is generally undamaged but some essential equipment has been removed which means that sawmill experts were involved.

"Whatever the Germans and Italians failed to take two years earlier was now seized by Greek nationals," Froso Haralambopoulos complains. "All the rest of my mother's dowry was taken away. One of the andartes even systematically bashed the marble steps up to the hotel with a sledge hammer. Then he smashed the marble tile floor in the entrance hall."

Handcuffed, the ten Germans were forced to walk that same night to Palea Giannitsou, a mountain village about thirteen kilometres away. The path winds up in tight bends to an altitude of over a thousand metres, and had the men and Gertrud Radwein not been in terror for their lives, they might have enjoyed the magnificent view at sunrise across the Sperchios valley and the grandiose snow-capped mountains behind.

The mood of the andartes was jubilant. Their "battle" at Platistomo Spa had been victorious. Their ruse had enabled them to detain all the men and "Madame". Not a shot had been fired. Lefterias would surely praise them for their success and the booty they had gained without any loss to themselves.

It was late morning when they reached Palea Giannitsou. The Germans were locked in a building in the middle of the small village, while the rebels waited for enemy reprisals. Look-outs had been posted on the slopes all along the valley from Lamia to Makrakomi. The telephone network still operated in most of the villages. It was therefore easy to warn the population of any advancing troops. But Monday passed quietly. No sign of any Germans, nor Italians. When evening came and there still had been no sign of the enemy, the guerillas decided to take the prisoners under cover of darkness to Kolokythia where the ELAS headquarters were set up. This meant walking back via Platistomo, Makrakomi and Sperhias.

"When they were led through Makrakomi," says Sefardim Koutsardis who was formerly a policeman in German service, "some of the women ran to Madame and the Germans, and offered them food and drink. The andartes let them do this."

Haydn confirms Koutsardis' statement:

The prisoners were led through Makrakomi in the morning. They were roped together, but Madame was seated on a donkey. Some of the villagers gave them cigarettes and water.

After many hours they reached the small mountain village of Perivoli. Here the villagers neither moved nor spoke. Their fear of reprisals was too great as they watched the sodden, weary men trudge along in the rain, linked together like slaves and headed by an exhausted woman on a donkey. The Germans could get no information from the andartes. All they were told was that they were being taken to Kapetan Lefterias in Kolokythia and that decisions would be taken there.

"An andarte told me much later," Sophia recalls, "that during the march to Giannitsou, Trude lost one of her sandals. He knew that she was always kind to us Greeks and was sorry for her, so he offered to give her his shoes, but she declined. She was a proud woman."

The Italian unit responsible for the protection of the outpost at Platistomo Spa briefly records the attack in the log book on 30 March, 1943:

Fig. 40   *Franz Meier in the Hotel Asklepios: "It's like being in the Wild West."*

A thousand bandits travelled through Makrakomi after capturing ten German soldiers there. They cut telephone lines to Lamia and disappeared to an unknown destination.

At the end of March 1943, the family of Franz Meier received his last letter, dated 19 March, 1943. He wrote to his mother, his wife and his two little "sweethearts":

My boss has approved the dates of my holiday and if all goes well I shall leave here between 6 and 10 April. It will take me two days to Belgrade and another one to Vienna. At any rate, I shall be with you all for mother's sixtieth birthday and for Easter. I have actually got twenty days leave. Let's hope that there won't be a general ban on leave and all goes well. Then I will be celebrating Easter with you, my dears, and with my two little sweethearts.

The bandits are all around us in great numbers and they are heavily armed. They were recently in the village nearest to us which is only ten minutes' walk away. A few have come up our drive. They told

*us expressly that they would do us no harm because we are decent
people and German. We are now living in their midst, and
unfortunately they are very numerous — nine hundred to a thousand
men. One has to take things as they come in life, and I personally do
not fear them any more, because I know most of them — their leaders
are almost all former Greek officers. They all know us too, so it is not
likely that anything will happen to us. They took our car one day, they
just nicked it but brought it back two hours later.*

It's like being in the Wild West.

The Attacks

Dimitris and Polixenie Psalidas from Kajitsa, a small village north
of Lamia, remember the six Germans well, who were billeted there to
guard the Aghie railway station down in the valley.

The village changed its name to Makrirahi after the war. It nestles
peacefully on the mountain slope surrounded by cherry orchards and
agouritsies, which are small trees covered in white blossom in April.
Wild roses grow along the roadside. The village is bathed in the spring
sunshine. It must have looked as sleepy when the six Germans
assumed their guard duties here in the winter and spring of 1942/43.

They were stationed in a cottage directly opposite Family Psalidas
and from there they had a view right down on to the railway station
about one kilometre away. "The Germans lived in this little house
when they were not down at the station," Dimitris says. "The minerals
extracted from the mines were loaded here for further transport to
Northern Europe."

Polixenie remembers Viktor Schendzielorz amazingly well.
Although she does not speak any German, she has not forgotten his
name. She was only thirteen years old and loved to play with the
Germans when they came back from work. "They were friendly and
well-liked and they had contact with everyone in the village. Viktor
always spent time with us whenever he could and he used to tell us
about his children."

Viktor Schendzielorz came from Gottesdorf in Upper Silesia,
which is now part of Poland. His comrades were Rudolf Zahout from
the Sudetenland, Oskar Kudlick from Kassel, Walter Kunz from the
Stallegg Estate in the Black Forest, Kurt Pfaue from Klein Biewende
and Wilhelm Franz from Uckersdorf near Herborn. Apart from Kurt

Pfaue, who was divorced and Wilhelm Franz, all the men were married and fathers of small children. They were all about thirty years old except Oskar Kudlick who was born in the first year of the century.

Fig. 41   From left to right: *Georg Prametsberger, Victor Schendzielorz and Rudolf Zahout with their dog Peter at Aghie station*

Wilhelm Franz was seemingly the luckiest of them all, as he had been granted home leave and was to start his long journey via Belgrade to Herborn on 3 April, 1943. But his luck deserted him. For on the night of 28 and 29 March 1943, three days before his scheduled departure, the partisans pounced. While four Germans were lying asleep in their spartan quarters and two others were working down at the station, the andartes stole down the mountainside from Palea Kajitsa and attacked the cottage and the station at midnight. They were led by Kapetanios Thanos and Ermis. There was no opposition. All the German soldiers were taken prisoner. Without doubt, the station guard must have been very lax, particularly because the station was in

172

the plain surrounded by flat land and anyone approaching it could therefore be seen several hundred metres away. The Germans must have been totally unsuspecting and seemed quite unaware of any threat to themselves or their station.

Fig. 42 (left) *Wilhelm Franz*
(right) *Kurt Pfaue*

Even Wilhelm Franz, a robust young man from Uckersdorf who had written to his sister "they will never get me", was overpowered by the partisans. He could not fire a shot: they surprised him in his sleep at his lodgings in Kajitsa.

Why had they not bothered to take any precautions? Nobody from Lamia had informed them about the aggression on hotel Asklepios nor on the sawmill on the previous day. Their relationship with the inhabitants, who were earning a good wage for doing reloading work at the railway station, was excellent. The soldiers had some of the village girls knit them sweaters. Kajitsa seemed a peaceful island of happy co-existence in occupied Greece. "No one in this village went hungry," Dimitris says. "Just a week before the assault, all six Germans were invited to a village wedding. We celebrated together till the early morning."

The soldiers' few belongings were immediately shared out among the partisans. Shoes, coats, guns and ammunition were loaded on mules and taken away. Kapetan Thanos had the railway station completely destroyed, doors and windows were smashed at the hinges, and Peter, the collie, was shot; that was, in fact, the only shot fired that night.

Fig. 43   *Rudolf Zahout in front of his lodgings in Kajitsa:*
"Greek women used to knit sweaters for us"

Two days previously, the partisans had attacked and blown up the mines at Kaniani and Topolia; and now the station at Aghie, which had been essential for the transshipment of minerals, had been completely put out of action. These two partisan attacks were so successful that no further minerals were ever mined nor transported till after the war ended.

"In the village we were horrified by the attack. We were frightened for ourselves," Dimitris says. "We expected that the Germans would take hostages as the Italians always did and that they would burn the village to the ground. We had no choice but to pack a few necessities and flee into the mountains and await the German reaction."

"But before they left," Polixenie interrupts, "the andartes seized a girl who had had dealings with the Germans, and burned a 'P' on her cheek. I shall never forget her screams." The old woman chokes with emotion although the incident happened so long ago.

"What does 'P' mean?" I ask curiously.

"*Prodothis,*" Dimitris answers, "traitor."

A gravel road branches off the main Lamia-Karpenissi road and leads to Agios Stefanos, which used to be called Nezeros. On the way there, the road passes through Kurnovon (now renamed Trilofo), which is at about eight hundred metres altitude and offers some magnificent views of the fertile Sperchios valley and the imposing Mount Timfristos north of Karpenissi. On the other side of the hill the road continues to the stations of Nezeros and Aghie.

Fig. 44   (left) *Maximilian Rossmann*
(right) *Karl Blachnik*

After the destruction of Aghie station, the commander of the regiment, Colonel Guksch in Lamia, ordered a scout patrol to "investigate this band". It departed on the first of April, 1943. Lance-Corporal Karl Blachnik and Maximilian Rossmann belonged to this company. Both were married, with children. Karl Blachnik (thirty-three) came from Evenkamp-Werne in the district of Münster, and Maximilian Rossmann (thirty-five) was from Ebene-Reichenau in Carinthia, Austria.

The andartes were well prepared under the guidance of Arthur Edmonds. They correctly assumed that the Germans would send out a patrol to investigate matters at Aghie. Kurnovon was an ideal place to ambush them. The andartes entrenched themselves at the end of the village close to the road to Nezeros, and let the scout patrol pass the village unchallenged; then they pounced. The company commander, Captain Sacher, wrote to "dear Mrs. Rossmann" on 8 April, 1943, that although "an experienced non-commissioned officer was in charge, and in spite of extreme caution, the patrol was surrounded by a ten-fold superior force":

Gunner Franz Thurner saw your husband fall but could not go to his aid because he was cut off by heavy machine-gun fire. The wound was probably not serious but he was lying next to his machine gun. Then the enemy stormed and he was probably taken prisoner.

Max Rossmann was wounded in his left leg and captured with Karl Blachnik once the German scout unit had withdrawn.

"Colonel Guksch personally wrote to the mayor, demanding the return of the missing men or else the village would be burnt," Captain Sacher wrote on 8 April, 1943. "So far, they have not been released and therefore the colonel's order is about to be carried out." He closes his letter on a comforting note:

I join with you and your children in hoping that your husband, and our good friend, will return soon and meanwhile we shall continue to try to discover his whereabouts. Other German soldiers responsible for railway security have also been abducted and it is not likely that these bands are going to harm all these people.

Sacher's kindly wishes are negated by his ominous postscript: "Personal belongings will be sent to you under separate cover." The Captain had actually written off his soldier Maximilian Rossmann.

I spoke to Maria Andonopoulos in Trilofo, an old woman dressed in shabby black, her face full of deep wrinkles. "A German was shot," she says. "Later in April the Germans came back." She fans the flies away from her face, standing under a magnificent olive tree in front of her drab little hut and scrutinises me before she continues. "Nobody was in the village. The Germans went through all the houses, and before they left, they laid fires and many houses were burnt down. As all the young men had gone into hiding, they took my father who was out with the sheep. He never came back."

"What are your feelings about the Germans when you think back to those days?"

Maria Andonopoulos shrugs. "There was a war," she says. She turns her back on me, shoos the chickens away from her feet, and without wasting any further words, she shuffles back into her cottage.

Just as those men who had been left to their fate in remote "defence industries" and lonely railway stations, many other German soldiers in Roumeli working at strategically important points but detached from their units were suffering the same treatment. As early as March 1943, the German Wehrmacht was not able to carry out Löhr's order of December 1942, "that guard troops must be strategically deployed so as to prevent any enemy approach to a possible target".

After these initial successes it was obvious that the rebels would go on to attack other insufficiently protected posts. Like the Italians before them, the Germans were now on the defensive and not in a situation to be able "to comb through areas surrounding the tracks to sniff out the bandits from their hide-outs". Neither did the guards protecting the railways defend themselves from "military bases" nor did they stay in "bulletproof living quarters" as demanded by Hitler and trumpeted by Löhr.

Instead of organising optimum security, the German and Italian leadership mutually put the ball in the other's court. The High Command South East reported to the OKW in early April 1943:

We have put in an explicit request for military protection of the industries which are important for the war effort in Greece to the Senior Commander of the Italian 11th Army, to which he replied that he was not in a position to provide such protection.

It would involve the scattered deployment of about one division, a force which the Senior Commander of the Italian 11th Army does not have available in view of the situation he faces with the bands. He considers that the best protection of these industries lies in actively combatting the bands.

Soon afterwards the German Commander was of the same opinion:

The question of providing adequate protection to the defence industries is still unanswered. As neither German nor Italian troops are available for constant surveillance, the best protection must lie in actively and terminally combatting the bands.

But before issuing orders to "terminally combat the bands", Löhr commented with frustration:

Experience so far has shown that even this aim will hardly be met, and it is questionable whether the failure of the Italian troops is a result of lack of goodwill or of incompetence.

So, unmolested by either German or Italian troops who could not decide on their strategy to combat the bands, the andartes attacked the railway station at Gravia south of Lianokladi. It was the night of 29 and 30 March, 1943; one day after the attack on Aghie, two days after the sawmill and hotel were destroyed and three days after the mines had been blown up.

Towards midnight the andartes, led by Fotis Parnassiotis, broke into the station and overpowered the lone soldier Rudolf Herrmann who surrendered immediately. Herrmann had learnt Greek quite well during his service in Greece and he was friendly with the villagers. He knew the EAM representative of Gravia, who put in a good word for him, so that Fotis Parnassiotis promised to do him no harm and to take him to their headquarters in Kolokythia.

The andartes found out from Herrmann, however, that two other German soldiers would be controlling the track, usually turning up in the morning for work at the station.

"In the morning, when two German soldiers walked to the station together, the andartes lay in ambush. They called to the Germans and when they turned to run into a nearby wood, shots rang out. The

178

andartes had old rifles and could not aim. But both Germans were hit in the back and fell forwards on to the path. One groaned terribly. His dog now sat next to him, but the andartes did not dare to cross the path to him because they were afraid that other Germans stationed at Gravia might have heard the shooting and would be hurrying along." Petsopoulos, who witnessed it all, remembers every detail and talks as though it happened yesterday.

Fig. 45   (left) *Rudolf Herrmann at Gravia station*
(right) *Horst Langer: "Souvenir from Salonica"*

In the afternoon Private Horst Langer walked down the same path to go to work at the station. "When he saw the two soldiers lying on the path," Petsopoulos continues, "he ran straight to them without bothering to take cover. The andartes were waiting for him, of course. They sprang out from their hiding place and seized him. He held his hands up and screamed."

"Did you understand what he was saying?" I ask.

"No, but he screamed most terribly, and the andartes laughed. He probably thought he was also going to be shot. But they only killed the dog. They left the two soldiers lying there. I heard that the second soldier, who had been moaning so awfully, died later, but the andartes took their clothes and their boots and guns."

"What about the villagers, didn't they do anything about the wounded soldier?"

"No, they had all fled to the mountains after the first attack in the night. The village was deserted. Nobody was there. They were terrified of reprisals and stayed hidden in the mountains."

Horst Langer was an employee of the Reichsbahn (State railway) and had only begun military service in February 1943. He had trained as a business assistant, and was married with four children who were seven, five, four, and three years old when he was captured. He had only just arrived in Gravia the day before, and had not yet had time to write his first letter from Greece to his wife. But he had a photo taken of himself standing on the promenade at the waterfront in Salonica and had written in awkward letters on it "Souvenir of Salonica".

The next ELAS target was the picturesque little railway station at Nezeros, located on a wooded slope some three kilometres north of the village and guarded only by five German soldiers. It lay close to the infamous Nezeros rail tunnel which, two months later, was blown up by Lambros exactly when a Wehrmacht transporter was going through it. Arthur Edmonds had made the dynamite available for this militarily senseless massacre. Within two days the tunnel was already cleared and fully operational. But three hundred human lives were lost in the burning inferno.

On the night of 3 and 4 April, 1943, Georg Prametsberger from Mühldorf, Upper Bavaria, and Richard Nickel from Elsenfeld on the Main were on duty at the station with two of their comrades. Although the men had heard of strikes by partisans in the close vicinity, they evidently saw no reason to be particularly worried. After all, their company commander had granted leave of absence to one of their comrades, so times could not be too dangerous.

Gunner Prametsberger and Private Nickel were about to take their turn doing guard duty in front of the station when the partisans attacked at midnight from the woods. Gunshots, trumpet blasts and blood curdling screams sent terror through their hearts. In the pitch-black night a superior force of andartes had crept down through the pines and immediately shot one guard behind the station. His comrade rushed at the andartes but he was wounded and died the next day when he was found by German troops who repossessed the station in a pillaged and destroyed state.

Fig. 46   *Lambros blasted the Nezeros tunnel which was again operational within two days. Over three hundred human beings died in the inferno*

Prametsberger and Nickel had no chance of fighting against so many and threw down their arms and surrendered. They were handcuffed in the usual way and were led away blindfolded.

The young workman Kapetan Thomá, who had conducted Chris Woodhouse back to the mountains from Athens, wrote in 1975:

As a result of all these attacks which were co-ordinated by a general staff and heroically carried out in the face of great danger, the ELAS personnel gathered up a great deal of war booty and about thirty German prisoners from the Nazi guard posts and garrisons and brought them to Kolokythia.

And the German Commander South commented on the attacks in his report dated March 1943:

In the period covered by this report, the activities of the bands in the Italian area directed against the Salonica-Athens line are disturbing. There have been several sabotage acts and attacks. The main thrust has been against the section Larissa to Lianokladi. Rail tracks and small bridges have been dynamited, assaults made on patrols and bases safeguarding the rails, one station, Aghie, was destroyed, and trains were shot at and rail men and train passengers have been abducted.

No regrets about the loss of life are mentioned in these army reports. But repeatedly promises were made that:

by increasing patrols and making small scouting forays in the areas endangered by bands, the continuation of work in the arms and defence industries can be assured, the attitude of the population can be controlled and a degree of peacefulness can be achieved.

However, this assertion no longer corresponded to the facts. The Germans had to concede that Tasos Lefterios and Arthur Edmonds had definitely been successful:

As the two bauxite mines at Topolia and Kaniani are inoperative, no bauxite is being mined in Greece until further notice. Since 28 March the chromium mined at Domokos cannot be transported onwards owing to the destruction of Aghie station by the bands.

182

Italian protection has failed completely. These bands are consistently led and they aim at interrupting German supply and communication lines. The main target at the moment seems to be the disruption of the Salonica-Athens line and consequently of all German supplies. It is doubtful whether the originally intended extension of the line Athens-Salonica into a dual track can be carried out due to the extent of the work involved. Many locomotives have been damaged. German rail men are exposed to enormous pressures because the Italians never provide the necessary military protection. The rail employees cannot take over line security as they are already stretched to carry out repair work to make the section operational again.

General Weygoldt, a general staff officer, at last described the unadorned truth on 31 March, 1943. His report was to have terrible, indeed fatal, consequences:

The resistance movement has had an enormous lift as a result of the successes of bands in northern and central Greece. The attacks on the mines at Topolia and Kaniani, the destruction of the sawmill at Makrakomi and the disruption of the railway line Athens–Salonica at various points all testify to increased activity by the resistance. So far, the German service stations have had one property after another destroyed. The remaining defence industries must now be protected by German troops to prevent their annihilation. Italian measures have been insufficient. Only a consistently led, big blow against the bands can offset the increasing danger to the occupying troops.

But what about the German soldiers who had been taken prisoner? Who thought about them? How would the partisans react to a so-called "big blow"? Were the prisoners all written off, just as Max Rossmann had been written off so quickly? Did these few human lives count at all for General Weygoldt in his safe haven in Athens?

No Warning

Lance-Corporal Georg Wunderle and Privates Helmuth Kohlhoff and Karl Kapp were to accompany their Paymaster Hermann Meyer on his drive to Platistomo Spa on Tuesday, 30 March, 1943. As arranged on the previous Friday, Meyer wished to speak to Erwin Kaufmann and Franz Meier about future supplies of provisions to his unit.

Fig. 47   *Helmuth Kohlhoff in front of his "Wanderer" at
Lianokladi station*

Karl Kapp from Nagold in Württemberg and Helmuth Kohlhoff
from Schwerin were both butchers by training. Georg Wunderle was
the cook of the 117th EBK. Before the war, Helmuth Kohlhoff worked
as a driver for a bakers' delivery service. He dreamt of opening a
haulage business of his own after the war. Karl Kapp was the only one
of the four men who was single. His father ran a farm and counted on
his only son to take it over after the war.

Georg Wunderle, who was born in 1910 in Schwerin, already had
a fourteen-year-old daughter called Anneliese, and Helmuth Kohlhoff,
thirty-eight, and his wife Anna had two little sons of three and five.
He drove the car; Hermann Meyer sat next to him while Kapp and
Wunderle made themselves comfortable in the back seats of the black
"Wanderer". They left the station at Lianokladi at about
ten-thirty a.m.

It was a grey, cloudy morning. The wind blew violently and
uncomfortably cold from the north-east in contrast to the week before

when the days had been full of spring warmth. Flowers and fruit trees were already in blossom in the Sperchios valley. The edges of the road to Makrakomi were dotted with red poppies. Here and there, lilac wound around the poor dwellings they passed on the way.

These were their last few days in Greece. The Gorgopotamos bridge had been repaired, and after the first trains had passed over it, the timber trusses had been strengthened and then further small bridges had been built or repaired over the Sperchios river and at Katharini. It was rumoured that the Rail Engineers were to be returned to Serbia where partisans had been busy blowing up several small bridges.

It was only a twenty-seven-kilometre drive to Platistomo Spa. Kohlhoff knew the road like the back of his hand, having travelled over it many times with the paymaster. Approximately at the halfway point, they reached Kastri with its fortress-like building, where the most westerly German unit was stationed. It was perched on a hill above the cemetry and overlooking the Sperchios river. As the winter snows had not melted yet, the river flowed slowly in its wide bed and extensive swampy area.

Six kilometres on from Kastri, down a straight road alongside the Sperchios, lies Makri with its eight hundred inhabitants who, two nights before, had hurried down the slippery, narrow path to the riverside to hide in the reeds and dense thickets growing in the marshy ground, in order to avoid any "atonement measures" as a result of the attack on Hotel Asklepios. So far, the villagers had got on well with the Germans. They worked with them at the sawmill and on the farm estate. Now, they cursed the andartes, their own nationals, whom they held responsible for their plight. No one knew how Lamia headquarters would react, but there was absolutely no doubt that the Germans would be at least as ruthless as the Italians.

Although it was damp and bitterly cold down by the river, almost all the villagers had fled there. Only a few old people who were too feeble to withstand the rigours of sleeping outdoors on the river banks had stayed in their cottages. But six village youths belonging to the ELAS-reservists had also stayed at home. They hid themselves around the market square in Makri, watching the traffic from Lamia to Makrakomi and Platistomo.

Dimitris Fekas, Constantinos Tsonis, Vagelis Tsagaris, Mantheos Iannocopoulos, Yannis Zuvuilis and Thomas Zigaras were all young admirers of the ELAS movement. They were thrilled with the success of the andartes at Makrakomi and Platistomo Spa. Psiloritos, the Cretan, had given them a vivid and detailed account of the victorious "battle" against the Germans at Platistomo Spa. And the youths were now eager to find out what was going to happen next and what the Germans would do.

To their great surprise, nothing happened on Monday, 29 March, 1943. No Germans, no Italians. It seemed as though no one was interested in the events at the sawmill and at the hotel.

Then suddenly, at eleven a.m., on Tuesday, 30 March, 1943, they espied the black car travelling along the straight bit of road from the direction of Lamia.

Forty-seven years have now gone by since the "Wanderer" drove through Makri. The maples and plane trees which shed their shade in the small market square are almost half a century older. But otherwise nothing much has changed. A travelling salesman drives up in an ancient Ford and noisily hawks his wares by loudspeaker. The bench is dirty, its wood rotten. Above me the wide branches of the trees seem to be swarming with little birds. Their twittering competes with the salesman's aggressive chatter. I play with a tall glass of cold Nescafe which I bought at the grubby taverna behind me.

Dimitris Fekas declines my offer. He is sitting beside me. "I don't remember anything," he says. He smiles in an irritating way. He is shy. Although he is old, he can't be senile, but he is scared. I try to calm his fear.

"In 1963 I met your neighbour Mantheos Iannacopoulos. He, you, Tsagaris and some others captured the Germans when they drove through this village in March 1943, isn't that so?"

"They came by car," Dimitris says, "everyone knows that. They stopped the car, pointed a pistol at the Germans and then took them to the mountains."

"Who did this?"

"I don't know. I wasn't there. They were other people."

"But Marika Youla, who lived in this street and says she watched the capture from her window, tells me, Mr Fekas, that you were there. I am not blaming you. After all, it was the Germans who invaded Greece. How many men were sitting in the car?"

"Four. There were four men in the car, and four Greeks stopped it. There, that's where the car was stopped." Dimitris Fekas points at a large, lone cedar growing on the right-hand side of the road.

"Where did the Germans come from, and what did they want?"

"They came from the Spa and they were travelling back to Lamia. Several Germans stationed at the hotel had been captured a few days before. Immediately afterwards almost the entire population left the surrounding villages and took to the mountains or to the riverside. Everyone was afraid of reprisals."

"How did the Germans behave when they were captured? They were armed, weren't they?"

"They were not armed. I was standing a bit further off. But they raised their arms and surrendered," the old man asserts. "I couldn't see it very well as I was standing further away."

"So why didn't the Germans just drive on? It seems rather foolhardy to have stopped. By then, they knew that their comrades had been attacked. Why do you think they stopped, Mr Fekas?"

The old man seems to gain confidence. He becomes more talkative. "Well, the Germans were simply signalled to halt the car. They didn't expect to be taken prisoner by us. I was twenty-three years old, the others were younger. We knew the Germans well. They often came to our house. They danced with my niece at Mantheos' wedding. They used to help us Greeks. Whenever we had any trouble with the Italians, we immediately appealed to the Germans to right the wrongs."

"Mantheos Iannacopoulos was the one to halt the car, then?" I ask, trying to sort it out in my mind.

"No, it wasn't him. It was Tsagaris. Vagelis Tsagaris stopped the car. He can tell you about it. He lives in Salonica now. He and Dinos Tsonis were both our leaders."

"Dinos Tsonis? Constantinos Tsonis from Lamia?" Marika Youla had mentioned the name of this former resistance fighter when I spoke to her in Lamia.

Dimitris Fekas nods and loses interest. He has no wish to talk any more. Someone calls him from the other side of the road. He still has that irritating smile. He never looked at me once during our entire conversation. He gets up decisively as though he has been waiting for an excuse, and shuffles across the dirty, sandy square and disappears

187

into his house without saying good-bye.

The Italian Comando Presidio in Lamia confirmed that by Sunday evening it had already been notified by its sources that the outpost at Platistomo had been attacked. According to the Italians, telephone contact had already been cut as of Saturday midday. At eight-thirty a.m. on 29 March, 1943, the Comando Presidio received a call from an unknown Greek source, supposedly from Makrakomi, saying that andartes had taken twenty-two German prisoners, six Italians and two interpreters; of these ten Germans were from Platistomo. By listening in to calls, the headquarters at Lamia heard of the incident in Platistomo on Monday morning and informed Lance-Corporal Baldowsky.

On Tuesday, 30 March, 1943, Paymaster Meyer from the Battalion of Rail Engineers at Lianokladi and three soldiers — Lance-Corporal Wunderle and Privates Kohlhoff and Kapp — set off for Platistomo, having had no warning of the incident, to pick up vegetables from there. He and his men were likewise attacked and captured including the car.

Lieutenant Haydn wrote this on 19 April, 1943. The "unknown Greek source" was the Greek agent Proedro Paleokori from Makri, working for the "Divisione Pinerolo". Already in the afternoon of 30 March, 1943, he informed Italian headquarters in Lamia by telephone about the "capture of four Germans". This message was passed on to the commander of the III Army Corps with the comment:

Although the German soldiers had been warned about the presence of rebels, they insisted on going into this area.

In other words, the German headquarters and Lance-Corporal Baldowski had been warned on Monday, but this vital information was not passed on to the 117th Company of Rail Engineers. Meyer's fateful trip only took place on Tuesday, a full day after Baldowski had reported to Major Sitzenstock, the town commander responsible for the outpost at Makrakomi. Why did Sitzenstock fail to inform the 117th Company of Rail Engineers? Von Falkenhausen's reply to this question sounds provocative. "The relationship between the Army and the Air Force was not too good. Maybe the town commander forgot, but it is quite possible that he just wasn't bothered to involve himself in the business of other units."

Sitzenstock died a few years ago in West Berlin. His wife refuses to talk as "it would not be to his liking". And the spy Proedro Paleokori is dead. He was uncovered by ELAS-andartes in Makri on 4 April, 1943, and, after a so-called trial, executed in Koloscopi.

———————

"When the car from Lamia drove past, we were hiding behind trees and houses around the market square." Dinos Tsonis speaks quietly and without emotion. This sixty-nine-year-old man recalls 30 March, 1943, very clearly, when he was twenty-one years old and triumphantly entered the ranks of the ELAS by making a spectacular capture of four Germans with his friends. After the end of the civil war in 1948, he was interned for sixteen terrible years on a remote Greek island. "In prison, I was so beaten up that at times I lost my hearing," he states matter-of-factly.

"We were all locals from Makri and knew of a hiding place to withdraw to if the Germans advanced with troops. Psiloritis had assumed they would and warned us. That is why almost the whole population — just imagine: eight hundred men, women and childen — had fled to the river!

"We were all surprised that nothing happened on Monday, and that on Tuesday only a car turned up. The andartes had look-outs placed on the slopes along the road between Lamia and Makrakomi who signalled the car's approach by trumpet blasts. Long before it entered the village, the car had been seen and we were warned.

"The car was travelling quite slowly. We saw they were uniformed Germans and knew that they would turn off to Platistomo Spa one kilometre down the road, and we assumed that they would go on to the sawmill at Makrakomi and then turn back. We were pretty sure that this would happen quite quickly as there were no more Germans at the sawmill and the Spa.

"My friend Vagelis Tsagaris was hiding in his house which is directly on the road. He and I were the leaders of our little group. As it was only a car, we decided immediately to halt it on its return journey and to capture the Germans. Vagelis volunteered to signal the car to stop. He knew the Germans and was the only one of us to have a pistol. But he did make one condition: 'If my Uncle Lukas is sitting in the car, we will let it go.'"

Fig. 48   *Hermann Meyer* (left) *with his comrades in front of Hotel Asklepios*

"Do you mean Dr Lukas Tsagaris, the doctor from Lamia who had studied in Germany and had a German wife?" I ask, interrupting Tsonis.

"Yes," Dinos continues, "Dr Tsagaris was known to have good relations with the German officers in Lamia and especially with the commander. After the Italians had taken hostages and shot them under the Gorgopotamos bridge in December 1942, he had been able to intervene successfully on several occasions to stop other Greek civilians from being shot.

"'If my uncle is sitting in the car, I will do nothing. We will let the Germans drive on,' Vagelis told us repeatedly. He had a healthy respect for his uncle. 'If he is not in the car, I shall shoot in the air with my pistol. That will be the signal for you to pounce.'"

"So, was your uncle in the car?" I interrupt.

"Hang on! Let me tell you," Dinos smiles at my impatience. "First of all, we took a vote, and when everyone agreed to the plan, we hid.

"Vagelis was waiting when the black limousine returned from Makrakomi driving at a moderate speed. He stood behind the big tree opposite his house and stepped out when the car approached. His right hand holding the old revolver was tucked in his coat pocket. He waved with his other hand. Instead of accelerating and driving past, the car promptly stopped and Vagelis saw that his uncle was not in it.

"And what happened then? Did he shoot in the air?"

"No, he didn't shoot in the air. In his excitement he forgot. The Germans got out of the car and when we saw that they were not armed, we rushed up and surrounded them. They seemed puzzled and astonished, but they showed no signs of alarm or fear of capture." Dinos suddenly breaks off and stares at me expectantly.

"What did they say?"

"We didn't speak their language nor did they understand us, but it was clear that they wanted to know what had happened at Makrakomi and Platistomo Spa. Their leader made himself fairly well understood with gestures.

"They were all tall men, particularly their Kapetan. I didn't even reach up to his shoulder. He repeatedly asked me what had happened to his comrades at Hotel Asklepios. We tried to explain that all the Germans from Platistomo Spa had been taken to the andartes in the mountains. He seemed reassured to hear this, but of course, we did not know what would happen to them. Meanwhile, we had done our duty and captured these Germans."

Dinos stops to drink his coffee, then he continues. "A man from Makri called Nikolaus Kaitsotis knew how to drive. So we put him in the driving seat and the four Germans in the limousine, while Dimitris, Thomas, Vagelis, Mantheos, Iannis and I accompanied them down to the river to Psiloritis."

"Do you mean you were all in one car?" I ask doubtfully.

"Yes, we stood on the sides, on the running boards of the car. Some of us were perched on the rear bumper. The car was thoroughly overloaded but it worked alright." Dinos laughs. "It was a good car. We all wanted personally to bring our booty to Psiloritis. We were terribly proud to have captured the Germans."

"What did the Germans say? What did the officer say?"

"Nothing. They were quiet, they seemed depressed. But the Kapetan did ask with amazement, when we got down to the river and he saw the eight hundred villagers, 'What! Are all these people partisans?'

"We all laughed and made him understand that they were not partisans but villagers from Makri who had been terrified of reprisals and had fled to the safety of the river banks."

The little man leans towards me as he continues his story. "You know, we were so young and thoughtless. We never worried about the consequences of our action. It was my idea to stop that car. It just felt like some madcap escapade. Well, Psiloritis, down at the river, ordered us to take our prisoners immediately to Gardiki where Tasos Lefterias was temporarily stationed."

In the early afternoon Mantheos Iannacopoulos, Vagelis Tsagaris, Thomas Zigaras and Dinos Tsonis again climbed on the running boards of the black limousine while Georg Wunderle, Helmuth Kohlhoff and Karl Kapp squeezed onto the back seat. Hermann Meyer, the "Kapetan" was allowed to sit in front. Thus, they drove back to Makri and on towards Makrakomi.

"One of the young chaps held a pistol to your father's head. We never understood why the Germans let themselves be captured by the youths." Alex Grivas said this to me in 1963 on the market square at Makrakomi. In spite of the years that lay between, he still couldn't seem to understand how a handful of youths could have dared to lay hands on the all-powerful Germans. But now, I could have enlightened him that it was Vagelis Tsagaris from the next village who had held the pistol to the German's head. And I could have told him why the German Kapetan had ordered the car to stop.

192

"Our driver turned left after the market square in Makrakomi, crossed the small stone bridge then up the straight to Sperhias, where he immediately turned right to head for Levkas," Dinos Tsonis intones pedantically.

The landscape is just as savagely beautiful now as it must have been then. On either side of the narrow road which winds along cutting through the mountainside, there are woods of maples, studded with oak trees and cypresses. In the far distance, the flat cupola of Mount Velouchi stands out, that mountain which Aris Velougiotis chose for his cover name. Although it is now the end of March, its peak is covered with snow and sparkles majestically at the end of the seemingly endless Sperchios valley.

The four Germans must have been assailed by doubt. Could it have been wrong to stop in Makri? They must have recalled Major von Falkenhausen, Gottfried Schawarzenbacher and Trude Radwein, who had been seized by partisans in this very area in October 1942 and whose story they had often heard. And now Gottfried and Trude were again being abducted. But, on the other hand, they knew these youths who had seized them and could not imagine, in spite of the threatening gun, that they would harm them in any way. In fact, one of the boys was Mantheos Iannacopoulos whose wedding they attended when he married Dr Tsagaris' nurse Georgia.

"The atmosphere in the car was quite relaxed," says Dinos Tsonis. "Shortly before Levkas, about halfway to Gardiki, we had to cross a ford over a tributary of the Sperchios river. But the car got stuck in the mud. Our driver had several attempts, then the German driver tried to cross the ford. Finally everyone got out, the Germans took off their jackets and helped us push the car across the stream. The German officer actually seemed ashamed that such a good car would not go through the water. Anyway, we all pushed, and thanks to our joint efforts, we managed to get to the other side."

"At this point, at least, the Germans could have escaped?" I interrupt Dinos' account.

"Of course they could," he confirms, nodding vigorously. "But they didn't want to escape. They wanted to be brought to the others. The German Kapetan felt responsible for the people captured at Platistomo. They had every opportunity to escape, for we had not even tied them together. Then when it started getting dark and it became too dangerous to continue by car on the rough road, we jointly decided to climb up the mountain to Levkas and press on from there by mule."

Levkas is perched on a hill, just like a castle fortress without the moat. Old cypresses adorn the village square, all leaning towards the church because of the prevailing wind. Clear as glass, mountain water murmurs through narrow ditches across the square. Yellow water lilies sprout out of the ditch in front of the wall around the churchyard.

"We were all hungry," Dinos continues. "The villagers were friendly and in spite of their bitter poverty, they gave us something to drink and some eggs. We fried these and the Germans ate them with relish. The villagers admired us for having dared to capture the powerful Germans. Some had never seen a German before, because they had not come here."

While the Greeks and their German prisoners ate fried eggs and even received some almonds from a sympathetic farmer's wife, Tsonis negotiated with some farmers for mules. He was anxious to move on as they wished to hand the Germans over to Lefterias that evening and return to Makri the same night.

Vagelis Tsagaris walked in front, Dinos Tsonis brought up the rear while Mantheos Iannacopoulos and Thomas Zigaras marched on either side of the Germans riding the mules. Night fell suddenly, but Vagelis knew the way to Gardiki like the back of his hand. Meanwhile, the Greeks were gaining confidence in the Germans' behaviour. A certain understanding for the situation of the other began to develop.

"They could have escaped ten times over, especially in the dark, between the trees and down the slopes. But it seems that they never even considered it. They spoke freely together. Of course, we didn't understand what they said. But they were calm and helpful and wanted to get on as fast as possible.

"We arrived late in the evening in Gardiki and asked for Tasos Lefterias. Somebody took us to him. When he stepped out of the darkness, he looked at us in amazement and praised us for capturing these tall Germans. His first question was whether we had not been afraid of taking such large men prisoner. Then he scolded us for not tying them up. We had been much too lenient there!

"In recognition of our feat, he gave the officer's revolver to Vagelis Tsagaris. It was a wonderful, handy little pistol, all shiny and beautiful. We were all envious of Vagelis. I can visualise it even now." Dinos Tsonis gazes thoughtfully at his empty coffee cup, annoyed with himself for not recalling its brand name.

Fig. 49   *Dinos Tsonis: "They could have escaped ten times over"*

Making use of the pause, I ask, "Did you not try to have a conversation with the Germans?"

"Oh, yes, I did. The officer spoke a few words of Greek. 'What is your task in the German army?' I asked him. He pulled a dictionary out of the left pocket of his uniform. He told me that he was responsible for the provisioning of the troop." Tsinos pauses, looking at me inquiringly.

"Yes, he was the paymaster, responsible for provisions. He was too old to fight at the front. He had nothing to do with the fighting troops. His unit was stationed at Lianokladi to rebuild the destroyed Gorgopotamos bridge."

Dinos nods. "When we handed the four Germans to Tasos Lefterias in Gardiki, the first thing he asked the Kapetan was whether he was from the Gestapo. 'No,' answered the German, and he laughed. 'I am not from the Gestapo. I am an officer stationed at Lianokladi.'"

Tsonis seems to be satisfied by my confirmation that Meyer did not belong to the Gestapo. Obviously some doubt had lingered, as Lefterias had voiced this suspicion. He again leans towards me and holds his hand out to me. I grip it. For a fraction of a second our eyes meet. I try to control my feelings thinking, "This is how he gripped his hand and said good-bye when he handed him over to Lefterias."

But Dino Tsonis was talking again. "On the following evening we met each other in Makri and celebrated the capture of the Germans. We described it all again and again to our friends. At some point, Vagelis even pulled out his old, rusty revolver and wanted to shoot in the air to show how he was supposed to give us the signal to attack. But the wretched old thing didn't even work! No shot came from that pistol!"

Constantinos Tsonis laughed at his anecdote. "It was a great day in my life," he said.

I met the physician, Dr Franz Tsagaris, the son of Dr Lukas Tsagaris, in his clinic in Lamia. Franz, too, studied in Germany and is married to a German, but he hardly works as a doctor any more. He is a deputy of the Government party "Nea Demokratia" and is an ultra-right member of the national parliament.

"Mantheos Iannocopoulos was one of the worst in those days. He skinned that German officer whom he captured in Makri together with my uncle Vagelis. Do you understand me, Mr Meyer?" he shouts with agitation. "He pulled the skin from that man's body, from the living body, just like skinning a sheep. Iannocopoulos was expert at it.

196

Everybody knows that here. He was a sheep farmer, a shepherd, he could take the pelt off any animal in a matter of minutes. His other expertise was staking. Do you know what that is, Mr Meyer?"

Fig. 50   *Dimitris Fekas* (left), *Vagelis Tsagaris* (middle) *and Dr Franz Tsagaris talking about the past on the market square in Makri*

"No," I mumble. I am speechless. This living-room, everything, suddenly seems unreal. This apartment looks just like in Germany: a sofa, two armchairs, dining corner, embroidered table cloth, landscape paintings, a stone mantelpiece with family pictures, father Lukas, mother Tilly, a sideboard with porcelaine and glass and innumerable framed pictures of happy children and grandchildren. His wife is trying to control the big collie whose wagging tail is threatening to knock the cup of genuine German Tschibo coffee off the low table.

"Before he skinned him," Tsagaris shouts, "he staked him." He dwells on all the "ss", making them hiss. "The communist pigs learned it from the Turks. They take a long wooden stick with a good point at one end and push it up the tortured man's arse." Tsagaris bellows the last word and points at his bottom. His wife is still trying to calm the dog down while she nods confirmation. "The stake is inserted in the anus and carefully pushed upwards. It comes out between the throat and the shoulder blade. As it does not damage any vital internal organs, the subject goes on living with the most horrific pain."

Dr Tsagaris looks at me inquiringly. He seems to expect some reaction. I don't dare ask how long such a person would have to suffer.

"My uncle, that madman Vagelis, and Iannocopoulos, Tsonis and the others, by their actions, caused our villages to be destroyed. My father tried to prevent it, but Vagelis wouldn't listen. That fool never achieved anything in his life except to get our country burned and bombed to bits. The ELAS-followers put Greece decades back, far behind the civilised countries of Europe."

CHAPTER EIGHT
In Captivity

Myers meets Lefterias

On the very same evening, 30 March, 1943, soon after the four Germans had been locked up in the schoolhouse in Gardiki, Tasos Lefterias prepared to welcome Eddie Myers in the small village. Myers had already become an almost legendary figure, added to which he had just recently been promoted to Brigadier by Cairo. He appeared with his liaison officer Arthur Edmonds who had so successfully carried out his instructions "to plan further sabotage operations in Roumeli". After the end of the war Myers wrote:

The following day, 30 March, Tasos, a young Cretan, arrived. I had some lengthy talks with him about the misbehaviour of EAM and ELAS. But the force of my argument was somewhat diminished by the news, received late that night, that ELAS andartes, in accordance with my recently issued instructions, had successfully attacked some chromium mines near Domokos and had put them out of action for many weeks. At the same time I learnt that another band of ELAS had captured a mixed bag of German and Italian troops in the plains west of Lamia.

In the course of their talks, Myers confronted Lefterias with the assertion that ELAS/EAM was an organisation infiltrated by communists. Chris Woodhouse had been able to confirm this suspicion when he found that the main office of EAM/ELAS in Athens was situated in the Communist Party's building and that the EAM/ELAS leadership were all members of that party.

Arthur Edmonds remembers how vehemently Lefterias denied this charge. "'The EAM has nothing to do with communists,' he lied to Myers. If a Greek had dared to make this accusation, Lefterias would have ordered one of his men to punish him severely. However, in this case, he had no option but to refute the charge and claim it was a lie. ELAS and EAM were still trying to dissimulate their communist background."

Tasos Lefterias did not divulge that Sarafis had requested to become a member of ELAS. Instead, the Cretan generously promised

Myers that General Sarafis would not be harmed until he was tried. He gave Myers the impression that he was acting as Sarafis' saviour, and thus cleverly avoided causing any rupture between himself and Myers. It was far more important to Lefterias to secure Myers' promise that the ELAS movement would continue to be supplied by vital air drops. The attacks on chromium mines and the enemy capture in the plains were his trump cards which testified that ELAS was serious about fighting the occupying powers. He dismissed the confrontations with other resistance groups as insignificant little skirmishes. Nevertheless, Lefterias, the communist, found it difficult to control himself faced with a barrage of accusations by the Briton.

Kapetan Thomá was also present in Gardiki at the time of this meeting with Myers. Later, he described Lefterias' mood after his talk with Myers:

He was seething with rage. Myers was only satisfied when he received confirmation that the andartes had blown up mines and captured thirty Germans. This showed what he really wanted. The lord and master can reproach his slaves and make accusations whenever they fail to work satisfactorily. This incredible British arrogance was the result of the utterly servile attitude of the Greek leadership towards the British.

While these talks were going on, the four Germans tried to sleep on the cold, stone floor of the schoolhouse. On the next day, 31 March, 1943, they were rudely wakened before sunrise. There was nothing to eat. It was cold, windy and rainy in the mountains and their clothing was inadequate. They were handcuffed together and ordered to follow a group of andartes who were marching to the ELAS headquarters in Kolokythia.

It is about thirty kilometres from Gardiki to Kolokythia. The narrow, stony path leads through the remote villages of Platanos and Kiriakohori, up, over two mountain ranges, down through two long valleys to Perivoli. The prisoners trudged through the hamlet of Nikolitsi, which seemed dead, with its few poor dwellings fashioned out of rough-hewn stone blocks and covered with jagged stone slabs. Holm oak, maple and fir-trees grow precariously on the slopes. Then the climb to Marmara starts after reaching the Vestrisa, a tributary of the Sperchios river, and then on to Kolokythia.

What thoughts went through the heads of those prisoners as they walked through this untouched, wild landscape? There was no hope of rescue. That was obvious. No German nor Italian soldier had ever penetrated this far because the area had been the stronghold of the Greek partisans since the beginning of the war.

On that same day Eddie Myers, accompanied by Arthur Edmonds and Tasos Lefterias, also marched to Kolokythia. Myers claims he never saw Hermann Meyer and his three comrades in Gardiki. This is hard to believe, for he writes in his book that on 30 March, 1943, in Gardiki, a Greek was brought before him who pretended to be Australian. Of course, the New Zealander and the Briton knew immediately that he was not Australian ...

...but a dupe of the Gestapo, and a pretty low-grade one at that. He had been sent up into the mountains by the Germans in Athens to pick up information about us. It was an incredibly poor piece of work. He paid the penalty of all spies.

If Eddie found time to question a "dupe" and have him shot, why ever would he not have questioned a German officer who could have given him detailed information about the reconstruction of the Gorgopotamos bridge, which would have been particularly useful as Cairo had already ordered him to investigate whether the viaduct could again be destroyed in a second operation?

The four Germans reached Kolokythia in the evening; by then Hermann Meyer must have realised that they were involved in a widespread action by the andartes. When the door to the schoolhouse in Kolokythia was pulled open and they were pushed inside, they found not only Trude Radwein and the ten men from Platistomo Spa, but also fourteen other soldiers who had been captured in various places in the preceding days.

Back to School

Jakob Eppelsheimer could hardly believe his eyes when Meyer and his three companions entered the small class-room. Eppelsheimer came from Haunstetten in Upper Bavaria and was a good friend of Hermann Meyer who had been to visit him at home during his last leave, making a detour when returning to Serbia from Mellendorf.

Sergeant Eppelsheimer was a stone mason of forty years of age and had only been certified "fit for limited duties". He was sent to Serbia on behalf of the Messerschmitt works of Augsburg as an inspector of industrial safety. He was moved to Greece in the beginning of 1943. Eppelsheimer was the only German national stationed at Topolia to safeguard the mining installation, which was the first target attacked under the leadership of Fotis Parnassiotis, Lambros, Tasos Lefterias and Arthur Edmonds. Arthur and his accompanying andartes disguised themselves as shepherds in order to reconnoitre the terrain and the railway stations around Lianokladi. Then Lefterias turned up with three hundred andartes and the attack on the mine took place two days after the conference in Marmara.

"When we attacked the mine on 27 March, 1943, the German immediately surrendered," Lambros recalls. "It was a miracle that he was not shot, but he pleaded that he had a wife and children so we took him away to Kolokythia."

Fig. 51   *Jakob Eppelsheimer* (left front)

The resistance fighters in Kolokythia had no experience in dealing with prisoners. In order to avoid German reprisals, they forced Eppelsheimer to write a letter to his unit, saying that he was alright,

202

that he would not be harmed and that he would soon be set free. This letter was deposited by night at the German headquarters at Lamia.

Fig. 52   *The village school in Kolokythia, seen from Leonidas Square*

The sergeant was the first to be imprisoned in Kolokythia on 28 March, 1943, and had to watch as, day by day, more prisoners arrived. First the eleven people from Platistomo appeared, then on the following day five soldiers were brought in, who had been taken after an attack on a freight train north-west of Lamia. "The train was completely burnt out, twenty-three wagons were smashed and the track had to be closed for twenty-four hours," the military report reads. This particular attack had also been executed under the guidance of Lefterias and Edmonds. Lance-Corporals Konrad Körling and Stahlberg, Privates Wilhelm Koller and Alois Holzmann and Gunner Franz Pelikan were lucky to be alive; they had immediately recognised that it was useless to resist and had surrendered to the andartes.

Then, in the early afternoon of 30 March, 1943, the six soldiers from Aghie station turned up, and in the morning of 31 March, Rudolf

Herrmann and Horst Langer, who had survived the attack on Gravia station, were delivered to the schoolhouse.

Two windows look out onto the school yard and Leonidas Square which is shaded by three ancient acacia trees. On one of their branches, young Kalambouras was hanged when Aris, Woodhouse and Zervas passed through this village before the Gorgopotamos operation. To the right, slightly above the rough-hewn stone school building, stands the rustic church. There was no bell tower. Instead, the bell hung on one of those large, strong acacia branches. From the square, the slope descends steeply to the west where most of the thirty houses of this mountain village are situated.

Just below the school, dilapidated huts and sheds stand higgledy-piggledy on the land belonging to Karageorgos, the farmer, where he keeps pigs, chickens, goats, sheep and his farm tools. His house, with its roof of rough stone slabs, is on the same slope as the school, but slightly lower. Between all the houses in the whole village, there is a myriad of fruit trees. In early April the cherry, plum, almond and walnut trees are in blossom and several apple trees are already budding.

The south-eastern window of the rectangular class-room looks out on the green valley below and across to the opposite slope which reaches about the same height as Kolokythia itself. It is densely covered by tall, dark green firs. Behind it, Mount Goumara is silhouetted against the sky, and further south-westwards, Mount Blia rises to 1,791 metres, forming part of the Vardoussia range.

At first, the Greeks had addressed all their communications through Eppelheimer. This role now fell to Hermann Meyer as the only officer among the prisoners.

One woman, twenty-eight German soldiers, and civilian employees were assembled in the room of only thirty square metres that night. It had been raining all day. They had had nothing to eat, and had no chairs, tables nor beds. Temperatures regularly dropped to freezing at night. It was dark inside, there was no lamp. The room had a rough wood floor. The andartes had removed all the school desks, chairs and the blackboard and stowed them in a room below. The prisoners could hear the andartes who were guarding them, stamping their feet outside. Fearfully, they tried to follow their conversation to discover their fate. Trude translated what they said, but the guards in front of their door did not seem to know more than they did.

It was truly an irony of fate for the teacher Meyer to be back in a schoolroom, albeit unwillingly. And when he was allowed outside to do his business in a hole in the ground under the apple tree, he could see directly into the storage room where the desks and blackboard were stacked.

Meanwhile the High Command in Athens, Salonica and Lamia had not been inactive:

In order to reduce the threat to the railway section under German protection, the High Commander South-east has decided to deploy a part of the 11th Air Force field-division (11. Luftwaffen-Felddivision) in central Greece to fight the bands. The High Commander requests the High Command of the Italian 11th Army for its support. He also demands that all defence industries working for the German war effort which lie within the command zone of the Italian 11th Army should be given proper military protection.

This demand for proper protection of the industries working for the German war effort came too late for the prisoners in Kolokythia and the men who had been shot or wounded in other attacks. But now the efficient German military machine was going to roll into action. The commander for Southern Greece received a cabled order on 31 March, 1943, to transfer urgently an Air Force rifleman regiment (Luftwaffenjägerregiment) to the area between Lamia, Lianokladi and Nezeros. And on 1 April, 1943, confirmation came through:

On the orders of the High Commander South-east, the 21st Air Force rifleman regiment (Lw. Jg. Regt. 21) with one train, one mot. Div. 11, 17 Pz. Rg. AR 11, one gun transferred temporarily to area of Lamia and Lianokladi.

Major von Falkenhausen protested in vain against the decision to put troops in to "comb through" the villages where the Germans had been captured. He knew how the partisans would react to any brutal intervention. "I told headquarters in Lamia to negotiate with the partisans. It was only because no military action was taken that I, Trude Radwein and Gottfried Schwarzenbacher were released when we were captured. I insisted that any kind of aggression on our part would only make things worse for the prisoners. But I was threatened with court martial if I did not keep quiet," the major recalls bitterly.

The leadership of the Italian 11th Army agreed to Löhr's suggestion to proceed together against the partisans. While the 21st

Air Force regiment was being sent to the Lamia area, the Italians marched a company to the bauxite mines in Amfissa where Eppelsheimer, Langer and Herrmann had been captured by Fotis Parnassiotis and Lambros. They also promised to transfer a strengthened regiment to the Lamia area to join up with the German 21st Air Force rifleman regiment to deal with the partisans.

In the meantime, twenty-nine Germans were shut up in prison by the ELAS movement. They were expected to be still alive, but apart from an initial message to the Italian headquarters, the andartes had made no further move and no one knew their whereabouts and no one seemed much to care how the andartes would react to the planned "cleansing operation".

At Andarte Headquarters

Although Arthur Edmonds and Eddie Myers were tired out when they reached Kolokythia late on 31 March, 1943, they demanded to be brought directly to Aris Velougiotis. The Archekapetanios was staying at andarte headquarters, a two-storey stone building in a green field somewhat below the village centre. From the large rectangular room, a wooden staircase leads up to the upper floor which is divided into two rooms by a clay wall.

A long, wooden table stood in the lower room. A fire burned night and day in the rustic fireplace. Aris was there, not only with his bodyguard but also his favourite white horse, which was not unusual for him.

Edmonds did not immediately recognise the andarte leader. The beard he had shaved off for his humbling trip to Athens had not regrown yet, but his manner showed nonetheless that he was one of the leading personalities in the mountains. Greetings were brief. Myers was still annoyed about the outrageous behaviour of ELAS towards Sarafis. He knew Aris well enough to realise that he could be capricious and quite capable, particularly if drunk, of giving orders to mistreat his prisoners brutally.

"Where is General Sarafis?" Myers demanded to know. "On what authority do you hold Sarafis prisoner? I demand that he is freed instantly."

"He is in Kolokythia and well looked after," Aris answered nonchalantly.

"Well, I wish to see him," Myers insisted.

But Aris was not able to comply. "A representative of the Central Committee of EAM who was formerly the Party Secretary in Athens has come to the mountains with me. His name is Andreas Tzimas. He is the Politikos of our movement. You can see him tomorrow and speak to him about Sarafis."

Myers was quite happy not to have to deal with Aris who was always unpredictable. He later described him as being "more Asian than most Greeks and all Greeks are Asian"!

The Brigadier met Tzimas the next morning, on 1 April, 1943. He was not yet forty years old and was already grey, but he had dyed his grey hair brown as a disguise. He spoke fluent French, so he and Myers were able to converse without the help of an interpreter. He had two cover names: "Evmaios" and "Vasilis Samariniotis".

Myers immediately voiced his indignation at Sarafis' capture and the insult to GHQ Middle East in Cairo by ELAS' highhanded disarmament of other national bands.

"Who took the decision to seize these men and how can you justify detaining them?" he questioned the politikos and threatened, as he had earlier threatened Lefterias, that Cairo would cease to supply ELAS immediately unless just retribution was made.

Tzimas, who was not to blame for the events in Thessaly, retorted angrily, "The British give preferential treatment to Zervas and EDES although our organisation is considerably bigger and is represented in every village. You have bribed Zervas with your British gold, but all he wants is to become the next military dictator of Greece." He blamed Britain for supporting the King who had recently arrived back in the Middle East from London.

Tzimas had touched on a raw spot and Myers could not refute all these accusations. He took refuge in his routine reply that "he was only in Greece for military reasons and not as a politician". His instructions as a soldier had been to support rebel movements in Greece which were faithful to the Greek King. As he had not been able to find any, he had to make do with the republican Zervas and the increasingly pushy communists.

Eventually Myers was able to direct the conversation to the topic of the National Bands Agreement. He insisted that Tzimas should sign it immediately and observe its rules strictly if he wished to have ELAS continue to benefit from British support. However, the politikos would not be rushed, but promised to study the paper and discuss it the next day.

Fig. 53   *Andreas Tzimas* (back), *the ELAS politikos with the fighting troops*

While the British Brigadier was having talks with Tzimas down at andarte headquarters, there was a disturbance fifty metres higher up in the village square. Within sight of the Germans' prison windows, several bearded andartes were driving some Italians before them into the square. They were tied together and, as usual, their boots had been confiscated. The partisans swung the Italian weapons in the air and showed off other booty which seemed to consist mainly of bandages and medicine.

The door to the schoolroom was pushed open and sixteen Italian soldiers were squeezed into the already over-crowded room. They looked deplorable. Many had a three-day stubble; their dulled eyes expressed total desperation. They had hardly been fed at all. Day and night they had been forced to march through the mountains and had slept outside, sometimes in the snow, and they were constantly threatened with death.

Inder Gill, the youngest member of Operation Harling, now lives as a pensioned general of the Indian Army in Madras. He remembers how ten of these Italians were captured on the road between Lamia and Karpenissi. "I had been given odd jobs to do like training groups of guerillas to use explosives, minor demolitions and the like. A platoon of Italians was ambushed. One Greek was killed and one of the Italians. The rest were taken prisoner but moved off separately under escort — where I do not know."

Three further Italians belonged to a unit which was ambushed near Nezeros. "About eight hundred rebels attacked this convoy," reads "Supergrecia's" message to "Comando Supremo" on 4 April, 1943:

The train was travelling to Athens with thirty-two officers and a hundred and thirty-one other ranks on board. It was derailed between Nezeros and Karia. But our men were on their guard and reacted swiftly. They were able to put the rebels to flight. Our unit, which is stationed at Lianokladi under German command, was immediately deployed in German tanks. But the guerillas had left the area. We have to report six dead, twenty wounded and three missing. Tracks of blood were noted, which leads to the assumption that the enemy also had some casualties.

And the last three of the sixteen Italians told their story: they were driving an ambulance from Kozani, and took a wrong turning somewhere because the guerillas had turned the signposts around. This led them to a bridge where they were ambushed and shot at in spite of the red cross on their ambulance. The three Italians surrendered immediately without returning fire.

Forty-five people now had to share the thirty square metres of the little schoolroom. Spirits sank lower and lower. Just waiting was terrible. No guerilla leader had been seen, and no contact had been made with the only officer among this destitute lot, Hermann Meyer. They could only surmise what the andartes would do to them. The Italians, in particular, feared for their lives. They knew how the partisans had treated their comrades in the past. It was rare ever to see an Italian prisoner alive again. But Meyer was hopeful for a good ending. His experience was that normally, when German soldiers had been taken prisoner, they were released within a few days. He was supported in this hope by Trude Radwein and Gottfried Schwarzenbacher, who had once before been through all this and had experienced the hell of not knowing what to expect.

In addition, none of the detainees could imagine that the partisans would dare to harm forty-five people. That would be out of all proportion and cause a terrible escalation of warring activities in this "pacified country" and for which the Greek population in particular would almost certainly have to pay a horrific price.

Friday, 2 April, 1943. Extract from the war diary of the OKW:

Lw.Jg.Regt.21(Air Force rifleman regiment) is rushed on 1. and 2.4.43 to Lamia area.

Myers, Aris, Tzimas and Lefterias did not know at this point, that the 21. Luftwaffenjägerregiment (Air Force rifleman regiment) was marching up from Athens, but they were certainly expecting some German reaction to their aggression. Nevertheless, the andartes and the British were confident that the Germans would not venture as far as Kolokythia, as well-trained mountain troops would be needed. And if the Germans did penetrate this far, it would be easy to move on to the next hamlet and hide or even to eliminate the prisoners.

The assembled leadership in Kolokythia was also aware that the prisoners were important pawns which could be used to their advantage. They decided to write both to the German and Italian headquarters in Lamia, stating that twenty-nine Germans and sixteen Italians were being held prisoner and to warn them against taking reprisals. The document was dated 2 April, 1943, and proposed that negotiations should be held with the "ELAS headquarters of Greece" to exchange prisoners. It ended with an ultimatum, saying that "if no answer is received within three days, we shall be forced to execute the prisoners".

These letters were given to a messenger with instructions to deposit them at night in front of the doors of the Italian and German headquarters in Lamia.

But this was only a marginal episode for Myers who had not come to Kolokythia to break his head over the fate of Italian and German prisoners. He had had promising talks with Andreas Tzimas, and when he returned to the rooms he shared with Arthur Edmonds, he commented to him that "Tzimas was an extremely clever and moderate man with whom one could talk without ideological limitations".

Brigadier Myers was all the more disappointed the next morning when Tzimas came to his cottage and declared that "he personally had no objection to the National Bands Agreement in principle, but that he objected to British Liaison Officers having a controlling influence over what should be an entirely Greek matter, namely Greek Resistance". He also objected to the name "National Bands" because "ELAS had existed long before any other partisan groups had been formed".

Still, Myers insisted that Tzimas should sign the agreement unaltered, applying the usual threat that he would otherwise recommend to Cairo to cease payments and supplies. Tzimas likewise stalled for time and used the accustomed reply, saying that he would have to submit the agreement to Athens for discussion with the Central Committee without whose authority he was not empowered to act.

Myers was extremely frustrated. He had hoped for better progress with Andreas Tzimas, particularly because he knew that, apart from Aris, other important ELAS officials and officers from the Athens leadership were present in Kolokythia. These were Evthymios Zoulas and Phoivos Grigoriadis, the son of an old republican general, Neokosmos Grigoriadis. Both these men had ambitions to become the "Stratiotikos", a vacancy which the ELAS urgently needed to fill with a professional military man, if the movement were ever to cast off the reputation of being a motley group of bandits and brigands and to acquire some standing for itself as a credible regular resistance army.

Finally, Myers changed the subject and asked Tzimas what his intentions were as regards Sarafis. Again, the Politikos was evasive.

"We are considering the matter and I will give you the reply later in the day. At any rate, I can assure you that we shall not harm him."

Meanwhile, Denys Hamson had arrived unexpectedly in Kolokythia. When Vlakhos was threatened by ELAS with revenge and fled, his BLO Hamson marched back to Avlaki and informed Chris Woodhouse accordingly. He was sent on post haste to tell Myers the story in his own words.

The brigadier was infuriated by Hamson's account and immediately summoned Tzimas to repeat his BLO's complaints about the behaviour of ELAS. Aris, Zoulas and Grigoriadis showed up for this meeting. The Politikos was unmoved in spite of the emotionally charged atmosphere. He listened quietly to Myers' reproaches and the repeated threat that supplies from Egypt to ELAS would have to be stopped.

"Whether ELAS in the mountains are under the strict control of EAM in Athens, whether they are acting independently according to the whim of their local commanders, your recent behaviour convinces me that you are primarily fighting against any competition by other Greek resistance movements and only secondarily fighting against the common enemy," Myers confronted them grimly.

Tzimas answered coolly, taking the wind out the brigadier's sails by saying, "Tomorrow morning, we will release Sarafis and his officers. This has just been decided. They can do what they want, go where they want, and form guerilla groups if they want. The matter of Sarafis' detention has all been a great mistake, our Kapetan in Thessaly, Koziakis, was indeed in error and we will see that he is severely admonished."

Eddie Myers was speechless. Andreas Tzimas had cleverly assumed that the Brigadier was only bluffing when he threatened to withdraw supplies, because it was obvious that sabotage against the enemy could only be carried out with ELAS co-operation. Four-fifths of the area was already controlled by ELAS, while EDES under Zervas was in charge of the remaining one-fifth only. Four to five thousand armed men belonged now to ELAS, just over four months after the Gorgopotamos bridge's demolition, while Zervas had only collected about one thousand andartes around him.

Nor was it in Tzimas' interest to lose the goodwill of the British. He stressed that ELAS wished seriously to fight off the enemy and

212

denied that they struck primarily at other andarte groups. He presented his facts. Had they not just successfully attacked the Germans? Had they not had great courage in demolishing strategic points held by the Germans? So far only the Italians had been attacked, but did this change of tactic not show their commitment? They were holding fifty enemy prisoners here in Kolokythia. They had kicked the enemy out of all Roumeli except for the garrisons at Lamia and Karpenissi. ELAS had done all this, what more could the British expect?

Tzimas ended the meeting, saying emphatically, "Since coming to Kolokythia, I have had many talks with Aris Velougiotis and Tasos Lefterias. They and I have but one concern, and that is to direct our war effort primarily against the Germans. I have called a meeting for 8 April, 1943, to assemble andartes from all the Roumeli districts. We expect about five hundred guerillas. I wish to speak to them and make our objectives perfectly clear: we are not fighting our Greek brothers, we are fighting the Germans!"

Myers was not convinced. Deeds meant more than words. But he realised that his National Bands Agreement was not going to be signed at the moment and that he had no alternative but to continue to subsidise ELAS. He decided to put an end to speechifying and asked to see Sarafis. He wished to support him to re-form his bands and to create a counter-balance to the communists.

Saturday, 3 April, 1943. Extract from the war diary of the High Command of the Wehrmacht:

Dense cloud. Storm. Lw.Jg.Regt.21 arrived at Lamia.

That morning, on Saturday, 3 April, 1943, the two generals met. Myers greeted Sarafis effusively and congratulated him on his release. Sarafis thanked him reservedly but did not make any mention of Myers' efforts to obtain his release.

To this day, Myers has not forgiven Sarafis for this discourtesy. "I am convinced that my intervention in Kolokythia saved Sarafis' life," the Briton says, "but I am prepared to give historians the last word."

Sarafis looked drained and weary. He pulled himself together and gave Myers a long explanation which he later put in his memoirs that were to be published in Greece, in English-speaking areas and the German Democratic Republic:

During the whole period of my captivity I had been studying the character of my officers more closely and I had become convinced that I had nothing in common with them. My place was not with them. There was no solidarity — just petty ambition and self-seeking and lack of any discipline or respect. I compared them with the guerillas who were guarding us, with the people we saw in the villages we went through and I realised that we were wrong in wanting to create a separate guerilla force, which would end up as the tool of the British, and that we ought to put ourselves at the service of the people. I compared the Zervas-Kostopoulos-Vlakhos bands with the ELAS forces and found the latter to be superior not only in discipline, courage and solidarity but also in their conduct towards the people, and even towards us, despite the fact that they had no professional military staff.

I saw that ELAS was a nationwide organisation, well loved by the people, and with tremendous strength; an organisation which, if it had the support of the politicians and the military, would develop into a unique resistance movement, which would draw to itself all that was sound and honest in the country and would serve the Allied cause better.

Fig. 54   *The two generals: Stefanos Sarafis* (left) *and Eddie Myers*

Without lifting his eyes to meet Myers' gaze, Sarafis continued. "I admit that my companions were astounded at my advice. How could they possibly join people who had imprisoned, bound and beaten them? Not only did I fail to convince them, but Kostopoulos, Andonopoulos and others began to plot secretly together."

The fate of those officers is known. Myers was horrified by Sarafis' lack of character! He could not understand how a high-ranking officer could so lose face and become a turn-coat, just "in order to save his skin".

"Do you mean to say that you are joining a resistance movement which, up to a few hours before, has threatened you with death, and from which, for many days previously, you have suffered insults? Did you not have to walk from the northern Pindus to Roumeli, not only under ELAS guard, but with your hands in chains, a mark of fallen authority and mockery to all whom you passed by the wayside? And now you want to join these very people?"

Sarafis listened to this homily without answering. Myers tried one last time. "ELAS is controlled by EAM which is communist. If you form a resistance movement in Thessaly, we will support you more than the others with funds, heavy weapons, grenades, machine guns, rifles and the like." But Sarafis was adamant.

"What is your actual job then going to be in ELAS?" the Brigadier inquired curiously.

"I have been offered the post of Commander-in-Chief of all ELAS forces in the field," the Greek General answered, smiling awkwardly. "But this needs to be approved by the Central Committee in Athens. I am to leave shortly with Tzimas for Athens, where the final decision will be made."

Myers was disgusted with the opportunist sitting opposite him, explaining away his change of allegiance. Nevertheless, he immediately realised that for ELAS, Sarafis' commitment to their cause was a terrific trump card. If Sarafis became the Stratiotikos, there might at last be some sorely needed military order among the ELAS forces in the field. His move would also signal to other ex-army officers who had been sceptical about ELAS that they too might consider joining.

Soon after this conversation with Sarafis, Myers and Hamson were walking through the village when they noticed a young man, "who looked unusual in that he had very blond hair". They asked who he was. "He is a young Frenchman," said the andartes. "He recently escaped from a German labour camp and joined us." "Bull" Hamson wanted to know more. As he spoke French fluently, he had the young man brought to him. "He broke down in ten minutes," he wrote later.

His French was mediocre. He was, in fact, a German soldier who had had occasion to learn French. He said he was a deserter. In point of fact, he was the first of many spies whom we were to catch posing as deserters. They never did us much harm, and, as in the case of our young "Frenchman", they got short shrift.

How the young man was smuggled in to Kolokythia by the Germans cannot be traced. But he was taken to the schoolhouse where the other prisoners were locked up on 3 April, 1943. He had been badly beaten and kicked, and his boots and clothes had been confiscated.

At the same time, Hermann Meyer was made to appear before the ELAS leadership. When he stepped out of the school with his interpreter, Trude Radwein, his hands were again bound by the andartes guarding them. A man on either side, they marched down the four steps in front of the building and descended the path leading to the andarte headquarters. The track zigzags steeply and it was slippery and wet because of all the rain. Although it was only a few minutes' walk, Meyer did not fail to notice that all around the building and the neighbouring houses there were hundreds of andartes encamped. Some shouted abuse at him, others eyed him with curiosity; many aimed kicks at him. It was like running the gauntlet.

Inside the building, he was brought before Lefterias and Aris, who came straight to the point and said, "We belong to the National Liberation Front EAM and in particular to its military arm, ELAS. Our purpose is to achieve freedom for our country. In the past, we attacked the Italian occupying army. You might remember that last October we captured a German major and a soldier with this woman who is your interpreter."

Aris pointed his finger at Trude Radwein. "She is now again one of our prisoners. The last time, we gave her her freedom and demanded that she and the major should take a letter back to the German headquarters. We stated in that letter that we would no longer

216

tolerate the occupation of our province by German and Italian troops. Sadly, we are forced to realise that your headquarters have taken absolutely no notice.

"Yesterday, we again wrote to the German and Italian headquarters in Lamia, explaining that you have been captured and are being held as prisoners of war. The Germans and the Italians have imprisoned our comrades in Lamia. We have demanded an exchange of prisoners and have set a deadline of three days. If we do not receive a reply, we shall have to resort to measures which shall be cruel."

Meyer was given no opportunity to reply. He was gripped by his arms and pulled out of the room. His meeting with the two leaders, Aris and Lefterias, had taken only a few minutes. He did not understand the words that were hurled at him by the andartes on the way back to his prison room, but he could harbour no doubt that they were prepared to go to extremes.

Deeply depressed, he told the other prisoners about the ultimatum sent to the headquarters at Lamia. They all knew that the Germans would not negotiate on principle with the "bandits". Nevertheless, most of them could not imagine that the partisans would dare to murder close to fifty Germans and Italians in cold blood. But, whatever their hopes and thoughts, they had no option but to wait for the three-day ultimatum to run its course.

"Most precious German blood is at risk"

Sunday 4 April, 1943. Extract from the diary of the OKW:

Mainly fair. Beginning the cleansing operation by reinforced Lw. Jg. Regt. 21 in Lamia area on 5.4.43.

The conditions in the enclosed schoolroom had become unbearable. The prisoners had had another dreadful night. Now they were silent and lethargic; some sat with their backs against the cold clay wall, others lay on the floor on the few coats the andartes had left them. The men were suffering from fatigue, from the cold and that terrible gnawing fear of the unknown. It was worst when they lay on the floor at night, pressed together like canned sardines. Every sound would jolt them out of their uneasy sleep and make them realise with horror that they were really living this nightmare and not dreaming it. Speaking to a comrade helped temporarily to soothe the panic which would still well up periodically from the gut.

A strong feeling of cohesion developed, a bonding between human beings. But gradually, many men grew more dejected and said that it would be better to put an end to it all, anything rather than this uncertainty. Trude Radwein and Hermann Meyer did their best to keep spirits up while he had plenty of time to recall the principles of the officer corps laid down by the "Führer":

The German officer is duty bound to use his unwavering belief in victory if any of his men should become weak and hesitant. Loyalty means fulfilling one's duty to the last. Loyalty is caring for one's inferiors. He who thinks first of his own comforts and needs, he who fails to help and advise his soldiers to overcome the distress and problems of everyday living, he who demands sacrifices which he is not willing to make himself, does not live up to his duty of loyalty. Loyalty is comradeship... Loyalty is respect for the grandeur of history...

But this cynical Nazi code of honour could hardly have been foremost in Meyer's mind that night, on 4 April, 1943, but rather questions about their imminent fate. He knew that Lamia headquarters would never enter into negotiations with the rebels. ELAS was regarded as a "bunch of bandits", it was not a "regular army" and consequently the imprisonment was illegal according both to the Geneva convention and the German standpoint. But why should the partisans care about legality? And what could he, Meyer, do to make his co-prisoners' existence more bearable? Was there any chance of getting out of there? He did not want to show his desperation about the fact that the partisan leaders had not let him speak. All he could do was to stop the group from sinking into utter despair.

He had been asked to repeat several times every detail of his meeting with the andartes and about the letter to the German Commander in Lamia, deposited already two days ago by now. The ultimatum would expire on the next day. What would happen then?

"The general atmosphere had reached a low point. They knew that they had very little hope of coming out alive. The andartes were becoming more and more aggressive, and I couldn't help remembering how they had given short shrift to Kalambouras. They

218

now kicked and spat at the prisoners whenever they were led outside."
This was said by Yannis Karageorgos, the son of a mountain farmer
whose curiosity led him to record all the events, added to which he
had access to andarte headquarters because he was the leader of the
youth group EPON. "The prisoners all behaved impeccably. Trude
and the German officer were always encouraging the others. They had
gained permission at least to wash themselves in the river. We
children would hide in the trees and watch the Kapetan when he went
down to the river. He was very tall; he stood head and shoulders
above the little partisans. We would pass hazelnuts and almonds to the
Germans. The andartes did not mind."

When Meyer returned from washing in the river Vestrisa in the
morning of 4 April, 1943, he was surprised by the news that four
further German soldiers had arrived. These were Maximilian "Max"
Rossmann with a leg wound and Karl Blachnik, both of whom had
been captured at Kurnovon, and Georg Prametsberger and Richard
Nickel whose lives had been spared when Nezeros station was
attacked. Max Rossmann was suffering from his leg injury. For three
days he and Karl Blachnik had been force marched through the
mountains. Whenever Max flagged, the partisans threatened to kill
him. So the Austrian gritted his teeth and pushed on. The wound had
been badly bandaged and cursorily cleaned, and now it was infected.
Trude Radwein tried to tend to it, but she was hardly able to relieve
his pain. There were no medicines nor bandages available to them,
although they knew that the andartes had taken all the medical supplies
from Platistomo Spa and had plundered the Italian ambulance. But the
andartes showed no inclination to help the wounded man.

Georg Lehmkuhl was also unwell. He suffered from malaria and
had a weak heart for which he had been receiving treatment since
Christmas 1942. He was now experiencing pain and attacks of fever.

Fleas and vermin pestered everyone. A change of clothing was out
of question. Food was sparse. They received maize bread and water
and at times some vegetables and hazelnuts and almonds. Many men
suffered from diarrhoea. Those from Platistomo Spa were very cold in
their summer outfits. Hardly anyone still owned shoes.

"They looked careworn and down-at-heel, with their unshaven
faces. Every time the andartes opened the schoolhouse door, they held
their noses because of the stench that came from the small room,"
says an eye-witness from Kolokythia, who is now a bent old woman.

She glances around timidly, as though fearful that someone might not allow her to speak, bends down and picks up a handful of walnuts and gives them to me furtively.

Monday, 5 April, 1943. Extract from the diary of the OKW:

Gusting winds, showers. Regt. 21 in place West of Lamia. So far no enemy contact.

Fig. 55   *German troops on their way to "cleansing operations"*

The reinforced 21st Air Force rifleman regiment had arrived in Lianokladi from Athens in the afternoon of 4 April, 1943. Three Italian companies stationed in Lamia and a further battalion were put under German command to help shield staff in charge of rail protection.

How would the Air Force rifleman regiment behave? Would they proceed with caution, bearing in mind that, as Löhr warned, "most precious German blood was at risk," or would they heed Hitler's order to "massacre every last man, whether in battle or in flight... as no pardon shall be granted."?

Wehrmacht headquarters in Lamia had, in fact, received the andartes' ultimatum and believed the prisoners to be alive, but Hitler's ruling made any negotiations about an exchange of prisoners out of the question. Major von Falkenhausen stood alone when he tried repeatedly to deter the leadership in Lamia from taking reprisals against those localities where the Germans had been stationed before their captivity. The old man curses and grumbles that "the 21st Regiment was a wildly jumbled group of men and those idiots just went off and created havoc".

This "wild group" left Lamia in the morning of 5 April, 1943, and marched in the next few days along the main Lamia-Karpenissi road in the direction of Makrakomi. The regiment was divided into three combat groups of about 3,000 men each. The soldiers knew that the partisans were an elusive enemy whose usual tactic was to fight from ambush with good rear cover and then to melt away in rocky crags and mountain terrain, using their superior knowledge of the area to their advantage. As long as the regiment marched in the wide Sperchios valley there was little fear of ambush, so it made good pace. A report was sent to Löhr saying "there is very little enemy resistance and the villages are deserted".

They marched past the most westerly German outpost, meaningfully dubbed "Stalingrad" by the partisans, which was close to Lianokladi station in the direction of Kastri. But there was no sign of andartes anywhere. The countryside was utterly deserted. The Greeks had posted their sentinels on either side of the valley who signalled the approach of the troops with church bells, trumpet blasts and messengers. When the troops marched through Makri, where a week before Meyer, Wunderle, Kapp and Kohlhoff had been stopped in their vehicle, there was not a soul to be seen. The whole population had left the village and had fled once more to the marshy land on the Sperchios riverside.

Oblivious to the fate of Meyer and his men in this very locality, the troops moved on and reached the equally deserted village of Makrakomi. There they inspected the wrecked sawmill. Sperhias, Platistomo, Grameni and Kurnovon were equally silent and deserted. At Platistomo Spa, Lieutenant Haydn wrote his detailed report about the destruction of the Hotel, the farm estate and the sawmill and the circumstances which led to the capture of Meyer and his three comrades.

As the population had disappeared, the Germans drew the cynical conclusion that each abandoned home proved that its owner had a bad conscience and was "contaminated by the bands" or was at least a collaborator. Consequently, "harsh measures were required" and the German soldiers could burn down the house without compunction.

At the same time, however, the aims of the operation had been scaled down to a minimum of the original intention of the Athens leadership:

Owing to our relatively small numbers and the evasive tactics of the enemy, our aim should not be the total destruction of the bands, but we should obliterate their organisational structures and fragment the groups, and strike at their means of provisioning and shelter.

Fig. 56   *Villagers escaping*

However, the 21st Regiment and their Italian "fratelli" failed to "obliterate their organisational structures" just as they failed to "fragment the groups", but they succeeded in wrecking the houses and terrorising the country folk. Neither the Italian nor the German troops dared to venture beyond Makrakomi, Sperhias, Giannitsou and Kurnovon and up into the mountain areas. The "cleansing operation" was limited to the villages along the Sperchios valley. It was not known that andarte headquarters were in Kolokythia, nor was any attempt ever made to reach that village.

Thus, there was no combat with the andartes, who had long since melted away into their mountain hideouts. A few old people who lacked the strength or willpower to flee with the other villagers stayed behind. They were brutalised, threatened, kicked, beaten with gun butts until they broke down and divulged the hiding places of their loved ones and neighbours in the surrounding woods, caves and marshes.

The villagers were soon found. "Suspected andartes and collaborators" were questioned immediately but no one was shot. The men were rounded up and marched away, amid the cries and protests of their women and children.

The "cleansing operation" in the Sperchios valley

Tuesday, 6 April, 1943. Daily report to the OKW:
Overcast, showers, gusting winds. The undertaking of the reinforced Lw. Jg. Regt. 21 is running smoothly, without much contact with the enemy.

———————

In Kolokythia, on the night of 6 April, 1943, a message was received that the German and Italian troops had marched as far as Sperhias and had searched and plundered all the villages in the Sperchios valley and abducted all the men. So, was this the German answer to the ultimatum whose deadline ended that night?

Meanwhile, Denys Hamson was making his way, accompanied by Nat Barker, from Kolokythia to Thessaly to take up his new post as liaison officer with ELAS there. They had to cross the main Lamia-Karpenissi road beyond Gardiki and found streams of villagers carrying their belongings and fleeing westwards from the Germans and Italians. "The troops combed the areas on either side of the road and searched all the villages," the British reported. In Sperhias they found that the local EAM Committee had collected a dozen armed men who were prepared to stand and fight if the enemy returned. This was truly a suicide commando considering the numbers and excellent equipment of the German force whose mandate was now to:

Destroy all abandoned villages. Shoot all inhabitants who can be shown to favour the bands. If weapons are found or sympathising with the bands is proven, martial law shall apply.

The justification for this brutal order was:

The Italian Army is passive and more or less ineffectual in dealing with the bands which are consequently flourishing. Robust measures are necessary. The longer we wait, the greater the force we will require to put the rebels down.

Back at the school in Kolokythia, the atmosphere was growing desperate. Most of the prisoners had now been incarcerated for more than a week. 5 April had come and gone in a state of terrible anxiety. But nothing untoward had happened. The andartes seemed calm. The prisoners had squinted through the filthy window panes to follow their every move, as each time anyone walked up the mud path from headquarters, they wondered if their last moments had come. But then they convinced themselves that the andartes had only been bluffing and drew new hope.

Suddenly, in the afternoon they saw the "terrier", Tasos Lefterias, scampering up the hill. His hurried movements did not bode well. Several andartes followed him. The prisoners were panic-stricken in the crowded room. For a moment the andarte leader was lost from sight as he rounded the side of the building. But then he burst in. Despair, anxiety and fear were tangible in the absolute silence. Only Rossmann remained lying on the ground and had a worm's-eye view of the beefy man standing menacingly close with his boot laces trailing. He was shouting, beside himself with fury. Trude was made to translate to Meyer while Lefterias aimed kicks at all and sundry.

Lefterias told the prisoners that the German troops had attacked and pillaged Makrakomi, Platistomo and Sperhias. He kept asking whether this was the response to his letter, but he gave nobody the chance to reply. He embarked upon a tirade of deep hatred against the Germans who had invaded his country, destroyed its villages, violated the women, massacred pregnant women, murdered children, shot, deported and beaten the men to death. But he did not include any mention of the Italians in these accusations.

He repeatedly slapped Meyer, who, like the other prisoners, refused to be provoked. Finally, he left the room and stormed back to his headquarters in the same state of fury as he had come.

In the afternoon of 6 April, 1943, there was a meeting of the andarte leaders in which Aris, Lefterias, Tzimas, Zoulas, Grigoriadis, Maniatis and Sarafis took part. Were Edmonds and Eddie Myers present too? They both answer, "I can't remember."

It is a fact, however, that Tzimas and Sarafis left for Athens on 10 April, 1943. Myers writes about his conversation with Sarafis:

Although I argued with him for some considerable time, I failed to make him change his mind, and later that day he left with Evmaios (Andreas Tzimas) for Athens to go before the Central Committee to be approved by them for his new post.

If this is correct, then Myers must have been in Kolokythia until 10 April, 1943. On the other hand, Myers contradicts himself as he also writes that he left Kolokythia on 6 April to return to his headquarers at Avlaki.

In any case, Arthur Edmonds was there, in Kolokythia, in the afternoon of 6 April, 1943, when the andarte leadership discussed their worrying supply situation and analyzed the Italian and German actions. The partisans were at least confident that the enemy would not advance past Sperhias and Marmara to threaten Kolokythia. The paths were impassable for mechanised units at this time of the year and air attacks were excluded as rain and snow clouds constantly obscured the sky.

But the enemy offensive had hit the partisans hard in that the advancing German and Italian soldiers had robbed the farmers in the Sperchios valley of all the food reserves which they held for provisioning the partisans.

In the meantime, over five hundred freedom fighters had gathered in Kolokythia. Andreas Tzimas planned to give his speech on the aims of ELAS on 8 April, 1943. Ever since his arrival in the mountains, he had been calling for this meeting. After talks with Myers, he was keen to assert himself as the representative of the Central Committee and personally to instruct the andartes to stop fighting other andarte groups but instead, to concentrate their efforts on fighting the real occupying power, the Germans. When Tzimas had come up from Athens to Kolokythia, he had found that in Gardiki, which was on his way, leaflets had been printed by the local EAM's underground press, calling for all-out battle against the Italians, but warning not to provoke the Germans. Tzimas immediately had the pamphlets shredded and pulped down!

And now, the prisoners fitted in well with his scheme of things: he would make an example of them. The leadership had agreed. They would show Myers and Edmonds that they had no compunction about ridding themselves of Germans. Five hundred andartes would see with their own eyes that they were serious about tackling the occupying enemy!

In fact, the presence of the German and Italian prisoners was becoming a burden which increased day by day. The ELAS leaders were not particularly surprised that they received no reply to their ultimatum as they knew from past experience that the Germans never negotiated with the andartes. But their sources had informed them that the Italian headquarters in Lamia was prepared to "do something" for its sixteen soldiers.

Lefterias used the usual rationalisation for making short work of the Germans. "The space is needed to lodge our own people. We cannot justify feeding another fifty mouths, even with minimal rations, while our own people are starving, while they are being attacked, beaten and robbed by the enemy, while villages are set on fire and innocent farmers are dragged off to labour camps or shot by execution commandos! There is only one solution: we must eliminate them!"

No one dissented. The ELAS leadership agreed unanimously to hold a "proper" court martial, in tried and tested manner, to hear the case in front of the assembled andartes on 8 April 1943.

Wednesday, 7 April, 1943. Extract from the diary of the OKW:
Broken cloud, weather worsening. Operation Lw.Jg.Regt. 21, two hundred and sixty taken prisoner so far.

While the German log only mentions prisoners, the Italian Commander for the Lamia area reported on the same day in somewhat greater detail:

Italians and Germans have made progress in their action in the Sperchios valley. Although we do not have precise information yet, it has been confirmed that automatic weapons and ammunition have been found. Hostages were taken, some of whom were executed together with bandits.

Fig. 57 (left) *Dr. Lukas Tsagaris*
(right) *Major Sitzenstock*

General Benelli from the Italian "Comando Operazione" showed how forcefully he intended to react to the abduction of his sixteen soldiers now fearing for their lives in captivity in Kolokythia by writing the following to the German Commander:

As a reprisal for killing six of our men in the attack on our convoy, the commander of the III "Corpo Armata" decided to execute twelve communists held in the concentration camp at Larissa.

The fate of the farmers and alleged partisans seized by the 21. Luftwaffenregiment is described by Dr Lukas Tsagaris (who nursed Baron von Falkenhausen back to health) in his memoirs, shortly before he died in the late nineteen seventies:

Disabled German soldiers were stationed at Platistomo Spa. One was lame, another had lost his hand and a third only had one eye. Their task was to conduct the forest operation and the sawmill in Makrakomi. These disabled soldiers helped the villagers and protected them from Italian attacks. Major Sitzenstock and I supported them. They adored me. One evening, in March 1943, the "brave men of the heroic ELAS" arrested and abducted these disabled German soldiers.

When the military in Athens heard of this attack, three SS Companies marched in and arrested about a hundred and seventy villagers in the surrounding localities. They were dragged to the railway station at Stirfaka near Lianokladi and locked in the wagons.

It was about four o'clock in the morning when Dr Tsagaris was woken by a translator who worked for the Germans. "Wake up, Doctor. You must help us. The Germans have taken a hundred and seventy hostages and intend to execute them at Stirfaka."

"I immediately informed Major Sitzenstock," Dr Tsagaris writes. "He contacted the SS Officer to find out why so many people had suddenly been arrested. The answer was that the Greeks who were to be executed represented a multiple of the number of Germans who had been abducted by the andartes."

In the evening Sitzenstock and Tsagaris met in his clinic. The German town commander was not hopeful about the hostages' fate. The doctor made the desperate suggestion that the rail wagons should be hitched to a train passing through and hauled to Salonica. "Then they would at least be out of the grasp of this SS Officer and we would gain time to think of ways to save them."

Major Sitzenstock was not averse to this suggestion. "Can we trust the German officer who is in charge of Stirfaka station?" Dr Tsagaris asked the major. He nodded. His name was Arpich, an Austrian.

So Sitzenstock immediately telephoned Arpich, who confirmed that he would help. He knew, in fact, that two trains were due to leave Lianokladi for Salonica in a short while and gave instructions that one was to be stopped and the wagons hitched up.

Simultaneously, Dr Tsagaris phoned his cousin Ilias Tsagaris in Salonica, who had made a fortune in the tobacco trade and who enjoyed good relations with the Germans. He asked his cousin to speak to Major Schubert in Salonica to request him to take the prisoners into his care when they arrived. Major Schubert agreed; in fact, he owed a favour to Doctor Tsagaris who had restored him to health when he lay wounded in the doctor's clinic after sustaining a wound in the Africa campaign.

When the train drew in at Salonica in the early morning, it was met by a small unit of German soldiers who unhitched the wagons with the Greek prisoners and shunted them to the camp at Pavlos Melas, on Major Schubert's orders. Dr Tsagaris writes:

The SS Officer's complaint arrived on Major Sitzenstock's desk promptly the next morning. An extended investigation into events showed that Arpich had given the order to move the wagons on. Arpich stated that he had drunk more than enough to slate his thirst and had been too inebriated to know what he was doing. He admitted that he could possibly have given the order to hitch up the wagons with the prisoners to the train bound for Salonica. Major Sitzenstock then ordered that Arpich be taken into temporary arrest. He also sent a telegram to Salonica insisting that the prisoners be returned to Stirfaka. But Schubert played the game, a game in which a hundred and seventy lives stood to be saved, and answered by return of post that "the water pipes in the camp required urgent repairs and he needed to keep the prisoners to carry out this work".

Dr Tsagaris is mistaken when he writes that SS units were involved — a typical but understandable mistake. After years of suppressing their memories, authors writing later about the war often believe Wehrmacht troops to have been SS units, the embodiment of all evil. The fact that the Wehrmacht and the Italian Army murdered no less brutally is often repressed. However, this does not change this exceptionally courageous action. Many of the Greek prisoners came from Makrakomi. All of them survived those terrible days. Not a single man was shot. After a short while in the labour camp they returned to their villages. None of the members of the Wehrmacht involved in this action was ever brought to task. The whole matter was dropped.

The andarte tribunal

Thursday, 8 April, 1943. Daily report to the OKW:

Overcast. Showers. Thundery storm. Operation Lw.Jg.Regt.21 reports no contact with enemy. Cleansing continues.

Never had the ELAS leadership assembled so many men! Over five hundred andartes had gathered at Kolokythia to be instructed directly by their EAM representative Andreas Tzimas, by Tasos Lefterias and their Archekapetanios Aris Velouchiotis about the future objectives of their movement.

This triumvirate had decided to use the occasion to bring the German prisoners to a public trial, thus enabling the assembled andartes to attend the spectacle.

Kapetan Thomá writes in his book about this gathering:

In deciding to join ELAS, Sarafis had been favourably impressed by its democratic spirit, a spirit which was not possible in a regular army. He was able to experience this personally in Kolokythia where five hundred guerillas from Roumeli were gathered.

For the first time, a representative of the Central Committee of EAM was sent to the mountains to discuss the problems of the armed troops in the Roumeli mountains. He was thus able to receive a first-hand account of the operation and combat of the soldiers and to hear their views and objectives regarding their fight for freedom.

Despite the bad weather, the five hundred andartes camped on the grassy area in front of the headquarters building. On the first floor, above the front door, there is a weathered wooden balcony from which Andreas Tzimas gave his speech. The Politikos underlined in his address that anyone, even if he was not part of EAM troops, had the right to form individual national resistance groups. And he confirmed the promise given to Myers that officers, such as Kostopoulos could go to Thessaly to establish their own resistance units. "This procedure is not only acceptable but also desirable, because it is not the aim of ELAS to monopolise the national struggle," Kapetan Thomá recorded.

But Tzimas' speech was interrupted by an andarte called Omiros. "But we must not allow Fascists to set up resistance movements which actually aim only to fight ELAS instead of the occupation." The word 'Fascist' was commonly used to refer to anyone who did not in fact belong to ELAS.

And another partisan called Psarianos who climbed a fruit tree, the better to be heard, shouted, "What about the revolution? Aren't we going to have a social revolution?"

This question caused considerable commotion among the andartes, as Thomá chronicles. Andreas Tzimas was very annoyed by the intervention and seemed suddenly to lose countenance and replied angrily, "No revolution, no way! Let that be crystal clear to all of you! Our sole objective is to free our country. When the war is over, the Greek people will decide on their government. But until the day when we shall be free, we need the unreserved commitment of every patriot able to fight. We must hold together, we must help each other and we must pool our resources. He who thinks otherwise and believes he can pursue his own political or personal aims is making no positive contribution to the freedom fight nor is he helping our nation."

The EPON leader, young Yannis Karageorgos was impressed with Tzimas' charisma and energy: "He was different from the other leaders who tended to rant on aggressively. Instead, he repeatedly explained to the andartes that they would lose support in the villages if they took on the role of brutal policemen, beating and killing people simply on the basis of suspicion. He ended his speech by urging the assembled andartes all to combine their energies to fight off the Germans."

This was a tactically intelligent speech, and it was in accordance with Myers' wishes, but history shows that the andartes did not act upon it. Only a few days later, ELAS attacked another independent partisan group, and at the end of the Second World War, such disputes degenerated into the civil war which claimed over 150,000 victims and only ended through British and American intervention in 1949.

Aris, who was still smarting from being called to order in Athens a month before, was content to toe the line as set out by his Politikos, who was theoretically his equal, but in practice his superior. But Aris did insist that a second meeting should be called that same evening in church, to which only the ELAS Kapetanios were invited. Lefterias was also in favour of this suggestion. He wished to take the floor to commit his Kapetanios to the policy of direct attacks on the Germans.

It fitted in the schedule to hold the trial of the German prisoners on the same afternoon, 8 April, 1943. Accordingly, they were led out of the schoolhouse to headquarters while their Italian comrades stayed behind in prison. In the simply furnished room of ELAS headquarters, all the prominent men were foregathered: the triumvirate of Aris, Tzimas and Lefterias, the new-arrivals from Athens Grigoriades and Zoulas, then Fotis Parnassiotis and Elias Maniatis. Among those present there was also Kapetan Thomá, the chronicler, and Brigadier-General Sarafis who wished to learn more about the "democratic procedures which governed ELAS".

The thirty-four Germans knew that the moment of decision had come when the schoolroom door was flung open. They were signalled to follow the armed andartes down the muddy path to the main building, in front of which they had watched the meeting take place. They had apprehensively peered through the branches of the fruit trees but the balcony from which Andreas Tzimas gave his speech was obscured from their view; nor could they know the content of the proceedings.

Hermann Meyer, who regarded the teaching profession as a vocation, had written when he was a young teacher, "If a teacher just does his duty, it means he has not done his duty." Similarly, he was now determined to do more than just his duty as an officer.

Aris, Lefterias and Tzimas, the three "judges," sat behind the long, rough wooden table. Andartes were packed in everywhere, on the stairs leading up to the next floor, and squashed into every nook and cranny. Trude Radwein squeezed in next to Hermann Meyer in order to interpret. Meyer ordered his comrades to stand to attention. Even the injured man, Max Rossmann, had to run the gauntlet in this crowd of andartes.

The hubbub stopped immediately when Aris addressed the Germans. He spoke about the suffering that Germany had inflicted upon Greece, about the killing of so many innocent people, and about the looted villages and the land laid bare. He deplored the fact that the assaults in the valley had devastated the peasants' very means of existence. He underlined that, so far, the Germans had been treated as prisoners of war but warned that this could not be sustained forever. He quoted the letter that the andartes had sent to headquarters in Lamia, and repeated the offer to exchange prisoners. Finally, he demanded that the death penalty by shooting should be carried out unless the attacks on innocent women and children in the Sperchios valley ceased immediately.

232

Aris' comments were repeatedly interrupted by shouts from the audience: "Death to the Germans! They have set fire to our villages and raped our women. Kill the pigs!"

But the Archekapetanios did not heed these shouts. He stood up to give more weight to his words, stared straight at the German officer and spoke directly to him. "I challenge you, as the officer of this group, to negotiate with your superiors in Lamia for the release of our ELAS andartes and to demand the immediate withdrawal of your troops in the Sperchios valley. In exchange, we are prepared to let your people go free."

Trude Radwein interpreted. Although very few of the andartes understood the hated language of the aggressor, there was again silence in the over-crowded room. Meyer took his time before he gave his answer. It was unambiguous. He refused to go to Lamia to bargain for the release of ELAS andartes or an exchange of prisoners. "Furthermore," he claimed, "it is the decision of the German leaders to occupy the villages in the valley. They must have their reasons. I must respect their decision and cannot attempt to influence it."

Instead of at least giving some semblance of accepting Aris' suggestion, Meyer demanded unreservedly and repeatedly that all the prisoners be released forthwith and stressed that Germans and Italians were being detained totally illegally. He was a German officer and, as such, he could not negotiate with rebels!

Kapetan Thomá wrote in 1975:

I still recall that exchange between Aris and the Hitler officer before they were condemned to death. I heard the man myself, that is, he spoke and somebody who knew German translated:

"I shall never negotiate with partisans."

"But if you won't negotiate with andartes," Aris insisted, "then you must realise that because of the conditions in guerilla warfare, the andartes are not in a position to run prisoner-of-war camps. You are playing with the lives of your men!"

"Do what you want," was the final answer of the German officer.

"Death to the murderers!" screamed all the andartes present in frenzied fury.

Fig. 58   *Aris Velougiotis and Kapetan Thomá* (left). *"Do what you want" was the final answer of the German officer*

The daily humiliation, the close quarters, the beatings, terror, fear, hunger and cold had all taken their toll on the prisoners. When they had first been captured, they initially suffered shock and were deeply traumatised. Not only did they fear death all the time but thoughts of their families, wives and children dominated their minds to the extent that it was difficult to make clear decisions; but they tried nevertheless to provoke the andartes as little as possible. After a few days in captivity, some felt better, their will to live revived. But the relentless, nagging fear of death gave them no peace.

Sleep was impossible despite utter exhaustion. Many were physically unwell, experiencing headaches and an excessive urge to urinate. The situation did not improve as the deadline for the ultimatum approached. On the contrary, faced with the reality of the death threat, coupled with the beatings and the undernourishment they endured, they began to sink into resignation and to accept their fate. They had nothing left but their resolve to hang on to their dignity and not to lose their self-esteem despite their humiliation.

234

"Do what you want!" Meyer flung his answer into Aris' face and thus sealed the fate of his companions. It was inconceivable to him, to leave his comrades behind while he went off to Lamia on a wild goose chase to negotiate fruitlessly for the release of ELAS prisoners. He also disregarded the fact that he could at least have saved his own life if he had accepted Aris' proposal.

Andreas Tzimas, though, was still prepared to compromise and insisted that a second letter should be sent to the Germans in Lamia showing unequivocally that the prisoners were still alive. The Politikos calculated that there would be no "cleansing measures" nor shooting of hostages as long as the prisoners were known to be alive. He, whom Eddie Myers had considered to be the only civilised man among the bands, commanded Hermann Meyer to write to German Headquarters in Lamia. He spoke German fluently and addressed the German officer in his own tongue. "Your life and the lives of your people are over. Only an exchange of prisoners can save you now. As you refuse to conduct negotiations yourself in Lamia, then at least write a letter to the German headquarters. I will have it handed in. An irrefutable sign of life from you should make your commanders in Lamia make contact with us."

Meyer was prepared to do this. Tzimas stressed that the letter had to be signed personally by every prisoner. So, a pen and paper and an inkstand were found and the German officer sat down at the long wooden table next to Tzimas, Lefterias and Aris and wrote:

8th April 1943

To the local commander at Lamia,
In the period between 28.3.43 and 3.4.43, we were captured through no fault of our own and have been held as prisoners of war. The leaders of antartis have declared the following:
If attacks are directed against the antartis, we shall be treated as prisoners of war. If, however, attacks continue against the civilian population (women and children), we shall be shot. We ask you to take account of our situation and to save our lives. We ask you to consider the offer of an exchange. There are at present thirty-four German and sixteen Italian prioners of war here.
The antartis leadership sent a letter concerning our situation to your office on 2.4.43. There has been no reply to this letter so far.

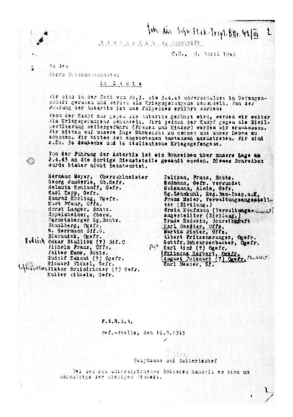

Fig. 59   *Hermann Meyer's letter of April 8, 1943*

Having drawn up the letter, Meyer was the first to sign it with his name and rank. Then he handed the pen to his three comrades who had been captured with him. They, too, signed with name and rank. On it went until everyone had signed. Max Rossmann added 'wounded' to his name, Franz Meier and Erwin Kaufmann mentioned that they were civilians, and Trude Radwein called herself a clerk.

When everyone had signed, Meyer pushed the letter over to Tzimas while Lefterias was already issuing the order to take the prisoners back to the school. "We have granted you a stay of execution," he growled, and added threateningly, "but if the Germans in Lamia don't reply within three days, you will be shot."

Towards evening a second meeting of the andarte leaders took place in the church. About thirty Kapetanios gathered in front of the altar on which Aris stood to speak. Lefterias and Tzimas were among the audience. Some of the andartes were perched on the high chairs on either side of the altar. It was a macabre sight to behold the heavily armed men beneath a picture of Jesus sweetly smiling from an icon high above them in the alcove. The sixteen-year-old EPON leader, Yannis Karageorgos, had slipped into the back door of the church and stood behind Andreas Tzimas when Aris Velougiotis took the floor.

"Aris," Karageorgos recalls, "spoke about ELAS being a democratic organisation where everyone was free to express his opinion. He reminded them that he had formed the first rebel group in Roumeli not so very long ago. He stressed that he would whole-heartedly support the aims set out by Tzimas and suggested that Psarianos and Omiros should apologise for the undesirable comments they had made in the morning." And Thomá recorded:

There was a strong feeling of harmony and satisfaction, so that eventually everybody agreed to follow the objectives as set out by Andreas Tzimas. Tzimas was impressed by the power that Aris exercised over his followers, by the devotion with which they listened to his words, assimilated them and thence forward identified with them.

Then Lefterias spoke. He knew that he did not inspire the andartes in the same way that Aris worked his charisma. But he needed to create a personal image for himself, distinct from that of Tzimas in particular. So he preached fire and blood. No one demurred; on the contrary, his speech was received with applause. He felt supported in his desire to give the odious Germans short shrift. The trial in the morning had not developed to his liking. He considered that the letter written by the German officer was a total waste of time and he was dead certain that the Germans in Lamia would take no notice of it.

Things began to go his way when his friend Maniatis, whom Edmonds described "as the worst communist fanatic", brought news after the "church meeting" that the Germans were continuing their advance in the valley and setting fire to all the villages. Houses were pillaged, women raped, children beaten to death and farmers shot. This news was a signal for Lefterias. He hurried past the guards, had the school door opened and commanded Hermann Meyer to come forward.

One of the sixteen Italian prisoners was a certain Gulielmo De Giulio, from a commando of the Forlì Division. He was freed on 18 April, 1943, and wrote the following:

7 and 8 April passed quietly. On 8 April, in the evening, we were informed that German troops had bombarded and destroyed a village. Many women and children were apparently killed in the bombing (I do not know the name of the village). Later, when the Germans entered the village, two young girls (according to allegations by the bandits) were raped and subsequently killed. Also in the evening of 8 April, an officer of Aris' band appeared (I was told later that he was a relative of the well-known Napoleon Zervas). He singled out the German officer and told him via an interpreter the details about the destruction of the village. Then he kicked and hit all the Wehrmacht soldiers except the woman and the wounded soldier. The behaviour of the German officer and his soldiers was worthy of praise, for they all took this rough treatment without batting an eyelid. After this brutal ordeal, the leader of the band ordered that their shoes and coats be confiscated. Then each German was attached by one arm to a chain. Before he went away, he also commanded that the Germans should receive no food and that they should not be allowed to sleep nor to lie down.

We were told by the guards that we would suffer the same fate as soon as Italian troops undertook any action against the bands.

It is true that Aris was a distant relative of Zervas and it is a fact that villages were destroyed. Makrakomi was indeed bombed. However, the destruction, the pillaging and the bombing took place not on 8 April, 1943, but — and this is only a small but vital difference — on 10 and 11 April, 1943. It is false that "two young girls were raped and subsequently killed". I could find no one in the villages who could confirm this.

Obviously, Lefterias and Maniatis had manufactured a lie in order to secure agreement by the ELAS leadership which assembled again at Headquarters later the same evening, on 8 April, 1943, to proceed to execute the Germans the next morning. They decided nevertheless to deliver Meyer's letter to Lamia. Thomá writes:

No one had an alternative proposal. The decision was not taken by Aris alone; the representative of the Central Committee was in full agreement. They were all of the opinion that the execution should take place.

Thomá does not mention, however, that Lefterias proposed to give those men who renounced Fascism and joined the ELAS-andartes a chance to live. Tasos Lefterias put the question himself to the Germans when he announced the death sentence in the school. "Either you join us or you will be shot tomorrow morning. You can choose between fighting with us against the aggressor or death."

Meyer immediately refused, the others took his lead. No one was prepared to take sides with the communist partisans. Unanimously, the Germans declined the ELAS offer. Lefterias could hardly believe his ears. He requested Trude Radwein to translate his words most carefully: "I repeat: whoever joins our struggle will be spared. All the others shall be shot tomorrow morning! Those who are not fascists will be spared, but those who refuse to renounce Hitler and Fascism shall be shot."

Without hesitation, Meyer answered his would-be executioner, "I shall never renounce my beliefs! Long live Germany! Long live the Führer!"

Lefterias was amazed. Not one of the thirty-four Germans seemed prepared at that point to give up his basic convictions to save his skin! Was it love of country, love of their Führer, Adolf Hitler? Was this a reaction to the psychological terror they had endured for days and to the beatings and humiliations? Or was it loyalty to their officer Hermann Meyer, who had selflessly refused to go to Lamia to negotiate and thus save at least his own life? Tasos Lefterias told Trude Radwein again to translate his offer.

"*Heil Hitler*, long live Germany!" The others now took up the cry.

The Politikos stormed out of the room abruptly and ordered the guards not to give them any food, to chain them up and take away their coats and shoes. They should suffer, they should not be allowed to lie down to sleep, they should stand till morning. He would arrange with Aris and Tzimas that the execution should take place the next day.

"When the Germans were faced with the certainty that they were to be executed in the morning, we could hear them moaning and crying in the room," says Yannis Karageorgos. "Later, they asked to go to the latrine ditch and this wish was granted. Everyone of them went and threw in valuables, rings, chains, watches and family pictures. They told the guards that they would not leave these to the andartes."

"The German officer was a fine figure of a man," says a poorly dressed old woman in Kolokythia. "I was then a young girl. He walked quietly, upright. He was much taller than the guards accompanying him. He took no notice of the jibes by the andartes. None of the Germans showed any emotion when they came out of the schoolhouse. But when they were all inside, during that final night, we did hear them lamenting, wailing and moaning. You could feel their grief. I could not understand what they said. But I still hear their voices."

Hermann Meyer, Oberzahlmeister, (Senior Paymaster), thirty-nine years old, born on 7 September, 1903, in Ülzen, married to Erika, three children, his four-year-old "Helgalein," his two-and-a-half-year-old "Hermannpinz", and his five-month-old "Steppke" Helmut, was led down the path while he slipped his wedding ring from his finger. It was a simple gold ring with "Erika" engraved in it, followed by the wedding date, "28.12.1937". He clasped it in his hand for a second then tossed it into the smelly hole. It was dark. He heard the plopping sound. It was now easier to throw in his watch and family pictures. The guard yelled brusquely. Others were coming. They hardly spoke, many were crying. Some slipped on the mud and picked themselves up on shaky legs. One after the other they went to the cesspit:

Georg Wunderle, Obergefreiter (Lance-Corporal), thirty-three years old, born on 18 March, 1910, in Schwerin, married to Anna, father of fourteen-year-old Anneliese.

Helmut Kohlhoff, Obergefreiter (Lance-Corporal), thirty-eight-years-old, born on 11 November, 1904, in Nienmark, Kreis Schwerin, married to Foolke, father of two sons, three-year-old Gerhard and five-year-old Hans-Dieter.

Karl Kapp, Gefreiter (Private), thirty-three years old, born on 13 July, 1909, in Nagold and resident in Calw. Father and mother never knew to their dying day what had become of their son. His sister lives in Nagold.

Georg Lehmkuhl, Regierungsbauinspektor (Governmental Construction Inspector), thirty-five years old, born on 13 June,

1907, in Oldenburg-Petersfehn, married to Martha, two sons. The man with the wooden pistol into which he had carved: "THOU SHALT NOT KILL!"

Franz Meier, Verwaltungsangestellter (Administrative Assistant), thirty-eight years old, born on 3 May, 1904, in Regensburg, married to Johanna, two small daughters, his "Herzepinkis" (sweethearts).

Erwin Kaufmann, Verwaltungsangestellter (Administrative Assistant), born on 12 August, 1910, in Hamm, Westfalen, had just returned from leave one day before his capture. His father Harry and his mother waited in vain till their death for a word from their only child.

Karl Hässler, Unteroffizier (Non-Commissioned Officer), forty-two years old, born on 10 January, 1901, in Sossenheim, married to Hedwig in Burg near Magdeburg. She died in 1985, still without knowledge of her husband's fate.

Martin Winter, Unteroffizier (Non-Commissioned Officer), twenty-five years old, born on 12 October, 1917, in Weida, Thüringen. His parents died still uncertain about the fate of their son. His sister lives in Augsburg.

Gottfried Schwarzenbacher, Obergefreiter (Lance-Corporal), thirty-five years old, born on 24 October, 1907, in Kleinard, Kreis Pongau. Two daughters. His wife Maria remarried, when she heard no more from him. She died in 1971 in Graz.

Albert Fritzenwanger, Obergefreiter (Lance-Corporal), twenty-two years old, the youngest, born on 21 December, 1920, in Krimml. His relatives live in Mittersill, Austria.

Karl Gross, Obergefreiter (Lance-Corporal), thirty-eight years old, born on 5 July, 1904, in Köln-Volkhoven. Frau Esch, his sister, lives in Düren.

Herbert Fritsche, Obergefreiter (Lance-Corporal), thirty-four years old, born on 22 July, 1908, in Berlin. His wife Margarethe never gave up hope that he would return one day.

August Pruchhorst, Obergefreiter (Lance-Corporal), twenty-nine years old, born on 18 January, 1914, in Klein Mentau, one daughter. His wife Dorothea remarried and now lives in Schwenningen.

Horst Langer, Schütze (Gunner), twenty-eight years old, born on 15 March, 1915, in Chemnitz, married to Dora, two sons (seven and four years old) and two daughters (five and three years old). He had only been sent to Greece a few days before his capture. His daughter Gerda writes: "Those years after the war were bad years of starvation, deprivation and poverty. My mother had four children, and no money... We cherish her always for what she went through."

Georg Prametsberger, Schütze (Gunner), twenty-eight years old, born on 14 June, 1914, in Hohenburg. His brother Josef from Mühldorf, Oberbayern, who never gave up the search, was told by the Red Cross in 1982 that "the prisoner can no longer be held captive anywhere".

Richard Nickel, Gefreiter (Private), thirty-eight years old, born on 30 September, 1904, in Ebersdorf, married to Hermine in Elsenfeld am Main. After the war she moved to Treuchtlingen.

Maximilian Rossmann, Gefreiter (Private), thirty-four years old, born on 7 October, 1908, in Ebene-Reichenau in Kärnten, Austria, married, one three-year-old son Kurt. His wife received a letter from Hauptmann (Captain) Sacher, with the fateful date of 8 April, 1943, saying: "it is not likely that these bands are going to harm all these people."

Karl Blachnik, Obergefreiter (Lance-Corporal), thirty-six years old, born on 17 June, 1906, in Evenkamp-Werne, Kreis Münster. He was a tailor living in Dinslaken-Lohberg. His mother had died an early death, his father was not interested in him, so he grew up in an orphanage.

Wilhelm Franz, Unteroffizier (Non-Commissioned Officer), twenty-nine years old, born on 7 March, 1914, in Uckersdorf near Herborn. His brother and his sister Anna still live in Uckersdorf and "have never given up hope of seeing our brother again".

Rudolf Zahout, Obergefreiter (Lance-Corporal), twenty-nine years old, born on 26 February, 1914, in Schlackenwerth, married to Berta, one severely handicapped daughter, exiled from Czechoslovakia after the war. "Always the uncertainty: did he die a natural or a violent death? Where is his grave or was he never buried?"

Oskar Kudlick, forty-three years old, born on 27 February, 1900, in Koberwitz, married to Ingeborg, who remarried and now lives in Bochum.

Kurt Pfaue, Unteroffizier (Non-Commissioned Officer), twenty-eight years old, born on 17 of March, 1915, in Klein-Biewende, one daughter. His ex-wife Magdalene obtained a divorce in 1940. She lives in Wolfenbüttel.

Walter Kunz, Schütze (Gunner), thirty years old, born on 25 September, 1912, in Unterrot-Brockingen, resident in the farm estate Stalleg in the Black Forest. His brother Wilhelm searched all his life for him and two other brothers who were also declared missing. "I spent all my money looking for my brothers."

Jakob Eppelsheimer, Oberwachtmeister (Sergeant Major), the eldest of the group, born on 5 February, 1898, in Laimbach in Oberbayern. His daughter Erna lives in Augsburg: "I can't understand why we never received a farewell letter from him."

Gertrud Radwein was about forty-five years old and came from Vienna. Sophia, her house maid in Hotel Asklepios, shows me a small tattered photo which she still carries about. She cries: "My mother gave me in writing to Trude for adoption. She was like a mother to me and my own people killed her."

I could only establish the name and rank of the others, viz. Karl Mesner, Private; Konrad Körling, Lance-Corporal; Stahlberg, Lance-Corporal; Wihelm Koller, Private; Alois Holzmann, Private; and Franz Pelikan, Gunner. I could not even find out Stahlberg's first name. One of these men was arrested by Denys Hamson and Eddie Myers in Kolokythia, the others were seized from a train in the vicinity of Lake Xinia.

Only two men did not go to the cesspit when they were led out of the school. These two were Rudolf Herrmann (thirty-five years old) and Private Viktor Schendzielorz (thirty years old), who, instead, spoke to the guards.

Herrmann was area manager on the railways in Zwickau when he was called up to serve in the Wehrmacht. He was of medium build; he had an oval shaped head with dark hair which he combed straight back without a parting. He enjoyed being in Greece, for he loved nature and liked the mountains and hills around Gravia where he was stationed. Here his first contacts with the Greek people were made. As so many other German soldiers, he was invited to their homes, celebrated their feasts with them and learnt a fair amount of Greek. A key experience for him was when he learned that the Italians had shot hostages after the destruction of the Gorgopotamos bridge. He was horrified by the barbaric methods used by the Italians to take revenge. His Greek friends described to him how alleged rebels and communists had been selected at random from the prison at Lamia and packed off to be shot under the bridge. Serious doubts about the war and the German involvement in Greece welled up in him. Although he was a member of the NSDAP (National Socialist Labour Party of Germany), he, like so many others, had joined because membership opened doors. He was keen to get on in his profession and he knew that promotion in the State Railways was much more likely if he was a party member.

Viktor Schendzielorz was a quiet man who had, however, conversed a lot with Rudolf Herrmann during their imprisonment in Kolokythia. On 27 March, 1941, he had been called up to serve in the Wehrmacht on the railways. One month before being taken prisoner, he had been on leave in Silesia visiting his large family, his six children Hubert, Helmut, Rosa, Günther, Manfred and Gerhard. He could not put Günther, the youngest, out of his mind. The baby was only born on 19 February, 1943, on the day of his departure. After a lot of wrangling, he had been permitted to see his wife and new-born son for a ridiculously short hour in the clinic.

'Six children, a wife who has no profession, parents and parents-in-law who all depend on my earnings,' the desperate man must have thought, 'and now I am to be shot.' What for? For principles, for Hitler, for Germany? He was never interested in politics. He was a worker, and as such he had only one aim: to earn enough for his family. To die for the "Führer", for the fatherland and all that, was not acceptable to him any more than to Rudolf Herrmann. For Viktor Schendzielorz, there was no other choice than to try to join the andartes. He and Rudolf had discussed this possibility for days, hoping that Fotis Parnassiotis whom Rudolf knew well might put in a good word for them.

While most of the partisans in Parnassiotis' group knew Rudolf well enough to favour him, Viktor made his plea by stating that he was not really German. He came from an originally Polish area, and had been obliged to wear the Nazi uniform. Fotis Parnassiotis promised to pass on their request to Tasos Lefterias but had them nevertheless brought back to the schoolroom.

Some of the faithful amongst those condemned to death requested to see the priest, Taslikis, but the Good Shepherd avoided making himself available. In fact, he was greatly bothered, as were some of the other villagers, that the Germans were to be shot in the new cemetry, Agios Markos. Until recently, the graveyard was next to the church, in the centre of the village, but, after years of argument, the community had decided to build a new cemetry on a hill overlooking the village. This beautiful site with its powerful pines lies about fifty metres above Kolokythia and provides stunning views all around to the peaks and valleys in the area. Before winter came, the villagers had excavated a large trench into which they had started to transfer some of the remains from the old graveyard. But now the all-powerful Lefterias had decided, without taking advice from anyone, to have the thirty-four Germans shot here. Priest Taslikis protested in vain. He pleaded that the Germans should be made to dig their own graves.

Standing, leaning against the walls, or squatting, the German prisoners wrote farewell letters to their families, but assuming that the andartes would never send them on, they hid them in cracks in the wood floor, pushed them between boards and beams in the ceiling or entrusted them to their Italian comrades. Later, children were to find these notes and puzzle over the strange-looking German writing.

The men must have been driven half-mad by a desire to see their wives and loved ones again. Perhaps Hermann Meyer wrote me a similar letter to that by the Greek Ilias Kanaris from Chalkis, who had written to his son Kosta:

MY LAST WILL

Tuesday, 6th January 1943

My dear son Kosta!
When you read these few lines, my dear son, I shall not be alive, because the Germans will have killed me. They have condemned me to death three times over and to three years imprisonment. My son, my little boy, I leave you behind as a two-year-old orphan, my strong boy, I have loved you so much but I did not have the luck to enjoy you and to play hide and seek with you as I played other games with you. When you are a big boy and you read this letter, I would like you to remember your father and the advice I shall give you, my clever little chap, my little "Palikari", my beloved son. Love your mother, your auntie Lulu, your auntie Andro and your uncle Cristoforos. My son,

never gamble with cards, never behave badly towards a woman in your life, be honest, sincere and truthful. Love your country and be a good Christian. Dear Kosta, my darling son, I bequeath you nothing, for I have nothing. I leave you in good hands, with people who love you and will care for you. Please forgive me, dearest Kosta, that I have left you fatherless while you are so small. I want you to always pray for me, my boy, for they condemned me, because I had two radios and transmitted messages and I belonged to an organisation and helped Englishmen to escape and had a revolver and I tried to strangle their interpreter and many other things, and I carried on espionage.

My dearest boy, I die as "Palikari" with your name on my lips, and in dying I shall cry: "Long live England, long live Greece and long live our allies!" My sweet son, my "Palikari", forgive me for leaving you an orphan. I shall die a "Palikari".

Farewell, farewell, farewell, my brave little man. I kiss you tenderly.

Your father, Ilias Kanaris.

Ilias Kanaris was shot in Kessariani near Athens on 24 February, 1943, with five other patriots.

Friday, 9 April. 1943

Extract from the war diary of the OKW:

Overcast. Operation by reinforced Lw.Jg.Regt. 21 proceeds according to plan, no contact with enemy. Localities abandoned by the population are being destroyed. Two hundred and eighty captured and put up in an assembly camp.

"I shall always remember the wonderful behaviour of those men," says Giorgios Kotsovolos, a shepherd from Kolokythia, in a voice charged with emotion. "It was cold and stormy. Heavy clouds obscured the sky. The Germans watched Lefterias hurry up the hill. They were shepherded out of the schoolhouse. The bell next to the church was rung, I can't remember why. But it somehow unnerved one of the prisoners. He started screaming and threw himself on the ground. His arms and legs were flailing about. Lefterias was enraged and ordered the guards to tie him up. They started hitting him. He immediately quietened down as suddenly as he had started screaming. I believe he was suffering from shock."

"Lefterias called me over to him," relates Yannis Karageorgos, formerly the EPON leader and now a tailor in Athens. "Our house is directly below the school and we children stood about on the square to see what would happen next. 'Get me a long, strong rope, and hurry up,' Lefterias ordered me. I ran into our stable and got the long rope which we used to lead the donkeys. He took it, handed it to the guards and told them to make the Germans undress first and then to tie them together by their hands. He praised me for getting the rope and being so quick."

Lefterias planted himself in front of the Germans, called Trude Radwein over and ordered her to translate. He again put the question, whether anyone would side with the andartes. There was an awful tension in the air. The Germans' eyes hung on Lefterias' lips. Even the noisiest andartes stopped conversing. The Germans did not understand the Cretan. Then Trude translated dutifully.

"The Germans listened to Lefterias with discipline and without any outward sign of emotion. But they categorically refused to throw in their lot with the andartes and to thus save their lives," the old people in Kolokythia still recount, shaking their heads. "Lefterias could not induce them to renounce their beliefs."

The Italians, left behind in the schoolroom, stood at the barred windows and watched the unlikely drama unfold in the muddy square. Children hung about. Andartes leant on their long rifles in relaxed attitudes.

"Did you understand exactly what I said?" Lefterias asked Trude Radwein, doubting the reply she relayed. She affirmed that the question was understood but offered to repeat it in German.

At this point, Viktor Schendzielorz and Rudolf Herrmann made themselves heard. Fotis Parnassiotis confirmed that Rudolf Herrmann had agreed to join ELAS and to fight against Fascism. "The other man is his friend. He is actually Polish and was forced to wear Nazi uniform."

Trude Radwein was told to ask the two Germans whether this was correct, and Herrmann and Schendzielorz confirmed obsequiously. Lefterias ordered the guards to free them and hand them over to Fotis Parnassiotis, who was to have full responsibility for the two men. "If they try to escape, it will be on your head," Lefterias warned him darkly.

"It was horrid," says Yannis Karageorgos despondently. "As EPON leader, I was attached directly to Lefterias. I had heard in the morning, when I was present in Aris' quarters, that the decision had been made to shoot them all."

"And when were they ordered to undress?" I ask the tailor.

Yannis is standing in his tailor shop behind the small counter which he also uses as an ironing board. An old rusty iron stands upon it. On either side there are large wall mirrors, making the room look bigger than it actually is. The former EPON leader can hardly speak because the images of those hours still haunt his memory. His daughter is sitting in one of the rattan chairs under the mirror, next to her mother. On the little table beside them there are some tattered fashion magazines. Yannis wipes his tears from his eyes.

"I can't talk about it. I don't want to say anything."

"It has haunted him all his life," his wife explains. "He finds it hard to talk about it and yet he needs to tell the story again and again," she explains, somewhat ambiguously.

On the road outside tyres squeal. A driver brakes, the other reacts too late; there is a bang. Mother and daughter turn their attention to the events outside.

"When was their clothing taken away from them, Yannis?" I insist.

"In the morning. Everyone had to undress. Everything was thrown on a heap. But they did not have to take everything off. They were left in their underclothes."

"What did they say, did they scream, did they sob, did they pray?"

"No, they said nothing. They were silent. They were tied one to another by their wrists. They had no chance of escape. All the guns were pointed at them. Some of the andartes had automatics. They had no chance at all, everyone was against them."

"But didn't a single man revolt against his imminent death?"

"No, the Germans were quite determined to face up to death. They were composed and made an enormous impression on the andartes."

"It was cold, wasn't it?"

"Yes, it was very cold. When they were led up the hill, it was snowing slightly, just a few flakes, but in the late afternoon there was the last real snowfall of the winter. I remember it well."

Kapetan Thomá was present, as well as Zoulas, Maniatis and Grigoriadis, the son of the venerated general. But these were the city boys from Athens, and Lefterias preferred to appoint a local Politikos to carry out the dirty job of leading the execution squad, so he appointed Fotis Parnassiotis. It was not an easy decision to make, for they were all — possibly with the exception of Aris — inexperienced in the business of mass murder. In the event, the young andarte Fotis Parnassiotis from the Parnassos mountains accepted command of the execution.

The disciplined Germans complied conveniently with the rules. They took off their uniform jackets. The slower ones were prodded into action with rifle butts. The jackets, then the trousers and boots which the andartes were rather keen on were dropped on the ground in the square riddled with puddles. Trude Radwein was rudely called "whore" for living with the collaborator Haralambopoulos. She was made to give up her black fur coat but was left with her striped summer dress. She had chucked her gold chain into the cesspit the night before. Max Rossmann was helped by some of his comrades to pull his trousers off his shot-up leg. Those who had divested themselves of their jackets, trousers and shirts, were immediately seized by the andartes. Fotis Parnassiotis had cut the rope into many small pieces and now he tied one hand of a German to the hand of another German. Meyer, attached to his interpreter Trude Radwein, led this string of prisoners.

They climbed up the four steps to the church. Those who might have wanted to make the sign of the cross one last time could not, because their hands were tied. The priest was nowhere to be seen. They followed the wall and passed the acacia tree with the church bell hanging on its thickest branches. To their right stood a marble memorial to another war, the strange Greek letters covered in a layer of moss. They walked on, beside the bubbling brook, winding its idyllic way down the mountain to join the Vestriza. The cherry trees, prolific in this village, were blooming already, but the strong wind was whipping off the delicate white blossom. To their left they could see a herdsman with his goats and sheep on a meadow which sloped right down into the valley. The tinkling of the little copper bells, which the animals wore around their necks, drifted up. The men tried to support Max Rossmann who had to stop from time to time, for he could hardly walk, but the excited andartes pushed them on with blows with their rifle butts.

It takes twenty minutes to walk up to the hill of Agios Markos, visible by its stately trees from the end of the village. "No one complained, no one spoke. We children ran along on either side of the prisoners. Hardly any of the older villagers came, but we children were curious and the andartes took no notice of us and let us come," Georgios Kotsovolos recounts, who is now a relatively rich man for Kolokythia. "I have two hundred and fifty sheep," he interjects inconsequentially. "We used to bring almonds to the school, and once or twice some cigarettes. The guards didn't mind us doing this. When the Germans were led up to the cemetery, we tagged along. They had given up hope entirely. Armed andartes were everywhere. I walked next to the German kapetan, he smiled and ran his free hand over my hair. He was tied to the woman with his other hand. He recognised me from looking out of the window when we took almonds to the school."

"He liked children," I said. "He was a teacher."

"Yes," said Kotsovolos. "Later on, Lefterias and the andartes said they would have freed them if only they had agreed to negotiate."

"What negotiating power has a prisoner got?"

"A lot," replied the shepherd. "Many Italians negotiated, joined the andartes and later walked free. The German officer flatly refused to go to Lamia to discuss a possible exchange."

In 1975, Kapetan Thomá wrote:

I was lucky enough to be one of the execution squad. No one can deny that what I say is true. Inexperienced as I was, I must admit that I felt an awful pressure on my chest and wished desperately to get away from a situation where I had to shoot any condemned man. I assume that the other partisans had similar feelings, because they were all honourable Greeks with human emotions.

But none of us will ever forget the provocative attitude of the Hitler officer, who constantly barked his Heil Hitler shouts at us, irritated us with his insults against Greeks, and his behaviour was imitated by the rest of the Hitler fascists like a bunch of robots. He was so fanatical that when I caught his eye briefly, he actually nodded to me as if to say: "What are you waiting for? Why don't you shoot me through the heart?"

Who knows what went through his mind and through that of all the others. Did they really believe that they were standing in front of animals, they, who themselves were like animals and who would have mown us all down if they had had a single machine gun. Maybe they believed that in dying a heroic death they would be clad in holy attire and go straight to Hitler's paradise for fascists.

The Germans were herded up the last few metres to the hilltop. They had to wade across the brook which was wider here. The icy cold water bit at their half frozen feet. They crossed the pine grove and were suddenly in the new village cemetery. And there was the newly-dug pit. It had been excavated in a five-by-five-metre square and was two and a half metres deep.

That morning Fotis Parnassiotis had selected a large number of guerillas to shoot the Germans. "One for each German," says Karageorgos. Parnassiotis had them stand about five metres away from the pit. He lined the Germans up directly in front of the pit. "They did as they were told," he boasts. The andartes chattered excitedly, it was suddenly chaotic, disorganised. They seemed more tense than the Germans. The snow fell thicker. Some curious villagers wishing to see the spectacle stood next to the condemned men. Unsuspecting children milled around. No one seemed to bother what this sight might do to a child's psyche. The Karageorgos and Kostopoulos boys pushed their way through to the front "so we wouldn't miss anything."

Meyer made things easy for the guerillas. Their lack of experience in shooting thirty-two people was compensated for by his order to stand to attention.

And they obeyed. They lined up in front of the pit. They stood shoulder to shoulder. The andartes backed up and checked their guns. Meyer stood next to Gertrud Radwein who had faithfully translated every sentence, every word that he uttered up to the last moments. Her left hand was fastened to Gottfried Schwarzenbacher. Lefterias gave her another chance to save her life if she would renounce the Nazis, but she still refused.

The andartes were equipped with a motley set of weapons, mostly of Italian and British make. Some had automatic guns which fired a volley at one pull of the trigger. Some were quite determined to shoot over the heads of the prisoners, for they could not square it with their conscience to kill defenceless, shackled human beings.

Fotis Parnassiotis stood to the side, checked both rows, the men who were to die and those who were to live. "I did not shoot, but I gave the order," he boasts. He is proud of his action, of being in charge of the death squad. "I gave the order to shoot."

"Lefterias was trembling when he raised his gun," says Kostopoulos, the shepherd. "The German Kapetanios screamed *'Heil Hitler'*. The Germans were all standing to attention. Although their hands were tied to each other, they tried to point their hands vertically downwards, along their legs. They stood straight upright, in line. In unison, as from a single mouth, they shouted *'Heil Hitler'* and almost simultaneously all the guns fired."

Those animals who invaded our country were shot by an execution squad of rebels. They all fell backwards except the fascist officer who fell forwards because the bullet hit him in the heart, as he wanted, wrote Kapetan Thomá.

"Lefterias himself shot him," says Kotsovolos. "He shot your father. He was so excited that he forgot to take the stopper off the rifle barrel which he had stuck on for protection. They all saluted and shouted *'Heil Hitler'*. If you ever see Lefterias, you can say to him that he was the man who shot your father. Lefterias wanted him to negotiate over the lives of his men. That question was asked yet again here, at the place of execution, but they all refused. They would have immediately been given back their clothes if they had agreed."

The shot. A little bullet. Legs crumple, a grotesque collapse. Out of control at last. That strong body, 1.80 metres tall and weighing eighty kilograms, slumped forward, slid down the slope and was pulled partially into the pit by his left arm, to which Trude Radwein was attached. She fell onto her back, like the others. His body lay partly on the slope, head up, legs and body in the hole. He looked as though he were standing. The bullet had pierced his chest and left shoulder blade. His eyes were open. Snow fell, mingling with the dirty grey of his underwear. Blood ran from the wound down his arm and contrasted sharply with the white snow and the grey underwear. He could see the mud-caked boots of the andartes. The shot had shattered his shoulder blade and gone through his chest but it missed his heart. Not an instant death. How long did he lie in the throes of death? Blood pulsed out of him with the rhythm of his fading heartbeat.

His comrades were hit "in the head, in the chest, in the left arm, in the face and the left upper arm, in the face and in the thigh, in the head, in the right arm and the right knee, in both arms, in the left lower leg and in the right knee". They all fell backwards into the pit as planned, but they were not all dead.

"It was suddenly quiet, very quiet." Kotsovolos lowers his voice in awe. He is standing exactly where Lefterias shot Meyer. "Then I heard whimpers and groans, some of the bodies twitched, some moved. The snow fell heavier. It was cold and the andartes turned, and ran back to the village. Their impulse was to get away. They could not stand being there a minute longer in this cruel place. Their work was done."

Fotis Parnassiotis is lying when he declares that there was a finishing shot for all those who were "whimpering". No one had the stomach to climb into the pit over the warm, and as yet flexible, bodies to complete the dirty job. And, in fact, it must have been difficult to do so because the hole was, after all, two and a half metres deep. Moreover, Lefterias and Parnassiotis seemed unconcerned about the Germans dying such a brutal, wretched death.

Who were the poor devils who lay groaning with pain, half buried and squashed by macabre, twisted limbs? Were these the ones who had "only" been hit "in both arms, in the left lower leg or in the right knee"? Or was it the man whose coccyx had been shattered? The bullet must have penetrated his abdomen and intestines before it splintered his coccyx. What infernal pain did this man have to endure and for how long?

Most were hit in the head and died fairly soon. But there is no doubt that many were wounded in the chest and suffered for many hours after Lefterias and Parnassiotis withdrew with their andartes. The impact of the shots and the metal splinters exploding within the thorax tore not only blood vessels but also broke through the lung and chest-wall, letting air into the small cavity between these two. Thus pneumothorax occurred, which means that the heart would have lost its rhythm but the sufferer would stay entirely lucid. An agonising, slow death.

Others suffocated in their own blood which accumulated in their mouths as they were incapable of changing the position of their heads. Many survived the hail of bullets but died of exposure. The temperature was close to freezing. They were without clothes and could not move and, therefore, died pitifully of cold, or bled until their extremities twitched spontaneously for the last time like slaughtered pigs in a hole measuring twenty-five square metres or 62.5 cubic metres.

Guglielmo, the Italian soldier, wrote about the last hours of the Germans:

The next morning two of the Germans were released from the chain. All the others including the woman and the wounded man were taken to a place about twenty minutes away and shot there. According to the bandits, the behaviour of the Germans was exemplary. At the last moment before they were shot, they shouted in unison "Heil Hitler".

The two Germans who stayed behind were Rudolf, a miner from the Gravia mine, and Viktor, a miner from the Amfissa mine. These two had asked the leader of the bands to be allowed to stay with the rebels in order to fight National Socialism and Fascism, and this they were permitted to do.

I personally neither saw nor heard anything of the shooting as we were all locked in the schoolhouse. Owing to a strong headwind we did not even hear the shots. But we did see the uniforms of the German soldiers later, as the bandits first robbed them of their clothes before they shot them.

It was about eleven o'clock in the morning when the andartes returned through the snowfall to the village. They hurried down the hill, for there was booty to be had. Lefterias had promised that they could share out the Germans' clothes, which still lay in a heap in front of the schoolhouse in Leonidas Square. Squabbles soon broke out. They particularly fought over the boots, but also the warm overcoats and the uniform jackets. Lefterias had ordered that all the identity discs and insignia should be handed to him so as to destroy them and leave no traces.

Aris' bodyguards pounced on Trude Radwein's black fur coat. There were loud howls as the men cut it up. In 1983 the former andarte Nikos Vlakhos wrote in the ELAS magazine "Ethniki i Antistasi":

Frau Gertrud owned a valuable black fur coat which was cut into pieces. Several cossack-style fur hats were made out of it.

254

Despite Lefterias' ruling, the children went on the hunt for identity tags and other small items which the andartes left lying in the mud. Many managed to grab a souvenir or two. The present Mayor Burchaz remembers that he got Hermann Meyer's braces which others had scorned.

Georg Tzivellekas was thirty-three years old when the Germans were murdered. He had grown up in Kolokythia, belonged to the KKE and, being the official representative of the EAM in Kolokythia, he was directly under Lefterias' orders. An old man now, he lifts his glass of chippero to me. We are in his kitchen. On the window sill above the kitchen table, there is a picture of Aris and Sarafis. I look at it keenly. My sceptical gaze seems to worry him. "That's nothing," he says, as though he wanted to apologise for something. He studies my face through his horn-rimmed glasses and relates,
    "After the shooting of the prisoners, we were terribly scared that the Germans would find out and bomb or occupy Kolokythia. So I decided to escape with my wife and five children and hole up in the mountains. On the way out of the village we passed the site of the execution."

But other people in Kolokythia say that no one fled from the village. Moreover, Tzivellekas would never have been allowed to go without Lefterias' permission. The true reason why Tzivellekas went up to the site of the shooting in the evening was because he wanted to look for clothes with his family. The poverty in the village was indescribable. People still went around barefoot in the mud and snow and there was no food, as the andartes had requisitioned it all.
    Instead of robbing dead bodies, Tzivellekas found to his unutterable horror, that two Germans were alive enough to have climbed out of the pit. "One was lying in the snow and stared at me without a word. The other was sitting on the ground, pushing handfuls of snow into his mouth. I shall never forget their bloodshot eyes. Two women from Kolokythia were in the process of taking off their socks."
    "What, two women were taking the socks off the living men?"
    "Yes," Tzivellekas confirms, nodding. "It upset me so, I ran straight back to the village."
    "The one who was sitting on the ground licking snow was wounded in the legs," confirms Yannis Karageorgos. "He must have gone mad.

His fingers scratched the earth and snow mechanically and pushed snow into his mouth. I couldn't eat for days although I was always hungry." Tears run down the tailor's cheeks. "I can still see it all so clearly, as though it were yesterday."

"I went to the headquarters, to Lefterias," Tzivellekas resumes having regained his composure. "I told him that two men had crawled out and that they seemed to have untied their hands. Lefterias was most displeased, in fact, he flew into a rage."

"What did he decide?"

"He sent off two andartes to shoot them both and throw them back in the pit."

"Was anyone else still alive when you were up there?"

"No, I don't know any more," says the old man shaking his head. His daughter is sitting next to him now and listens with deep interest. "Do you know," she says, "he never told us all this. Whenever the conversation in our family turns to the war, he always changes the subject. It upsets him so much, he always cries."

"We should have slit their throats"

Saturday, 10 April, 1943. The weekend! The sun shone for the first time for weeks. It had stopped snowing. The five hundred andartes and their leaders decamped. Andreas Tzimas and Stefanos Sarafis prepared for their laborious ride back to Athens, having completed their task. Like all great men, Sarafis wrote his memoirs after the war. This is what he said about the andarte assembly in Kolokythia:

I was greatly impressed by the way the assembly was held, by its order, discipline, freedom and simplicity, and by the sound judgement and maturity of thought shown by the guerillas. Far from endangering discipline, these assemblies actually strengthened it, because the guerillas felt that by giving their opinion they were participating in the decisions of the command. During these few days I had come to realise how much ELAS had achieved. It had taken a huge amount of booty (tents, medical supplies, food and military equipment) as well as eighty or so German prisoners who performed various tasks such as road repairs, sanitary duties etc. A fine fate for occupation troops in an enslaved land! On the morning of 10 April, Samariniotis (Andreas Tzimas) and I set out on mule-back with a small guerilla escort.

256

Fig. 60   (left) *Makrakomi's church destroyed*
Fig. 61   (right) *Karpenissi after bombing*

The General's lie, saying that the German prisoners performed road repairs, sounds awfully similar to declarations made by the Nazis who abducted their victims to so-called labour camps where they were in fact subjected to the most appallingly cruel conditions and death.

On that Saturday morning and on Sunday, the 21st Luftwaffenjägerregiment and the Italian units accompanying it ravaged the villages in the Sperchios valley:

The field regiment carried out reprisals on 10.4.43 and 11.4.43 in some villages, such as Makrakomi, Sperhias and Platistomo, by burning down some of the houses and confiscating cattle. The remaining male population, many of whom were in close contact with the Germans, were taken away.

Sophia Vassilki, the maid at Asklepios, returned to her mother at Palea Giannitsou after the Hotel was ruined. She recalls the extent of the brutality used by the 21st Luftwaffenjägerregiment. "Klemens Baldowski, who escaped capture at Platistomo Spa because he was out at the cinema at Lamia, came rushing into our village on 12 April, 1943, to warn us that German troops were on their way to search us. My mother and I did not run off to the mountains, as I had always got on so well with the Germans. My father had died a few years before, but his old uniform jacket still hung at the entrance of our little wooden house. When the soldier entered, he tore up the jacket, but my mother tried to stop him. He pushed her back. But she wouldn't do as he said, so he repeatedly rammed his rifle butt in her back. My mother could not move for the next six years, she was paralysed."

A corresponding report to the High Command of the Army says laconically:

We have increased patrols and undertaken small reconnaissance or offensive operations in areas at risk by the rebel bands and have thus been able to ensure that work in the defence industries can continue and that the population's attitude is more secure and a certain degree of peace is restored. As ordered, the villages of Platistomo, Kastri, Grameni, Sperhias and Kurnovon have been destroyed. In this operation, a total of four hundred and seven men were arrested. In spite of checking, we could not ascertain unequivocally that these men all supported the bands, but they were nevertheless rounded up for work at another location. Operation terminated on 13 April according to plan.

And on that same Saturday evening Jakob Eppelsheimer's superior found time and leisure to write some details to Frau Eppelsheimer about the capture of her husband. Although he could not know what had happened to Jakob on the preceding day, his letter could not have been composed in a more cynical manner:

I have been requested by your husband to send you his greetings. He writes that he is well and that the food and treatment are satisfactory. Your husband has informed us through a messenger that he is at present in the hands of Greek rebels who took him away from his assigned station. The Greeks have let us know through the villagers that he will not be harmed. We have taken the necessary steps here and hope to free him soon. The Germans are very popular with the Greek mountain people and there is absolutely no reason to worry about him. You will have to accept, however, that you are not likely to hear from your husband for some time. I will keep you posted and will inform you immediately he is released. Heil Hitler!

Frau Eppelsheimer had to wait a very long time for news of her husband. She made numerous requests, and four years after the war she was finally given a succinct message on 12 August, 1948. "There is no record so far that the subject was reported lost nor any indication of his whereabouts."

Shortly after Sarafis and Tzimas had ridden off on their mules, Aris and Lefterias were brought the unlikely news that two Englishmen had been seen in Marmara, the neighbouring village, and that the men were "filthy and half-naked" and were begging for clothing. They had been parachuted in and had lost all their belongings and clothes in doing so. Apparently they were dressed only in their underwear.

Lefterias cottoned on immediately. There had been no parachute drops in the previous night, because Arthur Edmonds would certainly have informed him. The fact that the men wore only underwear made the matter even more suspect. Tasos Lefterias immediately summoned Georg Tzivellekas as well as the two andartes whom he had sent up to Agios Markos, and asked them to confirm that they had indeed shot the two Germans dead on the previous evening and thrown them back into the pit. And he knew it could not be Rudolf Herrmann and Viktor Schendzielorz, as they were still in Kolokythia with Fotis Parnassiotis. It had to be two men who had escaped the massacre.

Tzivellekas and Lefterias and a group of andartes marched back up to the cemetery. They decided that they had to count the bodies in the pit. But that was not an easy task. The dead were lying on top of each other, their arms and legs intertwined with the limbs of others. In falling backwards in their death throes, their bodies had twisted into macabre shapes, they had grasped what they could and never released their grip. There was blood, excrement, tattered bodies everywhere. And now volunteers needed to be found to pull this incredible carnage apart to count the dead. Thirty-two bodies should be in the pit.

"Lefterias gave the command to jump into the pit and to count. But no one budged," says Tzivellekas. "Then somebody had the idea that the Italians should be made to do it. Tasos was quick to accept this proposal. So the Italian prisoners were brought out of the schoolhouse, and body after body was lifted, turned, piled on top or laid next to another body."

That must have been hard work. The corpses were now stiff. The rope tying them together had to be cut. It made the Italians feel nauseous, many threw up as it stank of excrement and death.

"They had to count them twice," says Tzivellekas and looks at me through his thick horn-rimmed glasses with an immobile countenance. "At last they were sure. Two men were missing. There were only thirty corpses in the pit."

"The woman?" I ask.

"She was dead."

"The officer?"

"I don't know." The old man found it difficult to answer.

"What did Lefterias do then? I can imagine that he was not looking forward to confronting Aris with this fact."

"Well, Lefterias was furious. He told the Italians to fill in the pit. And when we went down the hill together, he was swearing and said, 'Why didn't anyone listen to me? We should have slit their throats and we would never have been in all this mess'."

On the run

Did they have friends among the partisans, did they have the presence of mind to duck at the right moment, or did they have incredible luck? Karageorgos and Kotsovolos concur that many Germans had become good friends with some of the partisans wherever they were stationed. "These men simply could not bring themselves to kill their German friends. But they had to shoot, so they aimed above their heads." Apparently, many an andarte volunteered to participate in the death squad precisely in order not to shoot "his own" German friend.

The two Germans who escaped injury must have fallen at the right moment; they were pulled in by those falling beside them and dragged down backwards into the two-and-a-half-metre-deep hole. Dead comrades fell next to them and on top of them. Fresh blood spouted from innumerable wounds. They heard the cries of those with light injuries, the groans of the severely wounded and the death rattle of the mortally wounded and, above them, the nervous outburst of chatter from the partisans. The weight of the dead and dying bore down on them, they felt the cold emanating from the wet earth and the scantily reburied bones beneath them. Their hands were tied to dead comrades.

Although the andartes moved away from the pit within minutes, the survivors must have felt that it was an eternity. They could register movements in the pit, death tremors in the limbs of those whose wounds were fatal. Four of the men succeeded in freeing themselves from their shackles. They tried to hoist themselves out of the deep hole. Two of them had arm and leg shots. One of them stood upright on the corpses and pushed another up until he was able to grasp a protruding tree root and pull himself to the top. The knots attaching their wrists had been tied in nervous haste and it was not difficult to undo them. It was considerably more difficult to extricate themselves from the mass of stiffening human bodies. They had to push their dead comrades aside in order to get out of the pit.

While one of the wounded survivors sat in the snow a few feet from the pit, in a state of dazed madness, the other was so exhausted that he could hardly move further. His heavy wounds would not allow him to escape. He had been able to crawl just five metres from the grave when Tzivellekas saw him.

In the afternoon the two Kolokythia women came and took the socks off the man who was luckily either mad or in a severe state of shock and the critically injured man who was unable to fend them off. This was robbing the dead while they were still alive. What indescribable suffering had these women gone through to debase themselves to such an extent?

"I could only watch it for an instant," Georg Tzivellekas repeats, "but I cannot rid myself of the sight of those mens' red rimmed eyes, beyond tears, empty."

The German with major wounds knew that Tzivellekas would be back in the village in less than twenty minutes. He probably calculated twenty minutes to the village, ten minutes to find Lefterias, perhaps another five minutes to summon Parnassiotis' execution squad and another twenty minutes to return up the hill. So he had just under an hour to wait in this way for his murderer.

The other two survivors were unharmed. "One of the two was Gottfried Schwarzenbacher," says Sophia, the hotel maid. "The andartes told me later." This sounds plausible, because Gottfried was well known in the Sperchios valley and well liked. Some Greek friend must have shot above his head. His nickname "Kokino" is still remembered today in the villages around Hotel Asklepios. What must this man have felt when he undid the rope tying him to his lover who lay dead beside him and who had stayed in Platistomo Spa for his sake?

The other survivor was about twenty-five years old, 1.74 metres tall, and with blond hair.

The slope from the cemetery at Agios Marcos down to the river Vestrisa is incredibly precipitous. As fresh snow covered the ground and the men had no shoes, they must have slithered down, snatching at the trunks of pine trees, clinging to shrubs and undergrowth. They stepped on bramble which tore their skin, pushed through brushwood, stumbled over rocks and boulders until they reached the gently flowing waters of the river Vestrisa. The fruit trees and other broadleaf trees offered them scant protection from possible pursuers as the branches were still bare. They crossed the stream, stepping on the slippery grey stones in the river bed, and once on the other side they had to push through rotting fern which grew densely on the bank. They knew that if they went down river, they would soon be back in Kolokythia. So their only chance was to climb the mountain on the right side of the river in order to push on in the next valley.

Gottfried Schwarzenbacher and his companion must have been strong men. Otherwise it would not have been possible to climb to this altitude half-naked and shoe-less. Even in summer, well nourished and equipped, it is no easy ascent. But their mortal anguish must have freed some untapped energy. They succeeded in reaching the top of the partially snow covered, nine-hundred-metre-high mountain, south east of the river Vestrisa. It must have cost them an enormous effort and great suffering, because when they saw the huts and houses of Marmara huddled below, they decided to proceed directly into the village. They probably had no choice, for without warm clothing they would not survive the night.

When they reached the small village in the dark, they told the amazed and sceptical inhabitants that they were English on the run from the Germans. They asked for food and clothes. But there was an EAM presence in Marmara and its representative had knowledge of the execution of the Germans in Kolokythia. So the half-naked, wasted-looking men were treated with the utmost caution. The villagers became particularly suspicious when the "Englishmen" refused to be taken to Kolokythia. Nevertheless, they gave them food and clothes and then the Germans seized a favourable moment in the early hours of the morning to disappear. The EAM representative promptly sent a messenger to Tasos Lefterias to report.

The likelihood of the two fugitives reaching the nearest German garrison had to be extremely slim. ELAS and EAM were very well organised in this area. Many villages were still connected up to the public telephone network. The andartes and even the English used it regularly. Furthermore, the Greeks had the enormous advantage of knowing the countryside intimately, while Schwarzenbacher and his companion only knew that they had to head north to find Germans or Italians. And even that was not easy, because the risk of discovery was too great for them to use the dirt track between Marmara and Sperhias. They debated how they could escape this wilderness to reach the Sperchios valley and wondered whether they should separate in the hope that each man alone would stand a better chance.

The fugitives must have been too exhausted and fearful after their stop at Marmara to go far on 10 April, 1943. So they spent the day holed up in the dense brushwood just off the stony track from Marmara to Sperhias. They rightly suspected that the search for them was on and hoped that after a while things would quieten down.

In the evening of 11 April, they pushed on, stumbling along the mule paths in the pitch black night. But they soon realised that they were making very little headway without the help of an experienced guide.

As daylight broke they found it to be too dangerous to contemplate marching on. So they stayed in their hide-out, somewhere between Marmara and Perivoli. Finally, in the early evening, when dusk was falling, they pushed on. When they reached the Inacos river, Gottfried Schwarzenbacher decided to follow the main road to Dilofo. He wanted to continue during the night and was prepared to take the risk of being discovered. Perhaps he still remembered the area from the time when he had gone to reconnoitre it with Baron von Falkenhausen for timber exploitation.

The other fugitive was, however, too exhausted to follow the Austrian. He opted to stay another night in or around Perivoli in a barn, a deserted hut or a warm stable. Thus, the two comrades separated at the Inacos river.

The shepherd Ioannis Skoljas always lit a fire on cold evenings in front of his hut. He and his wife slept with the sheep in the stable which they had built out of brushwood. When the German saw the fire, he could not resist it and approached, hoping for warmth and perhaps some help.

"The German saw the fireplace where sheep are kept on the outskirts of Marmara," Yannis Karageorgos recounts. "He must have wanted to warm himself, but the shepherd and his wife were terrified by this stranger who suddenly loomed out of the darkness, roughly clad and down at heel. They did not know him so they were highly suspicious of him. They let him sit at the fire and then suddenly pounced on him. Together they managed to tie his hands behind his back, and that same night, Skoljas sent his wife off to Kolokythia to inform Aris that they had captured a stranger in front of their hut."

"How could they have been afraid of a half-naked, half-dead man?"

"The organisation had already warned all the villagers and shepherds in the area that two Germans were on the run. Everyone except the Germans themselves had been informed, but they, of course, knew that the hunt was on. The shepherd reproached himself bitterly; he regretted having seized a defenceless human being, but had he violated andarte rules and helped the German, he would have paid with his life. Nevertheless, he never got over it, and a few years later, he hanged himself somewhere near Marmara. He killed himself because he could never rid himself of that image of the German lying tied up beside him while his wife went off to get the andartes."

Shackled again for the second time within two days, the blond young man lay for a few hours next to a stranger who looked down at him with fear and terror. They could not communicate, for neither spoke the other's language. The German knew anyway that his time had come.

The henchmen arrived the next morning, Aris Velouchiotis, Kapetan Thomá and other andartes. The German pleaded for his life, he begged to be allowed to join the andartes now. "Now," they said, "now, you want to join us? Now, suddenly, after you turned us down three days ago? How can we trust you?" They deliberated among themselves and decided to kill him.

The young man was shot at the wall of the Marmara graveyard and his gold teeth were removed. In the nineteen sixties his remains were dug up and registered by the Volksbund Deutsche Kriegsgräberfürsorge (German War Graves Commission):

U 7561
Unknown
about 25
1,74 m
no personal items found
gold teeth broken out
blond hair

But what about Gottfried Schwarzenbacher? What happened to
Friedl, who had decided to press on to Dilofo in the night? The
distance between Perivoli and Agios Sostis is twenty-two kilometres
and about halfway, on the top of a hill, there lies the pretty village of
Dilofo with a stunning panorama. The Austrian skirted Dilofo, leaving
it to his right, and went on in the direction of Agios Sostis and Kato
Kalithea, two villages close together and only about ten kilometres
away from Kastri. From here the track falls steeply down into the
Sperchios valley. On a clear day one can see Lamia and the Aegean
Sea behind in the east, Makrakomi in the north and the imposing
Mount Velouchi in the west.

The view down to the valley and to Makrakomi, which he knew
well, must have instilled Gottfried with new hope. All he needed to do
now was to pass through the village of Mesopotamia which is halfway
between Kato Kalithea and Kastri, cross the bridge over the Sperchios
near Kastri and then he would be within reach of the German outpost
nicknamed "Stalingrad". But doubt assailed him. Would he be able to
cross that wooden bridge which would undoubtedly be watched by the
andartes? Swimming across was out of the question. Here the river
bed is so wide that even an excellent swimmer would have trouble in
the currents. Or would he have the patience to hide all day and to risk
crossing the bridge at night?

Initially, Gottfried Schwarzenbacher decided to push on as far as
possible in daylight. The river below him, the valley and the
comforting sight of Kastri on the other side had such attraction that he
took a gamble. He skirted Mesopotamia, the last village on the
Sperchios, and in the afternoon he reached the fields bordering the
forested swamp area on the riverside.

Fig. 62   *Kastri with its fortress "Stalingrad" on the river Sperchios*

Grigoris Tzivaros is now eighty-three years old. He is sitting in the market square at Kastri on a rickety old chair with a metal frame and dirty plastic seat. With deliberate movements he rolls a cigarette, and insists that I should smoke too. He subtly conveys the impression that he considers non-smokers to be inferior. His hands tremble; but, muttering into his bushy moustache and signalling with his canny eyes behind tinted glasses, he indicates to me that I should lick the side of the cigarette he has just rolled for me. The village seems to live on tobacco; it is processed here after being harvested in the fertile valley.

266

Fig. 63   *Greek priest with ELAS-andartes on their way to new
operations*

Finally the old man condescends to speak. "We were in the fields
on the other side of the river. I saw the man first. He was very
scantily dressed. He did not speak. He was lying in the field in a
furrow. I gave him my jacket and handed him over to the priest in
Mesopotamia."

"What! And that was it?" I react, stunned. "You simply took him
into custody, gave him your jacket and then handed him over to the
priest?"

"Yes, that's right," the old man nods.

"And the man just let this happen?"

"Yes, don't you see, I wanted to help him. I gave him my jacket.
He followed me. Then the priest from Mesopotamia came along the
path on his mule and he took him along."

Gottfried Schwarzenbacher never crossed the Sperchios river. He
was no more than a hundred metres, as the crow flies, from the safety
of the German garrison. He put his trust in the priest, in the hope that
the Good Shepherd would help him to cross the bridge. But the cleric

was hand-in-glove with the partisans and delivered the German to his Kapetanios Thanos.

Gottfried was interrogated and shot forthwith. His grave was found in the nineteen sixties. He died on 12 April, 1943.

His tragic flight was recorded by Kapetan Thomá:

Two Germans escaped death. The bullets missed them. They fell under the other bodies but were able to flee in the night. The Italian prisoners whom we held in Kolokythia were made to count and bury the dead the next day. They discovered that two were missing.

Half-naked, as they were, they reached Marmara where they posed as Englishmen who had escaped from the Germans. The villagers gave them some clothes and the Germans then tried separately to cross the River Sperchios and reach Lamia. But they failed. One was apprehended by revolutionaries under the command of Kapetanios Thanos who were guarding the wooden bridge across the river. He was interrogated and shot.

The other man was captured by partisans who were members of the reserve force. He was brought to Dilofo where we were stationed with Aris. He told us what had happened to him and begged to be accepted into the rebel army. But how could we trust him? He was refused and therefore executed like his comrades.

CHAPTER NINE
Missing

The Italian Soldier's Report

Concurrently with the action by the 21st Luftwaffenjägerregiment, the Italians had launched their own "cleansing" operation. A message cabled over the telex network and dated 12 April, 1943, runs:

ITALIANS INVOLVED IN CLEANSING THE AREA AROUND AMFISSA REPORTED TWELVE DEAD, THIRTEEN WOUNDED AND TWELVE MISSING. DURING THE ITALIAN OPERATION AT AMFISSA, FORTY-THREE BANDITS WERE SHOT DEAD AND TWO VILLAGES WERE BURNED DOWN.

Whereas German troops "only" took prisoners, their Italian allies shot forty-three "bandits" in reprisals. What was the reaction of Aris, Lefterias and Parnassiotis? Did they take revenge on their sixteen Italian prisoners, which they had threatened to do, as Private De Giulio recorded "as soon as Italian troops undertook any action against the bands"? In fact, Fotis Parnassiotis, who commanded the execution squad at Kolokythia, was himself the "politicos" of a guerilla unit in Amfissa. The appalling loss of life among his own ELAS troops would surely have been communicated to Kolokythia Headquarters by the following day.

But surprisingly the Italians were released from their death cell in Kolokythia on 18 April, 1943. They were blindfolded and brought at night to the main Lamia–Karpenissi road and left to be picked up by their comrades who had been alerted beforehand by the partisans. Had their freedom been bought as intimated by von Falkenhausen? I felt I had the answer to that question when Fotis Parnassiotis gave me this barefaced lie: "We never had any Italian prisoners in Kolokythia."

The facts are different. Supergrecia cabled their Comando Supremo on 19 April, 1943:

Fifteen of our soldiers who had been captured by the rebels in various attacks have been released near our barracks.

And Lieutenant Haydn recorded:

A letter dated 8 April, 1943, and signed by thirty-four German prisoners was found at the local headquarters at Lamia. There was also a letter dated 9 April, 1943, from Andartis headquarters which announced that the prisoners would be executed in three days if the rebels' demands were not met.

Lefterias, Aris and Tzimas, this cold-blooded triumvirate, drew up their cover letter on 9 April, 1943, some hours *after* the Germans had been shot:

ELAS Headquarters for Greece

9th April, 1943

We refer to our letter of 2 April, 1943, in which we informed you of the capture of Germans and Italians and to which we still have not received any reply. We enclose a letter from the prisoners and we point out once more that if we do not receive your answer within three days, we shall be forced to execute them.

The Headquarters
(Stamp and signature illegible)

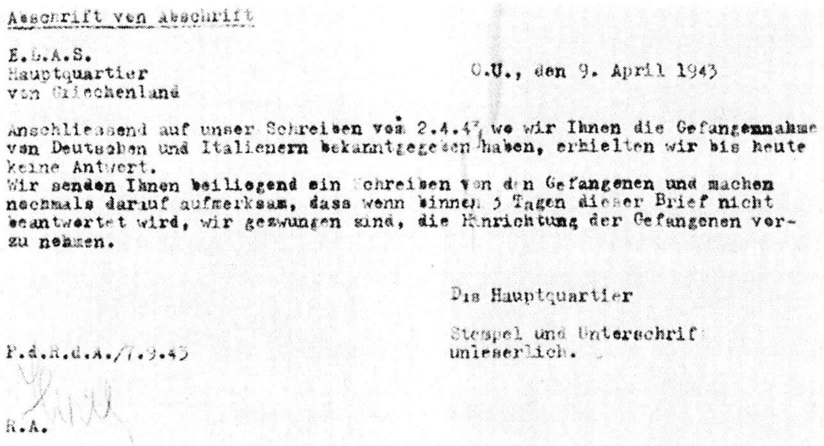

Abschrift von abschrift

E.L.A.S.
Hauptquartier
von Griechenland

O.U., den 9. April 1943

Anschliessend auf unser Schreiben vom 2.4.47, wo wir Ihnen die Gefangennahme von Deutschen und Italienern bekanntgegeben haben, erhielten wir bis heute keine Antwort.
Wir senden Ihnen beiliegend ein Schreiben von den Gefangenen und machen nochmals darauf aufmerksam, dass wenn binnen 3 Tagen dieser Brief nicht beantwortet wird, wir gezwungen sind, die Hinrichtung der Gefangenen vorzu nehmen.

Das Hauptquartier

Stempel und Unterschrift unleserlich.

F.d.R.d.A./7.3.43

R.A.

Fig. 64 *Official translation of the written ultimatum from ELAS. The document was not deposited at Lamia headquarters until 15 April, 1943*

The andarte leaders only had the two letters dropped off at German headquarters on 15 April, 1943, basically in order to delay German retaliation for as long as possible. However, these documents did not galvanise German command into any action at all as the field division had already moved on:

The field regiment left the Lamia area on 12 April, 1943. No steps were taken to free the prisoners, such as making counter-demands or an alternative ultimatum. Nor was any attempt made to penetrate the area of Evritania where the bandits are billeted and the prisoners were most likely to be held. According to sources in Makrakomi the entire area up to Makrakomi is again under the bandits' control. Some inhabitants have returned, others are still in hiding because the bandits have often been known to attack Greeks who are considered to be wealthy or friendly to Germans.

On 22 April, 1943, the Italian Headquarters in Lamia finally confirmed the cruel truth:

Our soldiers who were released by the rebels have reported that thirty Germans were executed by the rebels in Kolokythia.

And on 30 April, 1943, the Italian commanding officer, Brigadier-General Giovanni Del Giudice, wrote to the German commander "concerning the German soldiers captured and shot by the bandits":

Please find enclosed an extract of a report written by infantryman De Giulio Guglielmo who was released by rebels on 18 April, 1943.

Twenty-nine German soldiers and a woman were imprisoned in Kolokythia by the rebels on 3 April, 1943. Another four Germans arrived on 6 April, 1943, thus increasing their number to thirty-three (+ 1 woman = 34). They were treated like the Italian prisoners except that when Makrakomi was destroyed, a Greek officer called Zervas, slapped and kicked them all except for the woman and one soldier with a leg wound. Then he had their coats and shoes confiscated, he ordered them to be chained together, each by an arm, and told the guards not to let them sleep nor to feed them. On the following day the Germans, including the woman, were led out of the village and shot, with the exception of a miner called Rudolf working in Apostolia and another miner called Viktor working in Topolia, who had both requested and been permitted to join the bandits and to fight with them against Hitlerism and Fascism. The behaviour of the Germans, both during their captivity and their execution was admirable: no lamenting, no signs of fear. Before their death they all shouted "Heil Hitler!" The officer, in particular, was a brother to them all, comforting them and suffering the humiliations and beatings with a proud bearing, and whenever he was insulted the name of Hitler or Germany rose to his lips. They were all shot, but first their uniforms were taken away.

The commanding officer, Brigadier-General
Giovanni Del Giudice

But what happened to Rudolf Herrmann and Viktor Schendzielorz? We know that they were not actually miners but railwaymen who were captured at the stations close to the mines. And again, Aris and his band were mistaken for Zervas. We also know that pillaging and wrecking of houses in Makrakomi only took place after the shooting. Many former andartes declare now that "the Germans were shot because German troops set fire to the villages in the valley". That is simply not true.

The German command had the report by De Giulio and the letter of 8 April, 1943, signed by Hermann Meyer, copied and circulated to various military staff headquarters. Copies were still being made as late as 16 August and 7 September, 1943. Nonetheless, the German army never invaded nor hit Kolokythia. There was documentary evidence from the Italian soldier that thirty-two Germans had been shot, but who precisely were they? There were no bodies, so they were classified missing and their families were informed accordingly, but no one was ever told of the contents of the two letters nor of the Italian report.

In a way, this is understandable. De Giulio speaks of Rudolf and Viktor who were not shot but joined the partisans. There were two men called Rudolf among the captives. So was it Rudolf Zahout or Rudolf Herrmann who switched to the partisans?

The Wehrmacht made a judgement worthy of Solomon. It informed both Frau Berta Zahout, wife of Rudolf, and Frau Anna Herrmann, mother of Rudolf, that their Rudolf was missing.

272

Missing in Greece

In the summer of 1942 Hermann Meyer had been on home leave for the last time. Erika and he had gone together to visit his parents in Ülzen and her father in Dorfmark where they went for long walks on their beloved heath and took pictures of their children on the grass in front of the old chapel.

And now, it was almost the end of April, 1943. She had twice been to visit her father in Dorfmark in the last four weeks, for her mother — she never called her stepmother — had died on 23 March, 1943, after a long illness at the age of sixty-four. Erika's father was alone again, having been widowed years before when his first wife died in childbirth. He had then prevailed upon his wife's elder sister to come and look after little Erika and after a while, it seemed right to get married. Soon afterwards, Erika's little brothers were born, Gerhard in 1912 and Siegfried in 1914. But now they were both at war, Gerhard was serving in Southern Italy as a pilot and Siegfried was a young lieutenant at the eastern front. Her father continued to teach and was the headmaster at the village school in Dorfmark.

Since Hermann had joined up at the end of 1939, he and Erika wrote to each other very frequently, sometimes even daily. He would meticulously date and number his letters on the foldable tabletop in his "bunker", as he called his tiny train compartment. Suddenly, since the beginning of April, the letters had stopped. Erika had only just returned to Mellendorf after her mother's funeral and felt depressed and worried, but she tried to convince herself that letters had been late before. In the last few months she had often been unable to suppress her fears, and had written to Hermann complaining that he had now been away at war for almost three and a half years. It seemed that the "years of victory" had long gone. And Hermann, too, it seems, had begun to realise that the war could not be won any more after the Stalingrad disaster.

His letters cannot hide the frustration and despair he must have felt, and he could only offer words of encouragement to his wife who had to cope alone with her fears and the problems of raising three small children:

Fig. 65   *Summer holidays in 1942. Hermann and Erika Meyer
with their children Hermann and Helga in Dorfmark*

*My darling "Schetterchen", your letters of the seventeenth and
eighteenth made my day! I expect that, by now, you have taken new
hope. You have that wonderful spirit. Your most beautiful words were:
"everything will turn out alright, Daddy" Yes, Mummy. Everything
will turn out just fine. Yes, Mummy, I feel like you do, that just a few
hours together would make everything so much easier...*

274

Fig. 66 *The Oberzahlmeister in his "bunker"*

But the worries would not go away. The three small children did not give her much peace. Helmut had been born on 18 October, 1942, he was just six months old. She wrote about every detail of his birth, describing his delicate features in long letters to Hermann who had not even seen his youngest son.

Her friends, and especially her neighbour Lina Baumgarte, would say comforting words to her. "The war is over out there. Mothers and wives whose men are at the eastern front are the ones to worry. Greece is a holiday paradise in comparison!"

But suddenly there was no mail. Hoping and surmising did not help. Every morning she dashed out to meet the postman and every morning he shook his head apologetically. Finally she telephoned her father who appeared on her doorstep the very next day, and insisted on taking her back to Dorfmark with him.

News reached her there, by telephone. It was Mayor Bruns from Mellendorf. She dropped the headpiece as soon as she heard his name and screamed uncontrollably.

Finally her father took the message. "Hermann has been captured by bandits. He has been taken away into the mountains. They don't know what has happened to him. You are only being informed as a precaution. Our people have often been seized in this way and then freed within a few days."

Then the waiting started again, the sedatives from Dr Brütt, days and nights of uncertainty, then the letter from Captain Christ, the description of the capture and those words... "my duty to prepare you that the worst could happen". But there was also that other sentence which served to keep a gleam of hope shining through: "There is, however, no reason to fear at the moment that your husband is not alive." This was the sentence which inspired her to make her children pray every night before going to bed. "Dear God, make my daddy come home soon. Amen."

Her father-in-law, Hermann Meyer, whose bedridden wife never left her bed again after the news and died in July 1943, wrote desperate letters to Richard Wertheim, a soldier from Ülzen who was a member of the 117th Company of Rail Engineers. Wertheim replied on 15 May, 1943:

He left at ten a.m. At five in the evening they were not back. We drivers began to say we hoped they had not been attacked by bandits. We still waited, then our superiors tried to phone but could not get through. I was supposed to drive thirty men the next day to discover what had happened to our four men. When our office informed headquarters of this plan, they forbade us to go and investigate. Two days later 3,000 soldiers arrived and were immediately deployed. Many villages went up in flames... Altogether twenty-eight men were missing. A priest informed one of our military sections that our men were alive and were being held as prisoners of war... Let us hope for the best, Herr Meyer!

Heinrich Glüh, Erika's father, was in contact with Erich Klein, who had gone bravely into "bandit-land" to investigate:

I could not find any trace of the missing car... In this area similar cases have occurred in the past and hostages have been freed within four to eight weeks... We have not as yet found any concrete evidence. But there is no doubt that something will turn up soon. The matter will definitely be cleared up... I will naturally continue every effort to find the missing men — after all, we are all concerned for our paymaster and our comrades.

Eisb. Bau Kp. 117

Kapp Karl	Meyer Hermann
Metzger	Lehrer
13.7.09 B	7.9.03 T
Nagold/Württ.	Wellendorf/Hann.
Gfr.	Ozahlm. d .
Griechenland 3.43	Saloniki 3.43

Fig. 67   *List with snaps of missing persons compiled by the Red Cross in the nineteen fifties which was published under No. 05862 of the forces' postal services. Next to Karl Kapp details on Hermann Meyer but no snapshot*

On 30 June, 1943, she received the last letter from any member of the 117th Company of Rail Engineers. Richard Wertheim wrote that in the meantime the unit had been transferred a thousand kilometres further north:

*I shall probably have to wait another six months for my home
leave. Then I will be able to tell you and your father-in-law more than
I am allowed to write. I have not heard any more about your husband
who was, as you know, my school friend. I shall be in touch when I
am on leave.*

Neither Richard Wertheim nor any other comrades were ever in
touch again. The war ground on and the Meyer family and Hitler's
army had lost one member. Just a statistical detail, really, when one
considers that it is estimated — no one even knows for sure — that
36,652 human lives were lost every day on average. 60 million people
died in 1,637 days of war. In words: sixty million. So what was one
ridiculous little human life?

"'Missing', that is a cruel word," her brother Siegfried wrote from
somewhere in the field. "Hermann might have fallen, but then he
might well still be alive."

Then there were the dutifully comforting letters from friends and
acquaintances:

*When your initial suffering recedes somewhat, remember that our
thoughts are always with you. Your greatest help can only come from
your trust in the Lord and from your own heart. And if it should ever
beat out of kilter and lose its rhythm, then, dear Erika, take the hands
of your darling children. Look deep into their innocent eyes and your
turbulent heart will regain its calm.*

The teaching staff sent a communal letter of condolence, thus
saving themselves the disagreeable duty of writing individually.
"Hermann is a popular and respected comrade to us, the teachers. It is
incredible that he should have become the victim of a nasty,
treacherous war." They did not seem to bother to ask themselves who
had started this nasty treacherous war.

Gerhard, her brother, was the only one who dared speak the truth.
He had been shot down over the Mediterranean and picked up out of
the sea but he was psychologically scarred ever since. "Hermann is
dead, *c'est la vie,* don't harbour any false hopes."

At her insistence, Captain Christ confirmed on 1 June, 1943, that
"your husband, for whom I had a high regard, is still listed missing".
Becoming more practical, he added that "the Company has sent on his
personal belongings on 29 May, 1943".

A few days after Captain Christ's letter, a small plywood box painted blue with black lettering saying "Oberzahlmeister H. Meyer" arrived in Mellendorf. And later, only on 17 July, a certain Lieutenant Marquardt wrote, "Having been transferred out of the Greek area, I am only now able to send you the keys to your husband's case."

Thus, finally, having stared at the last token of her husband's life for several weeks, she brought herself to open the wooden case one night. Apart from a few personal belongings, it contained notes on his travels (he planned to write a guide book after the war), his camera and many slides of the country and its people, of soldiers and the destroyed and reconstructed Gorgopotamos bridge. The last photo shows him with two comrades and Thalia, Stravros Haralambopoulos' grand-daughter, in the grounds of Hotel Asklepios in Platistomo Spa.

Reprisals and hostages

Von Falkenhausen was suddenly called upon by the authorities to write a report "on the activities of the bandits" in the Lamia area. Having returned safely from that "bandit infested" district, where he had been conducting a search for the missing Germans, he wrote down his findings on 20 April, 1943:

The bandits are organised in tight military fashion under the command of superior Greek officers. Most men wear uniforms and are well armed. To civilians and would-be followers, they underline their national Greek character. Recently, however, communist ideas, apparently with the connivance of English or Russian agents, have taken on greater importance. As a result, there is some ambiguity in the population's wish to support and co-operate with this movement. For the most part, people only participate when threatened by the force of arms. Those who were employed by German or Italian military sections, in particular, have often been maltreated, killed, or at the very least have had their property appropriated. A large proportion of the civilian population has consequently fled to larger townships or has gone into hiding somewhere...

When villages are occupied by the bands, detailed lists of all the able-bodied inhabitants are immediately drawn up and they are warned that they must be available as soon as they are called up, or else they will be shot. Similar lists also exist for areas which are not entirely under bandit control...

As it became more and more certain that the thirty-four Germans would never come back, German reprisals in central Greece became more and more severe. The perverse logic of war, a seemingly endless period of cruelty and violence and intensified counter-violence resulted and escalated until the last German troops left the Greek mainland in October 1944.

Professor Constantine Apostolos Doxiadis, architect and engineer, who received a doctor's degree at the Berlin Polytechnicum, wrote in 1947 that "Makrakomi was ninety-eight per cent destroyed by the end of the war". Villagers say that it was attacked and destroyed seven times by Italians and Germans. This village, in particular, bore the brunt of a mad, destructive rage of the occupying troops after the disappearance of the thirty-four Germans.

Unimaginable brutality was used. The andartes continued to pursue their strategy of avoiding direct confrontation with the German troops, but they made sure that they regained control of the villages and countryside as soon as the German or Italian scouting patrols returned to their barracks. Neither side ever gained terrain or positions. But the country folk were made to suffer senseless killings and dreadful sorrows. And as the Germans never had sufficient troops to occupy the countryside effectively, their only strategy was to increase terror among the civilians in the hope of thus undermining the resistance movement. Naturally, this policy only served to inculcate the civilians with such hatred that the Germans lost any support they might once have had. Reprisal was now the only item on the agenda.

The desperate civilians feared not only the German occupier but also the British S.O.E. members leading their sabotage teams. Deputies of villagers would often appeal to the team leader not to carry out some act of sabotage as they would have to suffer German reprisals. Sometimes their pleas were met. On other occasions planned attacks were betrayed to the Germans, so that the element of surprise was lost and the operation had to be aborted.

Myers wrote that "it was a serious psychological error by the Germans when they bombarded villages. It only served to force men whose houses had been destroyed to go into the mountains and join the andartes".

Even Oberleutnant Waldheim, who was to become the Secretary-General of the United Nations and later the despised President of Austria, even he — who professes not to remember, not to know anything about reprisals, not to have had anything to do with them — wrote in May 1944:

Reprisals taken so far for sabotage acts and attacks have not had any noteworthy effect in spite of their severity because the duration of our operations is limited and the villages and areas which have been punished have to be abandoned again to the control of the bands.

As early as in November 1943, he expressed himself very positively in favour of the "prompt employment of reprisals", and that the "curtailed activity of the bands" was a direct result.

The barbaric factor of multiplication used to shoot defenceless and generally completely innocent hostages varied slightly in application. Almost all the shootings were carried out by the Wehrmacht whose communications passed over Waldheim's desk daily from autumn 1943. Whereas, originally, the decision over life and death was taken only by top military command, from July 1943 onwards every divisional commander could make his own judgement. As a result, the number of hostages killed increased.

When, for instance, andartes sabotaged the rail track close to Lithochoron in early July 1943, fifty Greeks were shot and four villages were burned to the ground. When a Greek policeman was murdered in Cumic on 13 December 1943, fifty hostages were taken from that village and shot. The Wehrmacht murdered thirty people in retaliation for the shooting of a Greek policeman in German service, and for a series of andarte attacks on 1 January 1944.

The Italian occupation force was no more squeamish. When the "Città di Savona", a vessel moored in Pireus harbour, was dynamited and sixty-nine horses perished but no humans were harmed, "counter-measures" were taken — by the Germans murdering ten, and the Italians murdering nine hostages on 17 June, 1943.

Fifty Greeks were shot near Heraklion for the death of one anti-aircraft soldier. The report on this event, dated 5 July, 1943, and sent to OKH (Army High Command), ended, "Further shootings threatened unless population helps to find the culprit within seven days."

In the beginning of June 1944, the SS destroyed the village of Distomon and shot two hundred and sixty-six inhabitants on the grounds that they had supported the partisans against the SS squads.

In contrast, "only" ten hostages were shot on 21 January, 1944, for the assassination of a Greek official. Obviously, a Greek was worth less than a German, even if he was in German service. Two hundred people had to pay with their lives because the German General Krech and his escort were ambushed and treacherously murdered. One hundred of the victims were actually shot by Greek units collaborating with the Germans.

Fig. 68   *Reprisals: A hundred hostages shall be put to death for the life of one German soldier*

Ten people were shot because a train was attacked. For the death of an SS officer on 7 August, 1944, six hundred hostages were taken and bundled off to the horrific Haidari prison near Athens.

A massacre was carried out by the LXVIII Armeekorps in December 1943 which was the culmination of a major purging operation started in October when twenty-eight villages were burned down and 918 Greeks shot. The town of Kalavrita was razed to the ground and the entire male population above fouteen years of age, a total of 696 human beings, were shot because of their supposed allegiance to the andartes. The German "Huguenot General" v.LeSuire was responsible for this massacre. "The Wehrmacht is still too considerate to this nation of pigs," this man said. His superior, General Hellmuth Felmy, who was formerly the commanding officer for Southern Greece, attempted to court martial him for this mass murder, but he was not able to assert his will. Towards the end of the war, however, after tens of thousands of innocent people had lost their lives Felmy came to this belated realisation: "All the random acts of revenge, the senseless shootings, the burning of entire villages and towns did nothing to help us but were to the advantage of the enemy."

Fig. 69   *Destruction of Distomon and murder of two hundred and sixty-six inhabitants by SS squads on the grounds that they had supported the partisans*

There are really no accurate figures of hostages shot by the Germans, but it is assumed that over 20,000 Greeks were murdered in the period between March 1943 to October 1944 and that about the same number were imprisoned.

Out of the 70,000 Greek Jews, only 10,226 were still alive in Greece after the German retreat from the country. On 15 March,

1943, two weeks before Meyer and his comrades were captured in Makri, the major deportation of the large Jewish community in Salonica began, the "Entjudung" (cleansing of Jews) of Greece. Cattle wagons, cynically marked "Weimar", the town of Goethe and Schiller, were used to transport 45,000 Jews to Auschwitz over a period of only a few days. Only about 2,000 of those deported survived. On 5 April, 1943, the Italian "fratelli" in Lamia were offered "eight hundred Jews for repair work on the railway station at Lianokladi"; these were "expatriates" from Salonica. But the Italians would have none of it. The arrival of "such workers would not be desirable as the German commander had not done anything to make Lianokladi safe". However, once the station area had been made "safe", the first Jews were sent along. Hermann Meyer's comrades guarded them. Nowadays there is a small marble stone at Lianokladi station which recalls the "five hundred Jews who were in employment here". For over a year now, the stone has been scrawled over with swastikas. No one seems to be bothered to remove that muck.

Professor Doxiadis estimates that during the entire period of the war, 390,700 Greeks lost their lives and, of those, 300,000 died of starvation. 1.2 million people, or eighteen percent of the Greek population, lost their homes during the occupation. Others estimate that over half a million Greeks died during the three and a half years under occupation, which is about seven percent of the total population. Added to this, another estimated 400,000 were suffering from tuberculosis, and over a third of the population had malaria by the end of the war. 3,700 towns and villages stood in ruins. 88,000 people lived in the country in hovels and 145,000 people lived in dereliction in the towns. There were 5,000 wrecked schools listed, without window panes, heating or basic installations.

The Axis powers lost over 20,000 men in Greece. Over 15,000 of these were German soldiers. Their burial sites were scattered in four hundred and thirty-seven communities and several Aegean islands until 1965, when an agreement on war graves was signed between Greece and the Federal Republic of Germany and, as a consequence, a cemetery in Maleme in Crete and another at Dionyssos-Rapendoza near Athens could be extended. These now hold the graves of German soldiers — 4,465 in Maleme and 9,000 in Dionyssos-Rapendoza.

Judgement on the Greek resistance organisations varies. Woodhouse praises the EDES movement, but has less time for ELAS.

For him, ELAS was always useless in combatting the Germans. "It was ideologically much more directed towards fighting its Greek brothers than the Axis powers. Apart from bringing terror and martial law to the mountains, the ELAS andartes achieved very little." Other historians commend the resistance movements for tying up over 300,000 Axis troops in Greece and thus making them unavailable for deployment in other war zones.

It is a fact that after the success of the Gorgopotamos sabotage, Hitler constantly sent further divisions to Greece. Even when the Allies had started to invade Sicily in July 1943, he continued to strengthen military presence in Greece as he still feared that the Allies would create a further front there. Thus, by October 1943, the number of German troops in Greece had swollen to 273,000 men. In addition, there were 54,965 Bulgarians, and 18,000 Italian combat and auxiliary troops stationed in Greece.

When Mussolini was captured in July 1943 and an armistice was signed between the Americans and the Italians in September 1943, the Italian occupation army was dissolved in what were, at times, chaotic and murderous circumstances. They surrendered without resisting to the LXVIII Armeekorps in the Peloponnese, but in other cases Italian units were overpowered ten to one by Germans disarming them. Italian soldiers and officers everywhere flogged off anything that could be converted into money. Not only arms, clothing, horses and machines were sold, but entire ammunition dumps and freight trains loaded with war equipment of every kind passed into the hands of the partisans. Even political prisoners were sold to their families for anything up to two thousand gold sovereigns per head (a gun cost one gold sovereign), and the ransom money was paid because of the threat that the prisoners would otherwise be handed over to the advancing Germans.

On the Ionian Island of Kefallinia, the Italian commander Gandin did not immediately accede to the German demand to lay down arms. Negotiations proved futile, so General Lanz, commanding the XXII Armeekorps, gave the order to attack, and in the resulting massacre 4,000 Italians died in the span of four days. Gandin and all his officers were shot on Hitler's orders. Survivors were sent off to the Russian front and were never heard of again.

Those who had once been "fratelli" now went on the long list of enemies of Germany. 265,000 had gone to Greece but only 220,000 returned to Italy, 30,000 served with the Germans and the rest were interned as prisoners of war.

That was the deplorable end of the proud Italian army which had started the war in the Balkans with its attack on Greece.

Return to Cairo

Chris Woodhouse says that Eddie Myers returned on 10 April, 1943, to Avlaki. During his four weeks' absence a great deal had happened. Several British and New Zealanders had been parachuted in. Woodhouse had made all the arrangements to put them up in accommodation which resembled the luxury of a four-star hotel in comparison with what Myers and his men had had to cope with only a little more than half a year earlier. Up to the liberation of Greece, two hundred and sixty officers and men were parachuted into Greece but there were two fatal casualties in the jumps.

John Cook reported to Myers on the creation of a partisan organisation in Albania, Tom Barnes on sabotage plans in Epirus, and Chris Woodhouse announced that he had now established excellent radio contact with Cairo and was in constant communication with the liaison officers who were already distributed all over Greece.

The restless General did not stay in Avlaki for long and in early May he set off again for Lamia where he wished to meet Andreas Tzimas in order to finalise the National Bands Agreement. On 10 May he reached the Lamia–Karpenissi road which was now completely in ELAS control. He was picked up at the arranged meeting place in the car confiscated from Hermann Meyer, and driven safely to Karpenissi and on to Sperhias. The general enjoyed a beautiful, warm evening in the garden of a private house there and wrote:

Vines growing up the pillars of the veranda were in bloom, and the garden was full of sweet-smelling spring flowers. After dark, lolling comfortably in garden chairs, Tommy, my host and I were sipping our ouzo when we heard an aircraft approaching. I recognised the note as that of one of our own Halifaxes, a type of aircraft which had at last arrived in the Middle East for our "Special Operations" squadrons, and which, as a result of our advance from El Alamein along the coast of North Africa, the RAF were now able to use to bring supplies from airfields in the vicinity of Derna, several hundred miles closer to Greece than the old ones in the Nile Delta. Two sorties were due for

Arthur Edmonds, one of them including in its load three sapper officers, who were being specially sent for our next attack on the railway. The aircraft overhead must be one of them.

Myers did not stay long in Sperhias. He set off into the mountains to Arthur Edmonds' headquarters at Anatoli, a tiny village high up in the mountains between Kolokythia and Mavrolithari to discuss with him and the three sapper officers what their chances were of blowing up the seemingly-unassailable Asopos bridge, which ran along a-hundred-and-one-metre-high and almost vertical mountain face, crossing the deep Asopos gorge and leading from the mouth of one tunnel to another on the other side. Having received confirmation that the Gorgopotamos viaduct was again in use since the beginning of January, Myers decided to destroy the Asopos bridge.

Donald Stott and a small party of volunteers succeeded in an extraordinary exploit on the twentieth of June, 1943, and placed explosives under the viaduct. Four men descended into the gorge by means of ropes, but found that they could get no further without additional rope. They left their explosive charges in a dry place and returned to headquarters to signal to Cairo for more rope to be dropped. Four weeks later they returned and using the extra rope they reached a path almost underneath the viaduct. Their luck was in. The German guards engaged in repair work had cut neat gaps in the barbed wire and had left a ladder leading up to a platform where they could reach the main girders. At two-fifteen in the morning the charges exploded and brought down the central span of the bridge. Photographs were taken by RAF planes, and, some months later, Eddie Myers was himself able to present them to Mr Churchill. "I still remember his gleeful chuckle," the brigadier recalls proudly.

The bridge across the Asopos gorge was rebuilt in only four weeks by the 61st German Rail Engineers Company, which worked around the clock under the most difficult conditions. All the debris hindering reconstruction and the materials required to rebuild the foundations for the girders had to be transported on steep mule tracks. But on completion, the supporting crane collapsed, apparently caused by faulty seals of the hydraulic jack, and as a result, part of the bridge crashed into the gorge. Major Sieber, forty German soldiers and Greek workmen lost their lives. A special transport from Germany brought new materials, and after another four weeks' work the bridge was operational again.

Fig. 70   *Reconstruction of the Asopos bridge; a drawing by a
Rail Pioneer, Professor Karl Pfeiffer-Hardt*

A few years ago Myers wrote in the New Zealand Royal Engineers
Journal, "With delight we learnt that one of these piers had collapsed,
causing the demise of several Germans." But the brigadier is mistaken
when he states that German units shot all their own guards because
they were convinced of treachery.

In Great Britain the destruction of the bridges over the Gorgopotamos and the Asopos are considered to be among the most gallant achievements of sabotage in the Second World War. In Greece, however, hardly anyone knows about the Asopos operation. Aris, Sarafis and Tzimas had refused to take part. They considered the undertaking to be too dangerous.

Not long before the successful attack on the Asopos bridge, Myers had received a coded message from Cairo saying that the Allies would invade Sicily in the second week of July, and that as from early June "Operation Animals" was to be carried out with as many sabotage acts as possible to distract the Germans from the intended invasion of Italy. The destruction of the Asopos viaduct had, therefore, been perfectly timed.

Hamson and Edmonds and their andartes were particularly successful in blowing up a number of smaller road and rail bridges: they laid mines, broke up roads, cut telephone cables and sabotaged sections of track to create a knock-on effect in disrupting trains. Operation Animals was a ringing success as Axis troops, who might otherwise have been sent to Italy, were drawn from northern Europe and the Balkans to fight in Greece.

Myers' endeavours to co-ordinate all resistance operations on the basis of his National Bands Agreement were finally successful. After interminable meetings a revised "Military Agreement" was signed by Andreas Tzimas on behalf of EAM/ELAS on 5 July, 1943.

Myers chose for their joint headquarters the small resort town of Pertouli in the Pindus mountains. He reckoned that he was now indirectly controlling 16,000 ELAS andartes, who, on their part, could call on the same number of armed villagers. EDES comprised about 5,000 andartes but were limited to the Epirus area and Evritania, whereas ELAS had spread quickly throughout Greece. However, the concept of a co-ordinated command centre for which Myers had laboured so hard was not to last longer than October 1943. The interests of the individual andarte organisations were far too diverse for the British to hold them together. "As soon as a British officer turned his back on EAM/ELAS, they attacked other andarte organisations instead of concentrating on the enemy," Eddie Myers deplores grimly.

After the invasion of Sicily Myers was informed that the Allies had no intention of moving the battle front to Greece. He consequently proposed, and obtained approval from his superiors, to hold a conference in Cairo with the participation of all the Greek interest groups. To this end, a safe airstrip was sought which would fulfil landing and take-off requirements.

Hamson took on this task with enormous verve. He was, after all, still keen to get back to the Middle East. He managed to complete an airfield in little more than a month in the midst of enemy occupied Thessaly, high up on a plateau. A large labour force of Greek villagers was employed to flatten the strip with shovels and pick-axes. As the landing ground took shape, it was camouflaged with branches resembling trees so as to hide it from enemy aircraft reconnaissance. At times as many as three hundred and fifty people were working on the plateau. Cairo supported Hamson not only with money for the workmen but also with drops of anti-tank and anti-aircraft guns.

A German sergeant who was captured by andartes and brought to Hamson for questioning paid with his life for seeing the airfield. Hamson could not risk leaving him alive. "I did not want to compromise our security in case the man got away."

The German prisoner seemed relieved to be questioned by the Briton who asked him about his unit and his service in Greece. He replied that he worked on the railway and had decided to go to the nearby village with four comrades. On the way there they were surprised by a guerilla unit. Two men died immediately, two fled and he, the sergeant, was taken prisoner.

"He said there would be hell to pay if he was not handed back very soon," Hamson recalls. "In all he was a little truculent. He was a typical Teuton, tall, blond, blue-eyed and hard — one of the Herrenvolk."

Hamson asked his men what guarantee they could give that the German would not escape. They thought his chances of escape were low. But "Bull" Hamson wished to take no risks. The German looked at the Briton imploringly and he, in turn, scrutinised him. Hamson thought how upside down things were: their similarities should have put them on the same side. But this was war. Hamson searched for some pretext to be rid of the man. "Turn his pockets out and let's see what he has collected in forty-eight hours' captivity."

"As I thought," Hamson recalls, "the German had more than a good handful of crusts. He had turned pale and looked at me appealingly." His fate was sealed.

The next morning Hamson saw his man Manoli at the airstrip. He was wearing the German's boots and on his right hand a ring gleamed dully. He told Hamson with a grin, "I told him I was going to bring him to the British officer, and he was quite happy. I shot him through the back of his head while we were walking through the forest. He never knew a thing."

It was an emotional moment for Eddie Myers when he heard the throb of aircraft engines through the darkness. Someone said it was a Dakota, a DC3. Myers could hardly believe that it had really worked out. He thought back to those bleak and discouraging weeks when he could recruit only six partisans, then the testing but successful attack on the bridge, the terrible march back over mountain terrain, those desperate days when they waited in vain for the submarine and then that awful trudge back and his illness which had brought him to the brink of death. But now he was about to leave in triumph, in the knowledge that, in just three quarters of a year, he and a dozen worthy men had built up a partisan army under the most difficult circumstances.

He was woken abruptly from his reverie. Two bonfires were being lit in the darkness. He could see the aircraft swoop and give the two pre-arranged signals. Despite strict warnings not to make any sound, the waiting men could not suppress a spontaneous cheer. The DC3 began to lose height, circled, and then flew off to make its final approach. Twelve andartes lying on each side of the strip simultaneously lit up their oil lamps, thus clearly defining the airstrip. The plane came in, making a perfect landing.

As it stopped, Myers looked at his watch. It was one minute past ten, one minute late! The stores were promptly unloaded by the andartes. Andreas Tzimas, Georgios Siantos, two further members of EAM, Pyromaglou, deputising for Zervas, and several other party delegates clambered into the plane with Eddie Myers and Denys Hamson. At twelve minutes past ten the DC3 took off, running only halfway down the strip before it left the ground. Their course was set for Egypt and just six hours later they landed at an airfield outside Cairo. Myers recalls:

*It was strange to feel the sand under my feet once again as, with
staff officers of S.O.E., we walked across the aerodrome buildings to
have a cup of tea. Half an hour later we moved on into Cairo, the
andarte delegates to go to a house which had been reserved for them
in Maadi, a garden suburb of Cairo, and I to the private flat of Lord
Glenconner, the Head of S.O.E. (Cairo).*

*After revelling in a delicious hot bath, I put on a dressing gown
and went to the shady veranda of my host's comfortable flat, where he
— and breakfast — awaited me. The noise of the distant trams and
other traffic in the crystal brightness of that early Egyptian summer
morning, still cool and refreshing, sounded strange after a year in the
rugged mountains of enemy-occupied Greece. The past year seemed
real enough. But the present comfort and security was like a dream.*

Fig. 71   *Still wearing their fur caps, the heads of Aris and
Tzavellas were exhibited for several days, hanging on
telegraph masts*

Myers never went back to Greece during the war. The Conference
in Cairo did not succeed in bringing agreement between the warring
resistance leaders of Greece. After the collapse of the Italian army, he

was informed while in Haifa at the S.O.E. training centre that civil war had broken out in Greece. He was deeply disappointed that the British Foreign Office did not consider him to be the right man to deal with the new situation there. In November 1943 Chris Woodhouse was officially appointed as his successor.

Many years later, Field Marshal Montgomery was asked whether Operation Harling had made a significant contribution to the victory over Rommel in North Africa. His reply was surprisingly negative. He had never heard about it until after the war. Certainly the operation came six weeks too late for the war in Africa because by the end of November 1942 Rommel had already been pushed back to Libya.

Eddie Myers is now retired and lives in Broadwell, a quiet, picturesque suburb of London. Chris Woodhouse spent a while in politics as a conservative member of Parliament for his university town of Cambridge, but then he returned to his original passion and teaches at King's College, London. Siantos, Grigoriadis, Maniatis, Zoulas, and Zervas are dead. Löhr was executed by Tito-partisans in a prisoner-of-war camp in Yugoslavia. Aris was murdered with his faithful but brutal bodyguard Tzavellas. They were ambushed during the civil war in June 1945 and their heads were chopped off. The heads, still wearing their "trade mark", the fur caps fashioned from Trude Radwein's coat, were hung for several days on two telegraph poles linked together with garlands. Sarafis died in the early fifties in Athens as a result of a car accident. Andreas Tzimas lived in exile in Bratislava, Czechoslovakia, where he died in the seventies without ever seeing his homeland again. Kapetan Thomá died in Athens in 1978 under his civilian name Hatzipanayiotou. Yannis Pistolis is in good health in Stromni, and Niko Bey died many years ago in his home town. Both received British awards for bravery. Dimitrios Dimitriou, alias Nikophoros, whom Woodhouse dubbed the "Greek Djilas", lives and works in Athens and has written six books on the Resistance. Themie Marinos achieved success in the Greek business world and was appointed vice-president of the state railways. But even he failed in peace-time to have a dual track built on the rail section between Athens and Salonica. In the seventies he received "the best possible present": Greek railway men gave him some magnets which had served to attach the explosives to the piers of the Gorgopotamos bridge. They had been found when repair work was undertaken.

Denys Hamson died after the war after an interlude in the French resistance. Edmonds worked in Greece for many years with the United Nations, "to repair at least a part of what I had helped to destroy".

None of the original party of twelve men who were parachuted into Greece, on those memorable moonlit nights in September and October 1942, came to any harm. They all returned to their home country.

And what about Tasos Lefterias? What happened to him? "After the civil war he emigrated to the USSR. But he was one of the first former communist leaders to return to Greece in the fifties," a former andarte in Roumeli tells me.

"Is he still alive? Where does he live now? Has he changed his name?" I can hardly restrain my urgency.

"No idea," he replies. "His wife originally came from Karpenissi. He was seen in Athens in the mid-fifties."

Homecoming

"Frequently," said the kind old gentleman, "nothing could be found anymore. The dead were buried in very shallow graves. Generally the ground was too stony to dig deep enough. Then the village dogs or foxes would tear up the remains. Identity tags were often lost too, so that when bodies were found, it was impossible to identify them."

A. Friemel was a representative of the German War Graves Commission (Volksbund) which had been kindly assisted by the Greek government in its painstaking work of collecting over 14,000 war dead from more than four hundred and thirty communities and several islands in the Aegean, "storing" them after 1959 in the monasteries of Xenia and Gonia, and subsequently, from 1974 onwards, giving them a dignified burial in the war cemeteries of Maleme in Crete or Dionyssos-Rapendoza near Athens.

Friemel was immediately prepared to follow up the information I had gleaned on my first visit to Makrakomi in August 1963. His colleague Argyriadis was sent to Makrakomi where Alex Grivas gave him the following statement on 9 December, 1963:

A black car belonging to the Wehrmacht passed on its way to Platistomo Spa, carrying the officer whom we knew (and who is, according to the photo, the Oberzahlmeister Hermann Meyer), the

*driver and two other passengers. The officer found the farm deserted
as the partisans had captured the Germans on the previous day.
Expecting the worst, they returned. The car was stopped at Makri and
the passengers arrested by partisans. They were taken to Makrakomi
at first. We all recognised the kind man whom we knew well and who
figures on the photo, i.e. Oberzahlmeister Hermann Meyer. We also
recognised one of the partisans who was Mantheos Iannacopoulos
from Makri, who told us later that the prisoners were taken to
Mavrolithari where they were allegedly executed but he denies any
knowledge of their graves...*

However, the supposition or intentional falsehood by Mantheos
Iannacopoulos led to the wrong track. There was no grave with
German soldiers in Mavrolithari. When I was finally allowed to
research in an institute in Berlin dealing with notifying families of lost
soldiers of the Wehrmacht (WASt), I struck lucky.

The yellowing index card read:

> *Meyer, Hermann, Oberzahlmeister*
> *born 7.9.1903*
> *Identity tag:-15-St.Nbl.Ers.Abt.1*
> *Unit: Eisb.Bau Kp.117*
> *Fp. Nr.: 05 862*
> *Date of death: unknown*
> *captured by partisans on 30.3.1943 near Makrakomi*

In the last letter written by Captain Christ to Erika on 1 June,
1943, he mentions the petition signed by the Oberzahlmeister and
other prisoners:

*In a letter dated 8 April, 1943, the thirty-four German soldiers in
captivity write that they will be treated as prisoners of war, provided
that civilians (women and children) do not continue to be targeted.*

Among the millions of perfectly organised files of the WASt, I was
able to trace an accredited copy of this petition of 8 April, 1943, with
the names of all the thirty-four missing persons. Christ's words are
almost exactly those of Meyer's text. The captain must, therefore,
have read Meyer's letter before he wrote to Erika.

Having now found the thirty-four names, I was able to look up
their index cards. That of August Pruchhorst had copies of the letters
by the Italian soldier, De Giuglio, and General Del Giudice stapled to

it, which were instrumental in the discovery of a grave in Kolokythia with the bones of thirty dead, and, right next to it, "grave II" containing four skeletons. The villagers said the second grave probably contained Germans who "had also been shot by partisans in 1943". The discovery in the second grave of the identity tag "EM 578 F.Ba.10" pointed clearly to Lance-Corporal Anton Prosch.

The Volksbund under H. Wolff took charge of the reburial. "The grave was five by five by two and a half metres; we had to move sixty cubic metres of earth." No finds other than the skeletons were made, but he confirmed that one of the thirty skeletons was that of a woman. Still, it was a mystery why only thirty skeletons were found, as the Italian soldier had specified that thirty-two had been executed. Wolff explained in the end that perhaps "animals had dragged some mortal remains away because of the shallow grave".

I had been able to track down Hermann Meyer's dental card, and I knew his exact height and furthermore that he had broken his left leg when he was young, so that the WASt was finally able to confirm on 28 July, 1966:

The Volksbund in Kassel has informed us that in their reburial work in Kolokythia, Greece, a skeleton among others was disinterred which bears the physical characteristics of your father, i.e. Hermann Meyer, born 7 September, 1903, in Ülzen... There can be no doubt that your father is one of the dead disinterred in Kolokythia...

On 14 December, 1966, the registry office in Mellendorf issued the official death certificate.

Friemel suggested that the "sarcophagus", as he elegantly described it, should "stay with his comrades". Meanwhile, the Greek colonels had seized power and Friemel intimated that he was facing great difficulties in having a cemetery built outside Athens. I was informed in the beginning of 1967 by the Volksbund that "Your dear father has been lodged with dignity in the new German memorial ground at Xenia monastery under reburial number 7568 until such time as he may be given a final burial".

As I insisted on repatriation, Friemel suggested writing to Bishop Damaskinos of Volos requesting permission to remove the sarcophagus. I wrote to the Bishop in 1969 but his Excellency never deemed it necessary to reply, and much less to do anything about my request.

———————

The monastery of Xenia lies between Larissa and Volos. Three wooden crosses erected on a hilltop in front of the monastery dominate the scene and can be seen from miles away. The road twists in hairpin bends up the barren hill. Never for a moment are those wooden crosses lost from sight on the long drive up.

The taxi pulls up in front of the whitewashed cloister walls. Children are playing in the inner courtyard. I see women and a black-robed monk who takes no notice of me. Chickens scratch the sand under a eucalyptus tree. A pig crosses the courtyard. The taxi driver stays in the car and smokes his cigarette. He can't be bothered to get out in the midday heat. At right-angles to the formerly white painted main stone building, there is an old barn with a door made out of roughly nailed planks.

Someone at last understands what I am after. I manage to explain that I wish to get to the German sarcophagi. "Yes, behind that door," says the man, pointing at the barn. I approach it. There is no door handle. I push against the planks, but they hold firm. Someone has locked the door.

So this is the "new German memorial ground" where the dead are lodged "with dignity" in the monastery of Xenia "which was founded in the twelfth century and is today a modern rectangular building dating from the first years of this century and which encompasses a beautiful chapel," as the Volksbund describes it sanctimoniously to thousands of bereaved families.

"Can't you open the door?" I ask, having gone back to the other decrepit building to find the man. "*Ochi,*" he says with that unexpected nod of the head, "we don't have the key. The people who bring the crates here have the key." I think of Friemel who spoke piously of sarcophagi.

Thanks to German thoroughness, each one has a "reburial number". The cases are stacked in numerical order. I am only a few steps away from U-7568. Through the door crack I can see innumerable, carefully-stacked cases in the semi-darkness of the barn. It looks just like a well run warehouse. Spider webs lace the cases, and I feel that I can discern rats or mice slithering through the darkness.

I press harder against the door. I shake it, kick it. It is midday and no one is around. The taxi driver seems to be totally uninterested in anything as long as I pay him. I throw my entire weight at the door, like the hero in a western always does with such success. It makes an awful din but the door resists.

But suddenly, people erupt from various doors that lead into this filthy courtyard. They are shouting and gesticulating. Some bearded monks in black robes approach threateningly and try to grab hold of me. I beat a hasty retreat. The taxi driver fortunately takes his cue, throws open the car door and somehow pulls me on to the front seat. It smells of stale smoke. He has stuck a postcard with a Madonna on his plastic dashboard. A rosary hangs from the rear mirror. Neither of us says a word all the way back, although his noisy radio remains switched off.

Three and a half years later, on 9 November, 1971, the manager of a specialist department of the German Funeral Business Ltd (Fachverlag des deutschen Bestattungsgewerbes GmbH) wrote "with best regards", that "the mortal remains of your father have been handed over today to the administration of Dorfmark municipal cemetery". Instead of writing "mortal remains", he could just as well have written "a case of tomatoes" or "a case of freight". As a conscientious businessman he should have, but failed to inform the authorities in advance of the time of arrival of the coffin (only best oak, of course, inclusive of value added tax), and left it to the local municipal administration to find out whom on earth these mortal remains could possibly belong to. Finally, Molle, the municipal administrator who was normally drunk, had a moment of clarity, rang up Erika and said, "Is this your husband?"

The grave digger had dug a child's grave for the chest "measuring seventy-five by thirty-five by twenty-five centimetres, oak wood, complying with specifications". The small coffin stood in front of the altar in the musty chapel. A metal plate engraved with his name was fixed to the front.

298

There was no organ music, no solemn speech, no friend, no decorations, no comrade who might have drivelled something like, "Hermann Meyer, you died for the glory of your country", no band, that might have played the Last Post — no, just us. It was unnecessary to have several men carry the coffin. It was so very light. I noticed the cemetery gardener lurking inquisitively behind the row of willow trees. He had never seen a funeral like it. We laid the little case on two thick ropes and let it down gently into the neatly dug rectangle. The earth was laced with grey black veins. Although the ground was very wet, clods broke off in the corners and rolled into the hole. Typical heath earth. Quite different from that hard, red-brown earth in Kolokythia.

In Kolokythia and at the Gorgopotamos

Eighteen years later, in summer 1989. Makrakomi has hardly changed. Alexis Grivas died at a ripe old age. Mantheos Iannacopoulos is also dead but his wife still talks animatedly of their wedding and how the Germans took part so gaily in their celebrations.

I have come back after all these years, driven by those terrible documents which would leave me no peace. I meet Marika Youla who saw Hermann Meyer's capture from behind the curtain at her window. She introduces me to Dinos Tsonis, talks of the family Tsagaris, tells me about the brothers Franz and Christos who both studied and graduated in Germany, of their uncle Vagelis, whose pistol failed to fire when the arrest was made. I arrange a meeting with Fekas at the bank in Makri, and he denies everything because he fears that I want to make him responsible.

Then I take a ride by car — past the recent monstrosity of a memorial to the andartes — from Lamia through Makrakomi, Sperhias and Gardiki to Kolokythia, driving through a magical mountain landscape with poor, unspoiled little villages, where the people wave amiably, incredulous that any foreigner would want to come here. Then, when it seems that the road is truly going nowhere and petrol is running out, one arrives at the end of the world, and Kolokythia.

Everything is steep in this village — so steep, in fact, that the car hardly makes it. Huge maple trees cast their shadows across the church and the village square in front of me. Two children are playing while their mother opens up the only shop on the square. I am still unaware that I am actually sitting in my father's prison. There is no school any more. Most villagers have gone to find their fortune in the towns. In the corner of the shop, close to the entrance, there is a rough chopping block with a skinned goat on it, and next to it, an axe and a slaughtering knife. I explain my business to her without divulging who I am. She says she knows an elderly man who lived in the village at the time.

His name is Yannis Karageorgos. He works as a tailor in Athens but spends the summer in his home village. He receives me politely, we sit on a wooden bench on the porch of his little unpainted cottage, and he scrutinises me. I ask questions. He answers. He knows so very much. But he speaks hesitantly. He takes me to Agios Markos. The outline of the large grave is still discernible. In the late afternoon, Mayor Burchaz and various other older men turn up at the square. They hang their shepherd's crooks on the wide branches of the mighty acacia tree. I think of young Kalambouras, whom Woodhouse, Aris and Zervas had hanged on this very tree. The old men study me curiously. I am introduced to Kotsovolos and Tzivellekas. Everyone talks at once and argues loudly about some detail. In some way, they were all involved. The shepherd, Kotsovolos, suddenly pulls off his old holey jumper and shows his scars from beatings, bullets and shrapnel. He grins: all thanks to the Germans! Then he shows off his German vocabulary, words that are known all over the Greek mountains: *"Raus, raus! Schnell! Fritz! Marsch! Scheisskerl! Schweinehund!..."*

They point out the school which is now a shop and taverna, and show me old rusty containers which have been left lying where the English dropped them. They mention the latrine ditch where the prisoners threw their rings before they were shot. They take me to the deserted and derelict andarte headquarters where tobacco plants are now being dried. They affirm that "all the andartes who were responsible are now dead".

"Even Lefterias?" I ask.

"He once came back here," one of them says. "He took another name. Apparently he lives in Athens. There was a film about ELAS, in which he figured. The British television people also came here and did some filming a few years ago."

They also confirm that two men escaped after the shooting but that they were subsequently caught. But they know nothing about Viktor and Rudolf who allegedly joined the andartes.

I put a series of photos at random in front of Karageorgos, all of German soldiers who basically look very similar with their rigid military countenances. "Do you recognise any of these men?" I ask him.

Even before I finish putting my question, he already stubs a large index finger on one of the many pictures and says, *"Afto ine o Kapetanios.* This is the kapetanios."* He looks at me questioningly.

"He is my father," I say.

———————

On 26 November every year the former andartes hold a reunion at the Gorgopotamos bridge. For many Greeks it has almost become a national holiday. It is the day when Greece dared defy the occupation for the first time, the day when ELAS and EDES fought side by side!

A large flat area has been especially prepared above the bridge to receive thousands of visitors and a stand erected for prominent people. Former ELAS fighters with their old banners are being bussed in from the surrounding villages. Vagelis Tsagaris steps out of one of the dozens of buses. He recognises me, but quickly melts away in the crowd, clearly unwilling to speak to the son of the man whom he took prisoner. Symbolically, a train rolls over the bridge below the spectators. A band plays some crashing music. Many former andartes are proudly wearing the old brown uniform of the ELAS fighters and the cap with the well-known E.L.A.S. logo. Pictures of Aris are visible everywhere, stuck on bus windows, with that distinctive cossack hat made out of Trude Radwein's fur coat. A helicopter approaches, hovers and lands impeccably on the prepared concrete strip next to the festival area, kicking up dust and finally spewing out a *bona fide* minister from Athens. Television cameras whirr while six men follow each other in giving long, totally forgettable speeches evoking the old fighting spirit and repeating the old slogans. One of them, called Spiros Bekios, receives rapturous applause. After the wreath is officially laid, a representative of EDES takes the floor, but no one seems to listen and very few people clap. Disappointed, the speaker steps down. It is obvious that ELAS/EAM/KKE is in control here.

Fig. 72   *From left to right: I. Gill, T. Marinos, E. Myers,*
Y. Pistolis, C. M. Woodhouse, M. Chittis and A.
Edmonds in front of the cave at Stromni in November
1992 on the occasion of the fiftieth anniversary of the
Gorgopotamos operation

I seek out Spiros Bekios, who was formerly called Lambros. He
still looks quite young. He wallows in memories of his biggest
operation, which was to blast the Nezeros tunnel in June 1943. He
asks me what I found in the German and Italian documents in the
archives about it and, in particular, how many men "bit the dust".
Bekios had laid the explosive charges he received from Arthur
Edmonds at both ends of the tunnel.

In fact, the Wehrmacht report of June 1943 said, "The carriages
were burning, ammunition on the train exploded and intense smoke
and repeated explosions impeded the rescue operation. About a
hundred passengers escaped injury while two to three hundred Italian
soldiers and seven Germans burned to death in the tunnel."

Spiros Bekios claims to know German soldiers "who raped
pregnant Greek women, slit open their bellies and then beat the living

baby to death. But," he said, without changing his tone of voice, "I also knew some nice Germans. There was one who fought in my unit. He was a German soldier who deserted and joined us."

"Who was he, what was his name?"

"There were two in our unit. One was Rudolfo and we called the other Telman."

"Rudolfo?"

"Yes, Rudolfo. He was my friend," Spiros says. "He joined us after we had decided on our National Day to make several attacks on the Germans along the rail track. I and my men destroyed the factory area near Topolia. That was on 27 March, 1943. A few days later, my friend Fotis Parnassiotis led an attack on Gravia station. That was where Rudolfo was picked up. We called his friend Telman, but I can't remember where he came from nor what his real name was. But, after being with us for a year, Telman tried to escape."

"If what you say is true," I say excitedly, "then Rudolfo's surname was Herrmann and Telman would have been a cover name for Viktor Schendzielorz. Rudolfo was taken prisoner at Gravia station in the night of 29 and 30 March, 1943."

"That's it!" Spiros agrees, nodding. "Rudolfo and Telman were both in my unit. We were in the mountains, in Agia Trias, our new headquarters in the vicinity of Karpenissi. One day, it must have been in spring 1944, Telman escaped. He thought he could make it through to the Germans in Lamia. But he did not reckon with our people who were stationed in every village. I immediately ordered that the whole neighbourhood should be searched. We knew every path, controlled all the roads and policed the whole area. I still cannot understand why he did it, because he had no chance of getting away. We caught him the next morning already in Mavrilo."

"What did you do to him?"

"He begged for his life. I remember it well. But he was dealt the kind of punishment every deserter deserves," Bekios says and looks hard into my eyes.

"What about Rudolfo?" I ask. "What was his reaction when his friend was murdered."

"Telman was not murdered," Spiros says angrily, his light eyes flashing with passion. "He got the true punishment every deserter deserves. As for Rudolfo, he threw down his gun and declared that he could no longer fight with us. We kept him with us nevertheless, and he did auxiliary work. He collected wood, made the fire, prepared the food, set up camp and carried our belongings. He was my friend. He owed his life to me. When the war was over we let him go."

Rudolfo, Telman and the bereft families

In long and painstaking work, using those yellowing index cards belonging to the WASt, I was able to determine the places of birth or the pre-war addresses of twenty-seven of the thirty-four people who had signed that letter of 8 April, 1943.

I could not find any details about Lance-Corporals Konrad Körling and Stahlberg, Gunner Franz Pelikan and the three Privates Alois Holzmann, Wilhelm Koller and Karl Mesner nor about the "clerk" Trude Radwein. I could not discover their dates of birth nor Stahlberg's first name. But I do know that five of these men were seized from a train near Lake Xinias and probably all belonged to the same unit. I was particularly keen to know more about Gertrud Radwein who was such an exceptionally brave woman. While I did get further information on her because I found Froso Haralambopoulos and the two former maids Nicki and Sophia in Athens, I was never able to discover any family in Austria.

My research was greatly hampered by the fact that Meyer's letter of 8 April, 1943, had been signed by each person in his own hand. The letter was copied on 16 August, 1943, and unfortunately the original was subsequently lost, but mistakes were made by the copier. He wrote Studlick instead of Kudlick, Schindrichter instead of Schendzielorz, Aioss instead of Gross and Puishart instead of Pruchhorst.

When the Berlin Wall came down, the Volkspolizei of the old German Democratic Republic was suddenly amenable to giving out information on old addresses. I tracked down the missing men, not only to both parts of Germany and to Austria, but also to Silesia which is now part of Poland and to Bohemia, now part of the Czech Republic.

All the families received letters like that written in April 1943 to Frau Eppelsheimer stating that "there is hope for the early return of your dear relative". They all received a comforting letter from the Wehrmacht and then had to live in uncertainty.

304

Josef Prametsberger, who is a qualified engineer living in Mühldorf in Bavaria, never gave up his search for his brother Georg, who was captured at Nezeros on 4 April, 1943. Finally, on 19 June, 1971, the district court Mühlendorf/Inn officially declared his brother dead (Akz. UR II 28/71); time of death: 31 December 1945. But still, Josef persisted. As a result of his constant queries, the Bavarian Red Cross asked him in 1982 "to contact our office in the next few days in connection with a wartime missing person". Josef relates that "it sounded as though they knew something important, like what had happened to my brother". But all they could give him was an assumption:

The result of all our investigations leads us to the conclusion that Georg Prametsberger most probably died in April 1943 during fighting which was taking place in the area near the greco-albanian frontier.

An identical hectograph from the Red Cross was sent to the family of the twenty-nine-year-old Wilhelm Franz, who was abducted from Aghie station only two days before his home leave.

Some of the bereaved families feel that the past should not be dug up. Kurt Rossmann, for instance, the son of the injured Max who was captured with Karl Blachnik in Kurnovon, "feels sceptical about it all". Family Fritzenwanger from Mittersill, Austria, thinks that "the whole business is best left alone". Or Frau Kuppler, Karl Kapp's sister says, "I just don't want to hear any more about it." She grieved so deeply for her brother and had to watch her parents go on hoping until their last breath that their son would return.

Other parents died without ever knowing, such as those of Erwin Kaufmann from Münster who was captured in Platistomo just two days after his leave. Hedwig Hässler died in Burg near Magdeburg in 1985 without knowing what had happened to the missing persons.

Gerda Köber, daughter of Horst Lange, the employee of the State Railways, writes:

An oral missing persons report was made directly to my mother towards the end of April 1943 by a Wehrmacht official. And that was it! In the German Democratic Republic, history was either taboo or completely misrepresented. Soldiers were by definition fascists, so that any research concerning our father would definitely have been punished.

Johanna Meier was expecting her husband Franz to come home to Regensburg on leave for Easter, but instead she received a letter dated 29 April, 1943, from Oberregierungsbaurat Grass, Athens:

Greek partisans attacked the service centre at Platistomo in central Greece on 28 March, 1943, and all the members were taken prisoner. So far, efforts to discover the whereabouts and fate of our comrades have not yielded any tangible results and I therefore have the difficult task of informing you that your husband Franz Meier is missing since that date. As soon as any news about his fate is available, you will be informed forthwith.

Martha Lehmkuhl was the only relative of those missing who went to the opening of the war cemetery in Athens in 1975. She insisted that her husband's name should appear on the memorial slab in the cemetery. "I have never been able to accept that he did not return. My father ran our business until my eldest son was able to take it over. So we bridged one whole generation. In Athens I found only his name on the memorial and I was disappointed to hear that his grave had not yet been found."

Baron von Falkenhausen had written to her on 12 May, 1943:

Although I do not know you personally, I feel a deep need to write a few lines to you... All our investigations have not supplied any conclusive results to date. I was the leader of the service centre at Platistomo, but I was on leave, having myself been captured and wounded somewhat earlier. So, I was spared the same fate because your husband was deputising for me at the time. I cannot tell you much about the attack itself as all our comrades were taken away... It is deeply painful, and I do not wish to deny you all hope, but the situation in general makes it difficult to expect that our comrades will return to us. They are not in the hands of a regular enemy, but of partisan bands, who are a law unto themselves... I trust that you will find comfort in accepting fate as so many other wives and mothers do, if in truth our last hopes are not fulfilled... Heil Hitler!

Dorothea Pruchhorst was the only relative to receive a report from the "Wehrmachtsauskunftstelle für Kriegsverluste und Kriegsgefangene" (Information centre on persons lost or missing in the war) on 15 August, 1943. She asked: "What suppositions can be made and what are these based on, regarding the fate of my missing husband." The reply read:

One week after the disappearance of our men, the local headquarters in Lamia received a telephone message. It was from Capitano Bardell, adjutant of the Italian infantry regiment stationed in Lamia. The Italians had been informed that the Italian captives had been set free and that our people had been shot. On the other hand, Greek civilians intimated that the prisoners had been taken further into the mountains. There are no other sources of information, as there were no witnesses of German or friendly nationalities at the scene.

Frau Pruchhorst, Frau Schwarzenbacher and Frau Kudlick remarried, as did Frau Fritsche in 1953. In that same year she had Herbert declared dead. She is now called Frau Räbel and still lives in Berlin-Weissensee. I immediately find her road, close to the lake. It is a grey street of terraced houses with the paint peeling off. Greyish white curtains veil the windows. The staircase is narrow and dim, it all looks seedy. I ring the doorbell.

Frau Räbel is in, the door opens; she was expecting me. She looks careworn and ill. I sit down in her clean and tidy little living-room. "You have brought me great sadness," she weeps, "for I always went on hoping he was still alive."

Her second marriage was apparently not a success. Her husband died about ten years ago. Since then, she has been alone, in bad health, and in her solitude she is apt to think longingly about old times. A year ago, she underwent a stomach operation and now she has shingles and is in pain. She is seventy-two years old.

"Herbert was a car mechanic. He planned to open up his own garage after the war. We had no children. When I first received the news that he was missing, I almost went mad. But I did not give up hope. In November 1943 I came home late from work at the factory. Bombs. Everything was burning. The whole house was on fire, our flat, just everything. I don't have a single memento of him, not even a photo."

"Was he a party member?" I ask hesitantly.

"Yes, of course, that is why I was so excited when you wrote to me soon after the fall of the Berlin Wall. I felt sure that you were writing on behalf of my husband, who wanted to contact me again once the communist regime had collapsed. I always thought that he had returned to Germany after the war but had stayed in the West, because he had been a NSDAP member and feared reprisals in the communist East. You see, he could have come back and started a new family. I would have forgiven him. I would have understood. But the pain that you are giving me by telling me that he is truly dead, that is harder to bear."

———————

Frau Zahout lives with her handicapped daughter in Halle, "like hermits". She was twenty-three years old when the daily letters from Rudolf stopped coming. In April 1943 the Wehrmacht sent her exactly the same letter as the one sent to Erika: "There is however no reason to fear, at the moment, that your husband is not alive." So, until this day, she never had her Rudolf declared dead.

"As compensation that he never came back, I receive a pension of a hundred and nine Deutschmarks sixty-eight pfennigs net," she complains. "My life is destroyed." Her daughter, whom she cares for devotedly, cannot speak, can hardly move, sits in her wheelchair, smiles and constantly wipes her crippled hands across her disfigured face. She takes an endless amount of time to open the locket which she wears around her neck to show me a picture of the father whom she never knew.

Rudolf and Berta Zahout came from Warta an der Eger, in the district of Kaaden in the former Sudetenland. "It is a wonderful area," says Berta, showing me her old photos. "When Hitler occupied the Sudetenland, Rudolf had just come home after two years of military service with the Czechs. Can you imagine, the Czechs trained him for Hitler's Wehrmacht! And in July 1946 we were made to emigrate with fifty kilos of luggage.

"In later years I came to the conclusion that my husband was no longer alive. But I still kept wondering whether he had died a natural or a violent death; whether he had been buried or simply covered up.

"I cannot understand how such war crimes can go unpunished. How could they just murder innocent people, just shoot them like rabbits? I have, however, heard that our people behaved no less cruelly."

———————

Gottesdorf, the place where Viktor Schendzielorz used to live in Upper Silesia, was renamed Groszowice after the war. It was unlikely that I would find any of his relations here but I tracked down his wife Lucie in Mannheim.

"My husband was abducted on 28 March, 1943, by bands, and has been declared missing ever since," Frau Schendzielorz says. "I have written everywhere, including to the International Red Cross, but I always received the same reply: Missing."

The old lady now lives on the top floor of an apartment block. It is almost a miracle that she manages to climb up the endless staircase to the fifth floor every day. But she does not complain. On the contrary, she is delighted to be in "the paradise" of Germany. After the war she submitted request after request to be allowed an exit permit from Poland. Finally, despite all the obstacles, she emigrated. "We Germans were treated like second-class citizens in Poland. We were not allowed to speak German nor to pursue our culture and we never had enough to live on. The period after the war was terrible. I never knew from one day to the next what I was going to give my children to eat. And now, here in Germany, they call us Pollacks," she complains bitterly. "But, of course, we are Germans!"

She shows me her husband's work book, who learned his trade with the master bricklayer Hermann Kügler in Oppeln, and subsequently worked as a maintenance worker in the rail district of Groschowitz.

"We had six children: Hubert, Helmut, Rosa, Günther, Manfred and Gerhard. They were all born between 21 October, 1936 and 19 February, 1943. My husband was called up on 27 March, 1941, and came back on his last home leave in February 1943. Our Gerhard was born on 19 February and my husband saw him for just one hour and then he had to leave. Can you believe it," she says, stressing her words, "he saw the baby for just one hour; they refused to prolong his leave for one more day!"

She shows me a letter from Captain Guntsch, dated 1 November, 1943:

... I must unfortunately inform you that in spite of tireless investigations there are no further details available concerning the whereabouts of your husband. Heil Hitler!

"Gerhard now works in Mannheim. He hardly speaks any German, but he is happy to be here. Only my daughter Rosa still lives in Poland."

"Have you still got a picture of your husband, Frau Schendzielorz?"

"We used to have one. He was standing next to an Italian wearing a funny hat with a cock's feather. It always made us laugh. But now I haven't even got a single photo of my husband anymore."

Later, Rosa, Gerhard and her grandson Waldemar and his girlfriend turn up. Only Waldemar is at all interested in the destiny of his grandfather. He wants to know everything. The new television set is switched on. It is carnival time. A man on a platform is speaking in a dialect which I find hard to follow, and certainly none of the Schendzielorz can understand a word. So I raise my voice and tell him how desperately his grandfather had tried to stay alive, how he had joined up with the partisans and how fear tracked him day and night as they were so unpredictable; how he finally could not stand it any longer and made a run for it, hoping desperately to reach his German comrades. I told him how he was found on the following day, and that he was brought back and executed in front of Rudolfo's eyes as a deterrent.

Emotionlessly, Rosa and Gerhard go on slurping Lucie's Sunday soup, while Waldemar makes just one comment. "So my grandfather was a traitor to his comrades."

I did not know that, in the GDR, offices are all closed on Wednesdays, including those of the state police. When I reach the large grey building in Zwickau I find that all the doors are shut. Finally, someone takes pity on me and lets me through to the janitor and then I suddenly find myself surrounded by three friendly policemen, who are amazed that someone has travelled so far just to find an address.

I knew that Rudolf Herrmann was born on 29 April, 1907, in Zwickau-Schedewitz. His index card at the WASt in Berlin quoted his last address as that of his mother Anna, at Karlsbaderstrasse 57 in Zwickau.

"That address does not exist anymore," says one of the men. "That whole area has been redeveloped. Nor is his mother's name Anna

Herrmann to be found in any documents of the town or country districts of Zwickau."

They let me go on sitting at the janitor's, and, because they feel sorry for me having come all this way, they agree to have just another look and see whether there is nothing at all to be found on Family Herrmann. After about half an hour the kindly fat policeman, in his sweaty grey shirt with its green shoulder flaps, appears again. He has at least found Anna Herrmann's date of birth. "Born on 28 August, 1878, but indubitably dead long ago," he says regretfully. But he is now hooked. "Let's find out whether Rudolf was married or had brothers and sisters," he suggests.

I do not know whether it is a new computer, a dusty index card or old Stasi documents, but whatever the source, I soon receive an answer that I never dared hope for.

"Rudolf Herrmann, born 29 April, 1907, died 4 January, 1978, in Zwickau."

"What did you say? He only died in 1978?" I ask, interrupting the fat man who is triumphantly reading out the fruits of his detective work. Bells begin to ring in my head. Rudolfo had actually made it through! He had managed to get home again!

Thoughts of my father flash through my mind. "Why didn't you do as Rudolf did? You could still be alive! Thirty-two out of thirty-four people let themselves be shot for Hitler, for the wrong cause, and left behind suffering and sorrowing mothers, fathers, wives and children, many children. Over ninety percent died a pointless death for their "Führer". And nowadays, when people are asked about their past, the vast majority declare that they had nothing to do with the Nazis!"

"Died 4 January, 1978, in Zwickau," the fat man repeated dryly, interrupting my thoughts. He does not realise how dreadfully depressed I feel. His expression clouds over. He expects gratitude for his fabulous success, and instead I sit there in the draughty janitor's lodge and look thunderstruck.

"Married to Wally, née Fischer, born in Frauenstein on 26 July, 1919, and now domiciled at Johannes-R.-Becher-Strasse in Zwickau." The words are written on the note which he puts in my hand before disappearing through the door to his office.

The road, lined with dreary uniform houses, named after the man who wrote the lyrics of the GDR's national anthem, lies in the north of the town. Frau Herrmann shows me an old album with pictures of Rudolf, a slim young man with his hair slicked back without a parting. "Yes," Wally Herrmann confirms, "the Greeks captured them at the station. The partisans took them and they were going to shoot them. My husband and another man deserted and then fought with the partisans. 'Two or three times I was made to dig my own grave', he told me. But time and again someone would stand up for him, and say, 'Rudolfo is OK.' He spoke Greek, you know. That saved his life."

Wally Herrmann talks in a detached way. She has dropped her guard a bit. "There was another chap who said, 'Come on, let's get out!' But you see, my husband was not one to take risks. He said, 'No. There is no point, we will never get out of the mountains. It's useless.' But his friend left just the same. In no time at all, maybe two days, they brought him back. And then they chopped off his head."

"That was Viktor, whom the partisans called Telman," I interject. "Do you recall the name, and are you sure that they chopped off his head?"

"Yes, that name sounds right. I tend to forget names. But I am sure that they chopped off his comrade's head, because he often related this. My husband came back from captivity in 1948. He worked here on the railway for two years. Before the war, he was area manager in Reichenau near Zwickau, where he had been trained. He was called up through the railways when he was thirty-four."

"Did he ever talk about his comrades being shot dead?"

"No, he never talked to me about that. But he told me about acquaintances of his from Zwickau whom he met in 1944 while they too were fighting with the partisans. In 1945 they wanted him to join them to go home, but my husband refused. He did not want to risk it, that was the way he was, you see. He used to say, 'I am content to accept my fate' and that attitude truly saved his life."

"Did he tell you about his war experiences?"

"Not really, he did not like to speak about them, because it always made him so emotional. He did relate that they carried bags and equipment endlessly up and down the hillsides, because over there in Greece, where the partisans hung out, it was very mountainous. You see, they did not do the fighting, but they were made to carry the stuff. And, my God, they were always barefoot, because the partisans

312

had taken their boots. We used to have a picture of him with a long beard and looking awful."

Wally leafs through her album and produces an application for a better job with the railways which Rudolf wrote in the nineteen fifties. She reads out loud:

We were employed at various railway stations in the Balkans and finally came to Greece. My unit was billeted at Gravia station. One day we were told that Greek civilians had been taken from the prison and shot as hostages. I decided then to join the partisans in order to avoid ever being made to shoot down innocent civilians.

"You see, that was the way he was, my husband," Wally comments.

Then, in March 1943, partisans came to us. I was alerted by a Greek acquaintance, so I went there and was accepted by them once I had declared that I wished to stay with them and to fight with them against Fascism. At first we were deployed at Karpenissi. I cannot remember the names of all the other places where we went. We finally got to Agrinion. At that point I was prevented by illness from going back to Germany with some compatriots.

"Do you know who these compatriots were, whom he met in Greece?" I interrupt.

"That must have been in 1944. They were people from Zwickau, who had formerly fought in Spain, called Lohberger, Reinhardt and Woresch. They are all dead now. But when my husband retired in 1972, they all came to visit him here in our flat, and Gerhard Reinhardt, who was the secretary of the Committee for solidarity with Greek patriots, even wrote an article for 'Die Zeit' about my husband."

The first time I met Rudolf Herrmann it was in the middle of a column of andartes. The Greek anti-fascists called him Rudolfo. It was January, and we were in the mountain village of Frankista in the Pindus. I was delighted to find a German co-fighter among my Greek comrades. At first I took him for a Greek: he had a full beard, his hair reached his shoulders, cartridge belts criss-crossed his chest and he carried his gun with the muzzle pointing downwards. These are all typical attributes of a Greek andarte. But no, this man was from Zwickau, born and bred! How the Greek partisans rejoiced with us and surrounded us! I heard with interest who this Rudolfo was. The

Hitler fascists had sent him to Greece as a military railway worker. Allocated to stations and sections of rail track, the railway man Herrmann gained more and more insight, seeing daily how the military leaders of fascist German imperialism were transporting all kinds of foodstuffs in long freight trains from the occupied south east to Nazi Germany. Rudolfo realised then how brutally the fascists were plundering the Greek people. He also noticed that the trains heading in the other direction were bringing weapons and other war equipment which were being used in a bloodthirsty suppression of the people's just struggle for freedom. Rudolfo became convinced that armed resistance by the people was essential against Nazi barbarity...

In March 1943, in Gravia, Rudolf Hermann discovered his true mates in the class war and he joined the national popular liberation army, ELAS.

"He was also in contact with Greeks who lived here in Eastern Germany," Wally continues. "They gave him an award in 1971." She shows me a garish red document with gold edging:

In celebration of the thirty years since the creation of the National Liberation Front EAM, Dr Stratis Tsiratsidis presents this award to comrade Rudolf Herrmann in recognition of his international contribution to the antifascist national liberation war of the Greek people, when he joined the forces of EAM/ELAS.

Centre of the Organisation of   *17 May 1971*
Greek resistance fighters

"What about his application for a job in the nineteen fifties? Did he get it?"

"They took it into account that he had fought with the partisans. He was given an office job at the station here. Then, in 1968, somebody looked him up at work. He didn't know what they wanted, but it turned out they recognised him as a victim of fascist persecution. That helped, of course, because they said that as he had gone through so much, he could achieve more in his career."

"Was he a party member?"

"Yes, he belonged to the KPD" (Communist Party, Germany).

"And in the Third Reich?"

"As area manager he was in quite a high position. There was no choice, he belonged to the NSDAP. You know," she says evasively, "he never said much. But he told me, 'Twice, I had to dig my own grave.' Each time a Greek stood up for him. On his sixty-fifth birthday some Greeks from ELAS came and congratulated him. One of them must have been in his partisan unit. They visited him around 1973, or so. They kept in contact. He was very pleased about the award."

"Did he ever mention a woman who was held prisoner at the same time as himself?"

"Yes, he did. She said, 'Things will go badly for us if the partisans get us.' And he answered, 'Then I prefer to join them.' So he volunteered. He said he would prefer to die later rather than sooner. He did not know Greek at first, he learned it down there. But he never knew what might happen next, it depended on their mood."

"He must have lived in constant fear. Did he never confide in you later, did he never tell you about a mass shooting?"

"You are right, he was always in fear. He did say that he saw a place where many had been shot. He told me that, but he never told me any details. He experienced that. It was cruel.

"You know, we loved nature and used to go for long walks. He told me he would like to show me that country, and he wanted to see one of those Greeks again. They played chess together. That man helped him a lot."

"When did he come home?"

"His mother, Anna, only heard from her son in 1946, from Africa. Earlier, the Wehrmacht had sent her a letter declaring her son missing."

"Why from Africa?"

"Well, in 1945 the partisans handed him over to the English. He said that he could have returned with the Germans, but he didn't dare to. He was cautious. He took no risks. The English put him in a prisoner-of-war camp in North Africa. In 1948 he arrived in Hamburg. He could have stayed there, but he wanted to return to his mother. He said he would never take a ship again in his life. The sea off Gibraltar was terrible."

"What does this mean, Frau Herrmann?" I ask, pointing to the abbreviation VdN in his papers.

"Verfolgte des Naziregimes" (victim of persecution by the Nazi regime), she says. "This was recognised and so he received a special pension, you see. But he has been dead now since 1978. He had bronchial trouble."

Return to Kolokythia

I requested WASt in Berlin finally to inform the relatives about the fate of the missing men based on my research, but I was stonewalled. Reddner, the head of the department for verification of graves ("Leiter Gräbernachweis"), continued to apply the same yardstick as the Wehrmacht once did, and therefore there was no definite "proof of death":

Although each body was discovered in one piece, there were no finds of personal objects, equipment, identity discs or military passbooks. The only other means of identification left would be to check distinguishing physical features (size of body, head, feet and any bone injuries). The document dated 8 April, 1943, and sent to local headquarters at Lamia, describes the persons listed therein as prisoners. No definite proof of death, naming each body, can be established to this day.

Von Lutzau, assessor of the Volksbund, however, did not agree with this analysis. He was prepared to "immortalise" the names listed in the letter of 8 April, 1943, on a commemorative plaque in Dionyssos-Rapendoza. "But," he warned, "it will take two to three years. For financial reasons, this can only be done every few years. And anyway, it was lucky it was not done before, as the name of Rudolf Herrmann would otherwise have figured on it too."

The name "Georg Lehmkuhl" appears on a metal plaque in the cemetery among "the immortalised names of eight hundred and forty-three soldiers who fell but could not be recovered". In the graveyard with the natural stone slabs the name "Anton Prosch" appears with dates, because he was the only one whose identity disc was found. Next to Prosch, in the same row, lie "the unknown Kolokythia dead". Not only have their names not been "immortalised", but the inscription over the entrance to the cemetery is irritatingly wrong. It says: "Here lie 9,905 soldiers." Gertrud Radwein was no soldier.

In the end, I order a memorial stone to be made in Athens. I have Anton Prosch and his three unknown comrades found in "grave II" inscribed on the stone too. They were shot in early summer 1943 after

316

many weeks in captivity in Kolokythia. They expected each day to be their last. Nikiphoros, now called Dimitrios Dimitriou, had taken them prisoner on 14 April, 1943, in the Parnassus mountains.

"We employed them as forest workers," Dimitrios Dimitriou relates. "Once, when I was sitting in my hut, I picked up a German radio transmission. Children's voices, light and clear, were singing. I ordered one of my men to bring the Germans along. I remember how frightened they were to enter the hut. They thought that they were done for, because I had summoned them. They stood in the room and I let them listen to the children singing their song. The older man among them started to cry when he heard their voices. When the song ended, I switched the radio off, turned around and asked him why he was crying. He said he had a nine-year-old daughter. There was suddenly complete silence in the room. You could have heard a pin drop. It was an emotional moment for us all. This man and the other Germans were later sent to Kolokythia and executed there. That was May 1943".

Fig. 73   *Anton Prosch*

Dimitriou pauses, muses and sips his whisky. "No, that is wrong. I saw them there again, cutting wood, in May 1943, before we moved our headquarters from Kolokythia to Karpenissi. But after that, they were shot because German soldiers had killed some of our people."

Anton Prosch was billeted at Amfiklia station with three comrades, and he was asleep when the attack took place towards midnight. He was suffering from a serious bout of malaria with a high temperature, and was due to go to the military hospital in the morning. Altogether, six Germans looked after the station where Nikiphoros overwhelmed them with four hundred men. One soldier was shot, the other five were abducted. One of the five was later found dead a little way from the station.

Anton Prosch's wife wonders:

Why did the partisans take my husband away with them? He was ill, so he must have been a burden to them, and did they not tend to shoot the sick and wounded? He was just a little private, he had no access to military secrets or anything. I don't even know if you can survive malaria attacks without medication. And then, in the end, they shot him and all the others, anyway.

I question Dimitriou about what happened to the fifth man. I get the set reply: "We did not shoot any prisoners. We delivered them to headquarters at Kolokythia."

"That may be, but in the grave only four bodies were found, not five. So it could be true that you had the fifth man shot after taking him prisoner. Do you remember what the reason was?"

"I can't remember," Dimitriou says and ends the conversation.

During my last visit, Burchaz, the mayor of Kolokythia, assured me with theatrical emotion, "Seeing that we are ashamed of what happened in our village and that your father was a good and popular man, we will agree that you may put up a memorial stone at the site of the shooting." But on my next visit, I hear from Dr Franz Vagaris — the member of the Greek parliament who told me that Hermann Meyer had been skinned and staked — Burchaz's conditions. I am told to pay for consolidating the path from the village to the Agios Markos cemetery, the path that the thirty-two took, walking to their death. I refuse in disgust.

The memorial stone is lying in the delivery van. We have come all this way to Kolokythia, arriving in the afternoon. The village seems

318

deserted at siesta time. Many former villagers now make a good living in Athens and come back in the summer months. The weather is mild but cool at night in the mountains. It is so peaceful here, like in an immense garden. The hills are covered in lush vegetation, and the houses are almost smothered by old, rampant fruit trees.

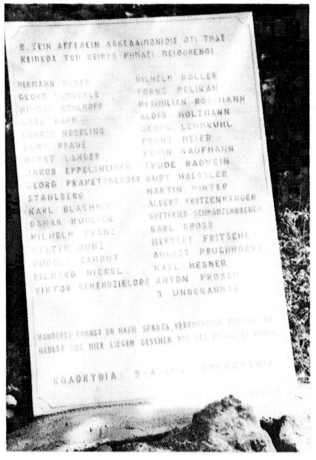

Fig. 74   *The memorial stone in Kolokythia*

In the evening the men gather in Leonidas Square and Karageorgos, the tailor, starts up the conversation. "We have founded an association of Kolokythians in Athens. There are about three hundred members. We are now building a village hall which is financed entirely from donations." He proudly points out the stone foundations of a building set on the hill above the former school and present taverna. But building work has been discontinued for some time.

Fig. 75   *"We hack away like gold diggers. The earth is almost humid"*

The old men are tough bargainers. I begin to think someone might damage the memorial stone. We agree that I shall pay a contribution towards the construction costs of the town hall. "That is a good deed," says the grey-haired Mayor Burchaz, who wore Hermann Meyer's braces after his murder. "There will be two special rooms — one for the doctor and one for the priest who come here once a week, and for guests like you who come to visit our beautiful village."

On the following day my son Christian and I dig in the earth below the school. This was the toilet, the hole under the apple tree. They all come and discuss whether it was here or there, and everyone thinks he knows better. Burchaz gesticulates and shouts down that it is madness to be digging now for rings, or anything else, for that matter. "The andartes fished out every last object after the shooting." I ask him how he knows. He does not reply and disappears. But I still hope to find just something; after all, there were thirty-four people who dumped their valuables here.

Towards late afternoon we give up. The earth we are turning over is still dry, light brown and stony. Then, the shepherd Kotsovolos appears with his divining rod and steps down into the long trench we have dug and soon turns around in triumph. *"Ine mavros,"* he says. "It is black" and dark earth trickles through his fingers.

We now hack away like gold diggers, kneading the dark, clotted earth in our hands. It is almost humid. With our naked fingers we sieve through this dark humus, which was once the shit of terror. All we find is a rusty Wehrmacht button and a few nails.

When we bid farewell in the evening, there is a show of emotion, and robust, Greek male kisses are generously shared out. Costas Karageorgos gives us a jar of best honey. Someone shakes my hand firmly and quickly presses a note into it. He gives me a knowing look but says nothing. I put on my spectacles and slowly decipher his scrawling Greek writing. On the back of a scuffed cigarette box, he has written:

> *Tasos Lefterias*
> *Papadakis Evangelos*

CHAPTER TEN

"No right to revenge"

"Myers is not like Waldheim"

I feel quite awkward about meeting Eddie Myers, because he is Jewish and I am German, albeit "blessed with being born late enough not to bear the burden of guilt for the atrocities," as Chancellor Kohl had put it naïvely on a state visit to Israel. But in no way do I want the famous brigadier to think that I am chalking up thirty-two human lives against six million, as some people brazenly dare to do by making comparisons with the persecution of the Jews. Nothing could be further from my intentions than to diminish German atrocities by putting them in relative terms.

He lives in the small village of Broadwell, in a yellow stone cottage delightfully positioned next to a green park. There is a brook which flows freely across the road; no bridge has been built over it. As I park the car, the brigadier, as his neighbours respectfully call him, comes hurrying out of his house. He has grey blue eyes and a long oval head. His left eye looks a little inflamed. He is extremely friendly and ushers me into his living-room, passing through the kitchen and the small dining-room, where old oil paintings of the family hang on the walls.

Eddie Myers sits down in a large wing chair next to the roaring fire. He is wearing a green army jacket with metal press buttons under his tweed jacket. There is no other heating apart from the open fire, and it is cold in the comfortably furnished room. I hand him my present: Hermann Meyer's photos of the demolished bridge. He is quite overwhelmed. Almost fifty years on, he is holding the pictures documenting the greatest deed of his life.

He starts to talk about the Gorgopotamos operation, grumbles about Hamson, praises Woodhouse, Marinos and Zervas, finds no good word for Aris and says he only vaguely remembers Lefterias and Kolokythia. But he is quite convinced that he saved Sarafis' life. Tzimas apparently wrote to him from Czechoslovakia a short time before his death. They had wanted to meet again, but it was not to be. "I am not aware of him having let me down seriously ever, although our political views were miles apart."

322

I keep trying to steer the conversation to his stay in Kolokythia, but the old man cannot, or will not, remember. I finally tell him of the fate of the thirty-four Germans.

"What a struggle," he says; then adds, "May I relate that to my wife?" He gets up, changes the subject and suggests, "Let me offer you a glass of whisky." Darkness has fallen, it is time for a drink.

"But didn't you interrogate the German soldiers when you were in Gardiki on 30 March, 1943?" I insist. "You must have been extremely interested in questioning my father who was an officer of the company which rebuilt the Gorgopotamos bridge. Particularly, because you were still planning to blow it up again if conditions were favourable. Gardiki is only a small village. My father was arrested on the evening of 30 March by Lefterias. On that same evening you met Lefterias for the first time, and he talked to you about the capture of the Germans. That is obvious from what you wrote in your book in 1954."

Fig. 76   *Kolokythia in April*

Eddie Myers has again made himself comfortable in his big wing chair. "Well," he says, "I can't remember those times so clearly. Also, I was only a soldier and not too well versed in political affairs. You should ask Woodhouse about that. But, how very interesting that your father and I should have spent the night of 30 March in the same village of Gardiki and then travelled on to Kolokythia the following day. Sadly, in answer to your question, I do not recall having interviewed any German prisoners in Gardiki on 30 March. So I missed getting some interesting, and possibly valuable, information from your father."

"So did you march to Kolokythia the next day with the German prisoners?"

"As far as I can remember, I travelled on to Kolokythia on 31 March with my interpreter and Greek guide alone. I certainly do not remember travelling with Tasos, let alone with a group of German prisoners."

"What about in Kolokythia? Didn't you even hear about the fifty prisoners? You were staying at Zissi's house which is within earshot of the school."

"It is very interesting to hear all this," says the brigadier, "but I have no recollection of ever being told of German prisoners."

"Myers may be old and he may have forgotten a lot," says Woodhouse the next day, "but, believe me, he is telling the truth."

The professor, having returned to his vocation, now teaches at King's College in London and has written several books about Greece and the Second World War. We talk about the time he spent in the Greek mountains and about his experiences with the ELAS andartes. Even fifty years later, Woodhouse cannot find anything favourable to say about the ELAS movement.

"I do not think I can recall a single incident when Aris fought the Germans, only the Italians and the other Greeks," he explains to me. "Obviously we did not want ELAS to attack other partisan groups. I am not sure whether Myers would have urged them to attack either the railway line or other objects."

I can hardly believe my ears and think of the countless attacks on German railway stations and installations which were targeted in Roumeli alone at the end of March and in early April under the aegis of Arthur Edmonds. "But," I interrupt him, "Myers himself writes about this in his book."

"Ah, well," Woodhouse clears his throat.

"He writes in his book that, in Gardiki, on 30 March, 1943, he reproached Lefterias for not fighting the enemy but wasting time and energy on attacking other groups of partisans. I asked Myers about this and he confirmed it."

"Well, this makes a lot of sense, obviously," says the professor, now launching into a lecture. "Attacking other partisan groups was wrong and had to be stopped. Attacking enemy targets on the railway line was something that was required on certain occasions for certain strategic or tactical purposes. You see my point? I mean, operations like Gorgopotamos had a significant purpose and then in the summer of 1943, in July 1943, when the Allies were about to land in Italy, there was a purpose in attacking targets all over Greece, to convince the German High Command that the Allied landings were coming to Greece. We always tried to work to specific tactical purposes. Not just to behave like bandits. You see what I mean?"

I think of Giovanni and of Nikos Kalambouras, and how Woodhouse was involved in sentencing the latter to death by hanging in Kolokythia. But I am too cowardly to confront him with this. Besides, I do not want to cut short our talk. He speaks so loudly that all his colleagues in the staff room cannot help but overhear.

"So, if I understand you correctly," I reply, "the difference between you and the partisans was that you selected your targets according to tactical purposes whereas the partisans attacked at random."

"I can quite see Myers saying 'stop attacking Greek partisans, you have more important things to do'. But I am puzzled that he should have urged them to attack targets on the rail road line, at that particular time, in April 1943, when there was no specific requirement," Woodhouse insists.

"But Myers had reproached Lefterias on 30 March, 1943, that, instead of fighting the common enemy, he was intent only on eliminating his political adversaries, and when Lefterias was able to counter that railway stations, sawmills and mines run by Germans had been successfully attacked — and this was done with the full knowledge and assistance of Arthur Edmonds who was directly under your orders, Mr Woodhouse — Myers was placated and withdrew his threat to stop supplying ELAS with those essential air drops. You must have been aware of all this as you were his deputy."

"Did you ask Myers about this?" Woodhouse avoids giving me a direct answer.

"Of course. When I spoke of Gardiki, he couldn't remember a thing. His only response was to smile. He remembers so many, many details, that it is difficult to accept that he cannot remember those days. That was, after all, his first meeting with Lefterias who then had Sarafis' life in his hands. So it was not just some run-of-the-mill meeting, but one of great significance for him. I cannot truly imagine that he has forgotten it."

"You know," Woodhouse interrupts, "he is over eighty years old now and he never understood any Greek."

"But he always travelled with an interpreter and he remembers so many other details."

"Well, I was at that time in our HQ in Avlaki. I only saw Myers again upon his return from Kolokythia. He is a completely honest man. If he says he does not remember, he does not remember. He is not like Waldheim who says he can't remember anything. Myers is a completely honest man."

In Putaruru

Arthur Edmonds, with his tireless smile, is now seventy-four years old. He looks sprightly, he is certainly not senile, his face is hardly lined, only his thick hair has grown grey with his years. After the war he stayed on in Greece working for the United Nations, "to help rebuild the country in which I helped to destroy so much".

He has finally agreed to speak to me. But even before we sit down at his long dining-room table, he asks me where on earth this place Kolokythia is. He knows who I am, for I had flown to New Zealand once before, but that time I was only able to locate his wife. Obviously, his tactic now to set the scene is to say, "I cannot remember."

These three words put in question the whole value of my long journey. This man does not even wish to remember Kolokythia, the ELAS headquarters in Roumeli where he was stationed as the British liaison officer! As a consequence, he has never heard of the capture of thirty-four Germans and sixteen Italians.

326

"But you were present at Kolokythia with Myers to negotiate with Tzimas, Maniatis, Aris, Lefterias and Grigoriadis about the fate of General Sarafis," I insist desperately. "That was a unique and significant event, an exceptionally important conference. You cannot have forgotten that."

"Fancy that," says Edmonds again and again, feigning surprise. "And I was there?"

"Of course you were there. You wrote it yourself in a manuscript for a book."

Fig. 77   *Arthur Edmonds in Putaruru. He is holding an Athens newspaper of 25 November, 1945, in which the destruction of the Gorgopotamos bridge is glowingly described*

"What! Did you read that?" he asks in amazement.

"Yes, I obtained a copy of the manuscript in Greece. In it you describe the conference with Tzimas and Sarafis in great detail. It also clearly documents that you and Eddie Myers arrived in Kolokythia on 31 March, 1943, and that you left the village again on 20 April, 1943. Besides, you were in Kolokythia several times before 1 April and after 20 April, 1943. Apart from your own records, various former andartes have confirmed to me that you were in Kolokythia at the time of the shooting of the Germans."

"Fancy that," the New Zealander murmurs. "I never knew there were Germans in Kolokythia. I swear that."

"Well, there were not only thirty-four Germans, but sixteen Italian prisoners as well. These were released on 18 April, 1943. Do you remember why the Italians were freed and the Germans shot?"

"No, I did not know at all that Germans and Italians were in Kolokythia. You know, our headquarters was a hundred metres away from the andarte headquarters."

"That is irrelevant. The village is so small. Everybody who is still alive and lived in Kolokythia in those days recalls the prisoners in the schoolhouse. The building is next to the church, in the central square. Every path in Kolokythia crosses this square. And you used to stay at Zissi's, the grocer's, whose house is situated very close to the school."

"I can't remember. It is really very interesting to be told all this after so many years." The man smiles unremittingly. It jars on me. His face has become impenetrable, like a rigid mask. But the old man is not playing the amnesia card convincingly, and the further away we get from Kolokythia, the more he remembers.

"Surely you recall the attacks on Aghie, Domokos and Kurnovon?"

"Yes, sort of. The Germans felt secure, the stations were guarded. But then it became uncomfortable for them."

"What about Asopos. Do you remember Asopos? That spectacular demolition of the viaduct? You planned it and you were responsible for carrying out the operation."

"Yes, that was a splendid operation. My men were so lucky that the Germans were just repairing the bridge and left a ladder standing. So Stott and his men could use it to climb right up into the structure to attach the explosive charges."

328

Edmonds is warming to the subject and slowly gaining confidence. He remembers a good many details and place names, he recalls Gardiki and Sperhias, the trial against Kostorizos and many facts regarding the Gorgopotamos operation. He complains bitterly about Hamson who was always trying to undermine his boss. And without prompting, he goes on to relate vividly how he dynamited a bridge near Kajitsa, an operation which he also describes in his manuscript:

With difficulty we suppressed our excitement at the anticipation of what was about to happen. The leading locomotive slid over the bridge at thirty-five miles an hour; we held our breath waiting for a half-inch fuse to burn and wondering if the improvisation would be effective — then there was a terrific flash and roar and the leading locomotive came to a sudden stop. One of the wagons had fallen into the gap and stopped the train — stopped the front part of the train, but the locomotive at the rear of the train continued to come on, crushing wagon after wagon into the gap. The explosion set fire to the wagons in the gap whilst the andartes, opening up with everything they had, set fire to another wagon. Then there was a terrific burst of flame which leapt hundreds of feet into the air.

The andartes fired fiercely for a few minutes until someone on the train returned a few bursts with a machine gun. One andarte, the bugler, quickly blew the retreat, turned about and ran as fast as he could to overtake his comrades who were acting in accordance with the bugle-call with all speed.

Edmonds eyes are shining while he grumbles about the "big-mouthed Greeks who turned tail and ran at the slightest hitch". He recalls every detail. "It was an indescribably exciting operation. I am proud of it because we had the enormous luck to have hit on an ammunition train."

The report which the German commander for Southern Greece received at the time says:

Thirteen wagons crashed down, twenty-seven wagons burnt out due to explosions. After the accident the train was shot at with two-centimetre anti-aircraft gun, one small machine gun and rifle fire. Section closed for three to four days. Number of dead not yet established.

"There were people in that train," I comment. "One of them was a general. Two hundred hostages were murdered to pay for his death:

one hundred were shot by the Germans and another hundred by Greek
units collaborating with the Germans. The Germans took their revenge
by having two hundred innocent people shot, Mr Edmonds!"

"Oh dear, fancy that!" Edmonds is staring straight ahead. He leans
across the table. I think I can almost feel his breath. "I thought there
was nobody on that train. I was always under the impression that it
was a goods and ammunition transporter."

"In that case, I cannot understand why you shot at the falling and
burning wagons."

Edmonds pays no notice to that remark. "Oh gosh, that's terrible,"
he says with concern.

"Do you remember Kapetan Thomá, Mr Edmonds? His real name
was Hatzipanayiotou."

"Yes, what about him?"

"Well, he wrote about the shooting of the Germans in Kolokythia.
He quotes my father's last words."

"Fancy that. You have done a lot of research. So what did he
say?"

"Heil Hitler."

"Gosh, I did hear about that. People talked about that in the
mountains. Fancy." For a second our eyes meet.

"And?"

"Yeah, I heard about it." Edmonds grins.

"And what else did you hear?"

"I heard that this German officer said 'Heil Hitler' before they shot
him. Yeah, he said that. He had everyone stand to attention to be
shot."

"Yes," I confirm, "and then they were shot. They died for the
wrong cause."

"Well, you know, he thought it was the right cause. Yes, yeah,
that's right."

"I asked former andartes whether you took part in the execution.
My question was not answered."

Edwards is not at all insulted. He makes a placatory gesture and
says, "No, no I was not there. You know, I was lucky enough never
to have to shoot anybody."

"But people remember that you were in the village at the time."

"Oh yeah?"

"Do you now recall that the Italians continued to be imprisoned in the school until 18 April, 1943, and that two of the Germans joined the andartes?"

"Oh really? Two Germans actually joined the andartes? No, I don't know anything about that."

"But surely you remember Lefterias and what kind of man he was?"

Edmonds becomes more talkative, because he could not stand Tasos Lefterias. He remembers him very clearly and refers to his own manuscript where he describes the fate of Arthur Hubbard, another New Zealander, who was an officer and a friend:

ELAS and EDES representatives had a convivial dinner on the evening of 10 October, 1943, and they parted at midnight the best of friends. Two hours later ELAS tried to round up the EDES-band. In their attempt they fired thousands of rounds of ammunition without any effect because EDES had been forewarned and had stolen out of the village.

Tasos with a force of ELAS andartes then set off towards Zervas' territory and reached Brianza one evening to find that the small EDES band that had been there, had left. Major Bill Jordan commanded the Brianza Mission station and was assisted by a school friend, Lieutenant Arthur Hubbard from Hamilton, New Zealand. That night, a burst of machine-gun fire swept one of the lighted rooms of their house. No one was injured but Hubbard went outside to see what was happening. More shots rang out and Hubbard shouted: "I've been hit." He had been shot through the stomach and it was obvious that he would soon die. "Fancy going out like this," he said, "shot by the people I've come here to help."

Next day it was established that some of Taso's men had shot Hubbard. Lefterias was full of apologies, but said that his men had mistaken him for an EDES andarte, and added that as he was bearded and in battle-dress, he looked very much like an andarte.

Edmonds gazes past me through the lovely bay window to his green garden with its glorious old trees. A few yellowing leaves have already fallen and lie on the lawn, a presage of autumn. It seems odd to think that in Europe the first delicate spring flowers are beginning to blossom. He gets up and shuffles off to his bedroom to get two old shoe boxes, and digs out a map of Greece from one of them. I point out Kolokythia, but even this does nothing to jog his memory. There are lots of old photos in his boxes which he willingly allows me to see: pictures of andartes but also plans and photos of bridges which he helped to rebuild after the war. One snapshot suddenly slips out of his hand, I glimpse two men with their arms raised, but he quickly tucks it away in the other box.

Fig. 78   *Arthur Edmond's unusual snapshot: arrest of two German soldiers near Sperhias*

"Oh, it's nothing much," he says when I try to retrieve it. But, then, I am suddenly holding it in my hand: two men in German uniform with their arms raised are being taken prisoner by partisans storming up a hill.

"Umm, it's nothing much," he says. "They probably posed for the picture."

"What do you mean? Even if it is posed, the uniforms are genuine. Where did they come from?"

Edmonds seems embarrassed. I cannot understand why. After all, there was a war and he was in it. Why should he want to suppress it? He looks at the picture and visibly squirms. For the first time he is now really ill at ease. The photo disappears under another heap, but I am obstinate and I fish it out again and turn it over. In a neat hand he has written "Sperhias" on the back. Suddenly, everything falls into place for me, because Sperhias was where some of those thirty-four Germans were taken prisoner, and Sperhias would have been in Edmond's domain at the end of March 1943. Who were these two Germans? Maybe Max Rossmann and Karl Blachnik, but it is impossible to tell because their faces are too small. One thing is certain: the German army never went back to Sperhias, so those two soldiers must have been among the prisoners of Kolokythia.

"I had a good camera, and took many good photos in Greece," Edmonds says.

"Fancy that," I say sarcastically and stop myself from saying any more, but I cannot help thinking that he had to be a callous, cold-blooded man to have photographed the arrest at all, knowing full well that these prisoners were doomed; he knew what the andartes' rules were and that Myers and Woodhouse had given instructions not to take prisoners.

"An utterly insignificant matter"

Everyone in Athens knows that a telelphone number beginning with "8" belongs to someone living in the elegant and rich northern suburbs. So, does this mean that the arch-communist and leader of the andartes, Lefterias, has transmuted into a capitalist, calling himself Papadakis?

The answer to this question comes from Hagen Fleischer who is the top German authority on recent Greek history and a professor at the University of Crete. "His wife is wealthy because she comes from a family of tobacco dealers in Karpenissi. You must understand that good contacts are of prime importance in Greece. He was also one of the first to return from exile in the USSR in the fifties."

Fleischer knows Papadakis very well, having interviewed him at length when he wrote his book "Im Kreuzschatten der Mächte, Griechenland 1941-1944" (In the cross-fire of the big powers, Greece 1941-1944). Originally, Fleischer had wanted Andreas Tzimas to write the preface because he considered him to be "a valuable and sincere eye-witness and a fatherly friend. However, Andreas Tzimas' untimely death, which filled me with personal sorrow, also created the problem of finding someone else who both fulfilled the editor's conditions and was willing to step in and be more than a substitute. I was very lucky to find Mr Vangelis Papadakis."

And Papadakis made full use of this opportunity to expound his views in eleven closely printed pages. "I do not expect you to agree with me on every point," he addresses himself directly to Fleischer in the preface. "All my life I have suffered for the right to freedom of thought, and now I would request you to consider my actions with an equally open mind."

And today I am going to see him. A friend contacted him and obtained his agreement to give me an interview. I was introduced as a German who was writing a book about the war years in Greece.

The Olympic Airways flight arrives in Athens with an enormous delay, and it seems to take a further eternity before the luggage rolls up. Sitting in the taxi, I really worry about whether or not he will still receive me, but we stop for a phone call and then press on, rushing along the coast towards Syntagma Square, darting through traffic jams and smog and finally we hit the exit road to Kifissia and, just as dusk is falling, we reach Demokratias Road in the suburb of Ano Pefki. The taxi stops in front of a low villa. I pay, get out and walk to the wrought iron gate sunk into the long brick wall surrounding the house. The gate opens easily and a path leads straight to the front door, across the garden where a thick watering hose is lying on the red earth. There is no name on the door, but at least there is a bell.

I hear a sound and turn. He is coming through the garden to greet me, gives me a welcoming smile and shakes my hand. I can still feel his hand in mine, the limp squeeze and the flesh warm and soft.

"Pleased to meet you," he says.

He invites me to take a seat on the veranda next to him. He looks young for his age. His thin, grey hair is combed back, his eyes are hidden behind tinted glasses. He is wearing grey, shabby trousers, an open-necked short-sleeved shirt and scuffed and worn leather shoes without socks.

I get up as his wife appears. She smiles, greets me and inquires whether I would like a cup of coffee. I decline, but do not want to appear impolite, so we compromise with a glass of water. She has dyed blond hair and seems tired and worn. She returns with the water and puts a slice of chocolate cake in front of each of us, which I really don't want but I smile my thanks.

I present myself to Papadakis and thank him for receiving me. He smiles in a friendly way. He seems a strong, stockily built man. His heavy hands and the sausage-like fingers with dirty nails look like those of a labourer, but his face is that of a civil servant. I just wish he would take off those impenetrable glasses.

"Well," he says, starting the conversation, "what I was given by Mother Nature is not strictly mine. In that sense, I can say neither good nor bad things about the war. My character is such, that I picked my way very calmly and quietly through those times and did all I could to help my country against the oppressor. I am talking about the resistance movement fighting for the liberation of our country."

He has obviously been trained to speak, a pupil of the communist élite school. He revels in hearing his own voice, and it is difficult to interrupt the flow of his speech in order to get him to come to the point.

"Mr Papadakis," I say at last, putting my first question to him, "were you present, when the British and Greeks destroyed the Gorgopotamos viaduct?"

"No, when that happened, I was just on my way to the mountains from Athens. I went to Roumeli which is the Gorgopotamos district. It is called Sterea Ellada nowadays. I belonged to Aris' group, but I was not present for the attack."

"A few months after the destruction of the bridge, in March 1943, some German soldiers working in the Makrakomi area were captured by partisans. Do you know anything about this?"

"Oh, yes. This particular operation could be called the first time that we attacked the Germans. I personally organised it. We hit a number of targets. We attacked Platistomo and Makrakomi, the guards at Nezeros, and we blew up various mines such as at Amfissa and others. The Germans were exploiting our natural resources, so we very efficiently stopped them from ever mining them again. About four kilometres from Lamia, we ambushed some Germans and were lucky enough to catch an officer. All together, we took forty-four German prisoners."

"I think there were thirty-four. What happened then?"

"Let me tell you," he says animatedly. "When we captured these people, I wrote a report and sent it to the German High Command in Lamia. I wrote that we were holding forty-four prisoners whom we would treat as prisoners of war provided that there were no reprisals against civilians. But, if civilians continued to be made to suffer, these prisoners would have to pay with their lives. The Germans burned down four villages one day after receipt of my letter and killed forty-two people in the neighbourhood of Lamia. That sealed the fate of the prisoners and unfortunately they had to be executed in the village of Kolokythia. Their bones have been dug up by the Germans and buried in the German cemetery near Athens. This has all been documented. There is no point in covering such things up.

"It is, furthermore, true that the fate of these people was determined by a number of other points, for which I was personally responsible. I was totally responsible for what happened. I made the decision. I had the forty-four Germans imprisoned in the school, and when I saw what the Germans' response was — I mean, the burning villages and so on — I asked the prisoners this question: 'Who among you is a fascist?'"

I interrupt him, "To whom did you put this question?"

"I asked all forty-four. I said: 'Who is a Fascist? Who among you is a fascist? Those who are not fascists will not be executed, although your commander gave us a negative response to our proposal.'

"It is unbelievable, but they all shouted in unison, *'Heil Hitler!'* To me this was monstrous. Four times I asked, and the interpreter translated. This reaction had a lot to do with their final fate."

Papadakis shakes his head violently. He still finds it incredible that anyone should have had that reaction.

"You know," he continues, "there was a lady among the prisoners who acted as an interpreter. I asked her to repeat it once more, in case they had not understood correctly, and the translated reply was the same again: 'Heil Hitler'!"

Vangelis pauses. I am sitting half a metre away from my father's murderer and I am mesmerised by his tale. It seems quite unreal, like in a dream. He still has no idea who I am.

"But I must point out that this was still at the beginning of the war. Our capacity to hold prisoners was very limited. And the attitude of the prisoners coupled with the reaction of their High Command led to the unfortunate denouement. I must also add that later we took many more prisoners and never did them any harm, neither to Germans nor to Italians."

"You say you also had Italian prisoners?"

"Yes, there were many Italians."

"Were there any Italian prisoners shut up in the school?"

"No. Only Germans with the woman."

"Two Germans were set free. They renounced Fascism and joined the andartes," I say, trying to jog his memory. Papadakis starts to slide about on his chair. He is beginning to dislike the conversation. He becomes monosyllabic.

"Ochi," he replies and nods his head backwards. "No."

I do so wish he would take off his glasses particularly as by now it has become totally dark. I can hear the traffic from the road. The headlights flit across the veranda windows and fleetingly pick out the outline of his face. He is now fiddling with a little metal chain between his heavy fingers. It is not a rosary. Through the veranda door, inside the lit room on the dining table, I notice one of those gold painted little bowls with black background which can be bought in tourist shops all over the Soviet Union.

"Yes, they did!" I insist. "They joined the andartes. One of them returned to Germany after the war."

"I know that two men escaped the execution. But we caught them later and shot them."

"How was that possible?"

"Well," he says with slight irritation and takes a deep breath. "I will tell you what happened. It is an utterly insignificant matter, so a few words should suffice. But as you are so insistent, I will start again from the beginning. It was a stupid incident, and we are wasting a lot of time over something which is really very unimportant. You see, there was a lot of snow then. The bodies were quickly covered by snow. We did not give a *coup de grace*. It was cold. This was our first operation against the Germans. Alright, I cannot put it down as a feather in our cap. I also must admit that, at that time, the German outposts were utterly unsuspicious and had not protected themselves adequately. Only at Nezeros did we suffer injuries and deaths. Anyway, those two Germans who got away were recaptured the following day. One of them had asked a woman in Marmara for water, if I remember correctly. He was probably off his head by then, but she promptly gave him away."

"Can you tell me how the German officer was captured?"

"He was taken between Lamia and Platistomo. He was riding in a car or maybe on a motorbike. I don't know why he was driving to Platistomo because he was not stationed there. Maybe he wanted to go to the spa."

"Do you remember the officer? What was his responsibility?"

"I believe he was in charge of provisioning his unit. Anyway, I spoke to all the Germans. I addressed each one directly. All I wanted from them was that they should renounce Nazism."

"Were the prisoners taken to Kolokythia via Sperhias and Gardiki?"

"Well, many were taken to Kolokythia. It was cold. It was snowing."

"How did you feed the captives?"

"They ate what we ate."

"Mr Papadakis, the prisoners wrote a letter to the German High Command asking that negotiations on their release should be undertaken. Are you interested in the contents of this letter? I found it in German archives."

"Is there the name of a woman on it?"

"Yes, Trude Radwein."

"She was married to a Greek." Papadakis leans forward as he says this and looks at me inquiringly.

"Yes, he studied medicine in Vienna. His name was Samothraki. She left him and went to live with Haralambopoulos, the hotelier. She was the hotel manageress, she never belonged to the Wehrmacht."

Papadakis lets me read Meyer's letter of 8 April, 1943, to him but suddenly interrupts brusquely, "That's all lies. They just yelled 'Heil Hitler'. I already told you that. They refused to write any letter."

I point out that the letter is a document which cannot be disputed and that Viktor and Rudolf were freed and taken on by the andartes once they had renounced Fascism.

"That may be so," he concedes suddenly. "But you must understand that I planned the different attacks on stations, trains and mines to commemorate our national day on 25 March, 1943, the day of liberation from the Turkish oppression which we suffered for centuries. That was the reason for the attacks. I called a conference in Marmara on 25 March, 1943. That village lies between Platistomo and Kolokythia. I invited all the leading people from Sterea Ellada.

We discussed our organisation, our plans for the future and our national government. By then, most of the villages in Roumeli had been freed from enemy occupation, and the police had joined us. There were only a few German-held spots left, and there were of course the Italians at Karpenissi. What we needed to do, therefore, was to flush them out of their last few holes in Roumeli."

"And what about their clothes, Mr Papadakis, the valuables that the soldiers carried with them, such as their rings, what happened to them?"

Papadakis focuses on me. He starts to get up. His voice is hard and irritated. "They took their clothes off. We needed them. I was telling you about my part in the freedom fight and you keep harping on about this shooting. We also fought the Germans at Makrakomi. Why don't we talk about that? We suffered terrible losses there."

"Yes," I agree. "But that was in November 1944. I wish to talk to you about the events in Kolokythia in April 1943. November 1944 was completely different, because Greeks and Germans confronted each other in battle and men on both sides fell in action. But in Kolokythia, people whom you yourself qualify as prisoners, were shot in cold blood. That was murder. You yourself called these people prisoners of war. What did Aris say, what did Edmonds say to this?"

Papadakis is standing in front of me, only inches away, while I continue to sit feeling numb and in a mental vacuum. He wants to end the conversation. I am quite unable to deal with the fact that my father's murderer is before me, just inches from me.

"Aris had nothing to do with it. It was my decision," he screams down at me.

I finally stumble to my feet and pick up my rucksack. "Before I go, I would like to show you a photo, Mr Papadakis."

"I don't want to see any photo." He shakes his head wildly and spreads his fat fingers.

I pull the picture out of my rucksack and hold it out to him in the twilight. "Do you remember this man? He was the officer among the Germans, the kapetanios who was taken prisoner on the way to Platistomo. He was my father. You killed my father."

Papadakis stares at me. For a fraction of a second, he is speechless. "You deceived me," he bellows while I find myself sitting on the chair again. "You should have told me straight away that your father was among those who were shot."

"I did it on purpose. That was the only way to exclude emotion, and to get you to speak the truth. Please try to understand that I needed to discover the truth about my father's fate."

We are now both standing. I accept that further conversation is useless, fruitless, and retreat into the darkness of the garden, find the stone pathway that leads to the wrought iron gate and turn around. He is just going through the veranda door into his living-room, but before I leave his property I yell threateningly, completely out of control, "I am coming back, this is not the last time that we shall meet, Mr Papadakis!"

I resolve feverishly to take legal advice to find out whether Papadakis can be prosecuted and punished for executing his prisoners.

The Greek lawyers informed me when I put the matter in their hands, that the execution of the prisoners was indeed illegal as it contravened the Geneva Convention of 1929, which had been ratified by Greece. However, the Penal Law of 1834 was in force in Greece during the war, and according to article 119 penal war crimes were expunged seven years after their perpetration. There could therefore be no legal action brought after 9 April 1950.

"No right to revenge"

My taxi driver is having trouble finding Neapoleos Street in the north-eastern suburb Agias Paraskevi of Athens. Rain is beating down, the street lights do not work, and the roads are transformed into gushing torrents. It feels like the apocalypse.

The building has six floors and looks drab. It is impossible to make out any name tabs in the darkness. On a hunch, I take the lift to the third floor and, opening the heavy metal door on to the landing, I find a slim man standing in the doorway to his dreary flat with his fat wife at his side.

It has been a long quest for me to track him down. His name is Tsokas, Thimos Tsokas. Half a century ago, he called himself Fotis Parnassiotis. He has finally accepted my wish to see him. His curiosity about meeting the son of the man whom he had shot was greater than any scruples he may have had about the act.

We are still in the entrance hall, when he says, "So you are the son of the officer?"

"And you the leader of the firing squad?" The directness of my question does not faze him.

"That is correct. But I, myself, didn't shoot."
"What did you do instead?"
"I gave the command."

Fig. 79   *Fotis Parnassiotis* (right) *in German uniform jacket:*
"I commanded the execution squad"

"So you stood between the execution squad and the Germans and gave the signal to fire the mortal shots."

"Yes, but I, myself, didn't shoot," he repeats. "Lefterias was not in charge of the squad. It was I and my men. It was not easy for them."

What a sense of power! He describes how he gave the order for the death salvo. He is still proud of that deed! He relates how the Germans were arrested and how he led the attacks on the Topolia mine and on Gravia station, and again and again, he refers to the fact that Rudolf and Viktor owed their lives to him. "Lefterias and Aris asked me if I would take full responsibility, should they betray us. 'Are you willing to lay your head on the line?' they asked. 'Yes,' I said. 'Alright then,' Lefterias said, 'if those two escape you will pay with your life.'"

It is understandable that Tsokas prefers to talk about his life-saving deed than about the murder of thirty-two Germans. He is sitting in his stained armchair, gesticulating excitedly and avoiding tricky questions and at times, if expedient, he lies. His hands are slim and he has long fingernails. His black hair, without a single grey streak, is perfectly parted on the left side. His thin face is full of wrinkles, but although he is now seventy-seven, he does not look very different from the single photo I found of him as an andarte. Like Lefterias, he was a law student, joined the KKE, and was then rapidly promoted to being the Politikos of his andarte group. Dimitrios Dimitriou says, "Like myself, Parnassiotis was arrested in 1944, incarcerated and only freed again in 1952. But while he was Politikos, he was under Lefterias' orders."

Tsokas remembers Gertrud Radwein and calls her "Trudie", not Gertrud or Trude. He does not show even the slightest pinprick of remorse that this woman was shot. In fact, he laughs as he relates how her fur coat was cut up after the shooting to make their fur hats. He is irked that I already know about this and that he is not the first to tell me the story.

His round little wife scrutinises me inquisitively. "May I butt in and ask why you want to know all this?"

I struggle to reply, while I am flooded with memories of those empty, fatherless days of dashed hopes for his return after the war and, in particular, I remember a dream: I am walking up a barren hill with sheep grazing peacefully. At the summit of the hill there is a large wooden cross. I am a little boy wearing short pants with braces, a bright short-sleeved shirt and sandals. It is summer time. I can only see my back, but it is me, turning my back on myself. A man is walking next to me. He is tall, he gives me confidence, comfort and a wonderful feeling of well-being. I can only see his back, but I know who he is. He is wearing a grey tweed suit. We are walking straight into the fiery ball of the rising sun. I am not afraid of the gleaming sunrays and can look into them without harm. I wish he would take my hand in his. But he does not. I wake up and I am crying.

Only some days after that dream did I suddenly realise that the hill was the one on the way to the monastery of Xenia.

"Have you ever cried in your sleep?" I finally answer her. She is puzzled and assumes that I did not understand her question. But he is talking again.

"We made a proposal to the Germans. We told them to send a note to their commander whose troops were occupying Makrakomi. If he didn't burn the houses, we would let them go free. But the German officer refused to write the letter."

"That isn't true," I interject. "The Germans wrote a letter. Every single person signed it, but it was only deposited at German headquarters one week after the prisoners were shot. It entirely contradicts the facts to say that the Germans were shot because they refused to write that letter."

Tsokas leaps up and accuses me of being a little know-all. He loses his temper, and suddenly deep-seated hatred flows from him. "We detested the Germans, I hate them all, I hate you, you are a Fascist, just like your father."

The fact remains that the hostages lost their value to the partisans as soon as the German troops attacked the Greek villages, which was Löhr's response to Lefterias' first letter of 2 April, 1943. Andreas Tzimas, Aris Velougiotis, Tasos Lefterias and Fotis Parnassiotis murdered unarmed prisoners for revenge and in order to secure Eddie Myers' goodwill. "There was a war on," Mrs. Tsokas comments succinctly, and she is right.

Vengeance is not what I seek, but I am convinced that a reappraisal of events must necessarily involve raking over painful memories on both sides. I needed to meet Tsokas. And even more, I now need to see Papadakis again to get some answers to so many questions which have been accumulating in my head. But he is elusive, his wife protects him, pretending he is in hospital. However, private detectives who advertise their services in the Athens newspapers soon find out that he is perfectly well and at home in Ano Pefki.

I must see him again; he draws me like a magnet. I wish to talk to him in daylight, look into his grey-blue eyes. I want to, well, what do I want? To get my own back? A word of regret? Some understanding of my sorrow?

I could stage-manage a perfect drama if I were to bargain with Vagelis Tsagaris for the pistol which he received as a prize from Lefterias for handing over Meyer and his three comrades in Gardiki. Another alternative for an act of vengeance full of symbolism would be to use the old nineteenth century Mannlicher rifle, which the taverna-keeper at Gardiki has kindly presented me with. Who would ever trace the original owner of that old gun? That would surely be a hopeless task. And it would be easy to take my revenge. I would not be noticed in the busy street in Ano Pefki. I could wait for her to go shopping, then step through the veranda door or through the bedroom window at the back. Or maybe just ring the door bell. I know they live alone on the ground floor. Two hours later I could be out of the country.

The wrought iron gate is not locked, just pushed to. The garden looks unkempt with straggling thick bushes. I walk straight up to the door. The front windows along the long veranda where I first met him are veiled with white net curtains. No one seems to be at home. Not a sound. I press the unnamed bell. I feel anxious, like a burglar, but I refuse to go back now. Inside the house, I hear footsteps shuffling to the door. He is obviously wearing slippers. The sound of steps on the stone floor is only just discernible through the heavy, wrought iron door with its glass panel. He pulls it open and I look upon him. With the glinting sunlight behind me, he does not recognise me immediately, and before he can react, I quickly say, "Hello, Mr Papadakis, I have come back to..."

Interrupting my greeting as he recognises me, he tries to close the door, but I slip past him into the house. He recoils, staring at me with hatred and incredulity. "Get out of my house! I didn't invite you in."

344

I glance past him through the wide entrance to the living-room, where a colourful couch stands out against the light stone floor. A copy of a Dutch landscape with a drawbridge is hanging on the wall above. A commonplace print. In front of the couch, there is a little glass table with the Russian bowl I noticed on my last visit. The room looks impersonal and unused. No doubt they only sit here on special occasions. "I would like to ask you some questions."

Fig. 80   *Vangelis Papadakis in his house in Ano Pefki: "You have no right to revenge"*

He retreats further. Stepping backwards he crosses a long hall and goes into the bedroom behind, without turning his back to me. A double bed, neatly made up with a brownish blanket, two night tables and a large wardrobe fill the room. The curtains are drawn, the walls are unadorned and painted yellow. Papadakis is tall and big, much bigger than I remember. He is a strong man with a bull neck and greying hair. He sinks onto the bed, snatches up the telephone and searches about frantically among some tatty notebooks.

"That's it, I'm calling the police," he spits out the words in a state of great agitation.

"Mr Papadakis, I would like to ask you a few questions, but if you wish to call the police, please do so. But you should realise that in that case, our conversation will take place in the presence of the police and your picture will appear in all the newspapers tomorrow."

"I can't bear to look at you. You are a fascist, like your father."

"But, Mr Papadakis..."

"Listen to me, just listen and shut up..."

"Just a moment, please, Mr Papadakis..."

"You came here a while ago, saying that you were writing about the resistance movement and that you were collecting information about it. But you did not speak to me about the resistance. Instead, you only spoke of this one occurrence."

Papadakis is talking without looking at me. He is still fumbling nervously in the pile of papers on the night table.

"That is correct, yes, what you are saying is true, but I have..."

I look down on him, sitting on the edge of the bed, but he interrupts, "You cheated me. You took me for a fool. I can't bear to look at you."

"Why don't we discuss my questions instead of you shouting at me?" I suggest reasonably.

"I have nothing to tell you, dammit, nothing!" Lifting his head, he turns his light eyes on me, blazing with contempt. He is holding his notebooks in his hand, and at this point, I realise that no conversation will ever be possible.

I turn nasty. "In my country, every child knows the telephone number of the police. Why don't you? It must be on the first page of the telephone book."

Papadakis gets up, runs past me up the long, dark corridor and rummages around on some shelves at the end for the telephone directory. But he either cannot find it or does not wish to. For a moment, the house imposes its stillness on us, and I feel certain that he is not going to call the police, that he is putting on an act.

"I would like to tell you, Mr Papadakis — or would you prefer me to call you Lefterias, as we are talking about the past...?"

"You are not going to tell me anything, you know nothing and you are going to tell me nothing, do you hear?"

"I don't want to annoy you, I just want some answers, please be reasonable."

"I have said all I wish to say. I have nothing to add. Just go and tell your story to the papers!"

"Mr Papadakis, you must understand how much I care about this matter. After all, you are the person who has my father on his conscience."

"Did I say that? What do you expect me to say? I have said it all."

"I have three further questions. Why did you—?"

"No more questions."

"Why did you free the Italians?"

"I won't listen anymore."

"Why did you give the Italians their freedom?"

"All those who were not Fascists," he suddenly answers in an objective tone of voice.

"You freed all those who were not fascists?" I repeat.

"Yes," he affirms, "I released all those who were not Fascists."

"In that case, what you wrote in the preface to Hagen Fleischer's book is sheer mockery, just hot air! 'All my life, I have suffered for freedom of thought'. If that is true, then you should never have had the others shot."

Papadakis stares at me incredulously. I sense that he cannot comprehend what is happening to him on this sunny morning: this unexpected visit, this brutal journey into the past. I recall that Arthur Edmonds described him as "terrier-like when angered". I believe Papadakis has not understood what I just said.

"Would you at least tell me whether Tzimas and Sarafis participated in the firing squad?"

He again ignores my question and shouts, "No discussion! No conversation! Enough!"

"Alright. But why do you look at me with so much hatred in your eyes?"

"Because I hate you!"

"So you hate me. But why? For what reason?"

"Because you cheated me. I am an old man and I am tired of being cheated."

"You murdered my father."

"I can't find the number of the police. When the police come—"

"I am now imagining how you first beat and then shot my father. I am thinking about how, after the execution, you had to go back to the site to shoot those two wounded men who had crawled out of the pit. Do you remember that you commented to Tzivellekas that you should have slit their throats?"

"Oh, get out of here. Get out. I never cut anyone's throat. We were at war. We were warriors. We didn't murder Germans or anyone else. You Germans, you were the murderers. They murdered my brother-in-law. Both my brothers-in-law were murdered by your people."

"I am sorry—"

"My brothers-in-law were killed by you, shot, not in battle, no—"

"But you killed prisoners, Mr Papadakis, people whom you yourself described as prisoners of war. They had no defence. So how do you regard that?"

Papadakis cackles cynically. He has sunk down on the edge of the bed again and is stirring about pointlessly in his papers. His head is bent above the brown blanket and I look down on his naked bull's neck and, in my mind, I see Viktor Schendzielorz in this position when he was beheaded by Spiros Bekios or Fotis Parnassiotis or one of their henchmen.

"Well, what about Trude Radwein?" I say. "Do you remember the name, the name of the lady from Vienna? She was a hotel employee, not a Nazi soldier. How do you regard that? How can you justify killing an innocent, defenceless woman?"

"I have had enough of this, just get out of my house, go to the police. Who do you think you are! You have no right to revenge. You attacked my country."

No right to revenge. That is what they all say, the former andartes, officers and soldiers, British, New Zealanders and Greeks, all alike, their standard response to any more probing, and therefore disagreeable, question I put to them. "You have no right to ask these questions. You were the ones who attacked. You waged a war of extermination. You invaded our land, devastated it with war and sowed unending misery. You are responsible for millions of murders." Having won the war, having made such terrible sacrifices to achieve victory, they conclude that they have the right to define the rules: "You have no right to sue for a just judgement of your father's fate because he was a Nazi and belonged to Hitler's criminal regime. *You have no right to research into the destiny of each individual.*" That is taboo.

And yet, how can you cope with multiple murder without reappraising the destinies of each individual involved? And why should this be the exclusive right of the victors? Personally, I am convinced that if there ever was a just war, then it was the war waged against the Nazis.

Papadakis has got up. He looks much stronger and more powerful than his seventy-four years might imply. His barrel chest propels me into the hall, pushing me out in front of him. He aims a kick at my shins and yells, "Bugger off, you bastard. Get lost, leave my house instantly, dammit! I don't ever want to see you again."

He grabs my pullover. He is strong. I am carrying my rucksack in my right hand. My camera slips out and falls on the stone floor. I bend down to pick it up, but I never take my eyes off the man. I hear my knees crack. Papadakis still has a hold on my pullover and he is pushing me, which I let him do, because I know that it is over, pointless, fruitless.

"Let me go, don't touch me." I, too, am shouting now and I think of how he beat and kicked my father and his comrades before they were shot. He pushes me out of the door and tries to slam it shut but I put my foot in. He keeps repeating the movement again and again. I finally withdraw my foot, because I realise that it is but a useless provocation. The door crashes into the lock, but the glass panel does not shatter. I am trembling as I stand in front of the closed door, still stupidly trying to glimpse him through the frosted glass.

"I simply had to see you again. That was really all I wanted. You did it. You have to live with it, and I have to live with it. We both have to live with it."

Abbreviations

BLO.	British Liason Officer
B.M.M.	British Military Mission
C.A.	Corpo Armata
EAM	National Liberation Front
EBK	Eisenbahnpionierkompanie (Company of Rail Engineers)
EDES	Greek Democratic National Army
ELAS	National Popular Liberation Army
EPON	United Panhellenic Youth Organisation
Hiwi	Hilfswilliger (Voluntary helper)
Kawi	Kampfwilliger (Voluntary fighter)
KKE	Communist Party of Greece
KPD	Communist Party of Germany
kv.	Kriegsverwendungsfähig (useful to the war effort)
NSDAP	German National Socialist Labour Party
NSV	National Socialist Welfare Association
O.T.	Todt Organisation
OKH	Oberkommando des Heeres (Army High Command)
OKW	Oberkommando der Wehrmacht (Wehrmacht High Command)
S.O.E.	Special Operations Executive
VdN	Verfolgte des Naziregimes (Victims of persecution by the Nazi regime)
WASt.	Wehrmachtauskunftsstelle — Office dealing with notifying families of lost soldiers of the Wehrmacht.
ZK	Central Committee

Bibliography

1. Antony Beevor: *Crete, The Battle and the Resistance*, John Murray, London 1991.

2. Spiros Bekios (Lambros): *Selides Apo Tin Ethniki Antistasi*, Velouchi, Athens 1976.

3. Berichterstaffel des O.K.H.: *Das zweite Kriegsjahr*, Wilhelm Limpert Verlag, Berlin.

4. Hanspeter Born: *Für die Richtigkeit*, Kurt Waldheim, Schneekluth, München 1987.

5. Marco Picone Chiodo: *Sie werden die Stunde verfluchen*, Herbig Verlagsbuchhandlung, München 1990.

6. Constantine A. Doxiadis; *Such was the war in Greece*, Series of Publications of the Department of Reconstruction, Athens 1947.

7. Dimitrios Dimitriou (Nikiforos); *Gorgopotamos, Fitrakis*, Athens 1975.

8. Dimitrios Dimitriou (Nikiforos); *Antartis Sta Vouna Tis Roumeli*, Athens 1965.

9. Arthur Edmonds: *With Greek Guerillas* (Manuscript), 1954.

10. Ehrentafel für die Eisenbahn-Pioniere, Kameradschaft der ehemaligen Eisenbahn-Pioniere, Frankkfurt an Main 1976.

11. Dominique Eudes: *Les Kapetanios*, Librairie Artheme Fayard, 1970.

12. Hagen Fleischer: *Im Kreuzschatten der Mächte*, Verlag Peter Lang, Bern 1986.

13. Eleni Fourtouni: *Greek Women in Resistance*, Thelphini Press, New Haven, Co. 1986.

14. Hermann Franz: *Gebirgsjäger der Polizei*, Verlag Hans Henning Podzun, Bad Nauheim 1963.

15. Gesellschaft für Literatur und Bildung: *Die Wehrmachtsberichte 1939–1945*, Eisnerdruck, Berlin.

16. A. Gerolymatos: *Europäischer Widerstand im Vergleich*, Siedler Verlag.

17. Vageli K. Gormova: *Istoria tis Makrakomis*, Makrakomi 1990.

18. C. Hadjipateras, M. Fafalios: *Crete 1941 Eyewitnessed*, Efstathiadis Group, Athens 1989.

19. Nicholas Hammond: *Venture into Greece*, William Kinter & Co., London 1983.

20. Denys Hamson: *We Fell Among Greeks*, Jonathan Cape, London 1946.

21. Gianni C. Hatzipanayiotou (Hapetan Thomá): *I Politiki Diathiki Tou Ari Velougiotis*, Dorikos, Athens 1982.

22. W. A. Heurtley, H. C. Darby, C. W. Crawley, C. M. Woodhouse: *A short History of Greece*, Cambridge University Press, 1965.

23. John Louis Hondros: *Occupation & Resistance*, Athens Printing Co, New York 1983.

24. John L. Hondros: *The Greek Resistance, 1941-44*, University Press of New England, Hanover and London 1981.

25. Edna J. Hunter: *The Psychological Effects of Being a Prisoner of War*, Hunter Publication, San Diego, Ca., 1974.

26. Friedrich Husemann: *Die guten Glaubens waren*, Munin Verlag GmbH, Osnabrück 1986.

27. Boaz Kahana, Zev Harel, Eva Kahan: *Human Adaptation to Extreme Stress*, Plenum Press, New York. N.Y., 1988.

28. Themie Marinos: *Apostoli Harling — 1942*, Papazisi, Athens 1992.

29. Piero Malvezzi/Giovanni Pirelli: *Letzte Briefe zum Tode Verurteilter aus dem europäischen Widerstand*, DTV, München 1962.

30. E. C. W. Myers: *Greek Entanglement*, Rupert Hart-Davis, London 1955.

352

31. Prokopis Papstratis: *The British and the Greek Resistance Movements EAM and EDES*, Spokesman, Nottingham.

32. Janusz Piekalkiewicz: *Krieg auf dem Balkan*, Südwest Verlag München.

33. Harald Pölchau: *Die letzten Stunden*, Röderberg Verlag, Köln 1987.

34. Ralf Georg Reuth: *Entscheidung im Mittelmeer*, Bernard und Graefe Verlag, Koblenz 1985.

35. Heinz Richter: *British Intervention in Greece*, Merlin Press, London 1986.

36. Heinz A. Richter: *Griechenland im 20. Jahrhundert*, Romiosini, Köln 1990.

37. Stephanos Sarafis: *In den Bergen von Hellas*, Deutscher Militärverlag, Berlin 1964.

38. Percy Schramm: *Kriegstagebuch des Oberkommandos der Wehrmacht*, Manfred Pawlak Verlagsgesellschaft, Herrsching 1982.

39. Errikos Sevillias: *Athens – Auschwitz*, Lycabettus Press, Athens 1983.

40. E. D. Smith: *Victory of a Sort*, Robert Hale, London 1988.

41. Maj. Gen. Stephanos Sarafis: *ELAS: Greek Resistance Army*, Merlin Press, London 1980.

42. J. M. Stevens, C. M. Woodhouse. D. J. Walace; *British Reports on Greece 1943-1944*, Museum Tusculanum Press, Copenhagen 1982.

43. Loucas Ch. Tsagaris: *Mia Zoi Enas Agonas*, Lamia 1985.

44. Apostolos Vakalopoulos: *Griechische Geschichte*, Verlag Romiosini, Köln 1985.

45. Georgiou Vassos: *1940-1945: Istoria Tis Antistasis*, Verlag Ailos, Athens 1982.

46. Helen Vlachos: *House Arrest*, Verlag Andre Deutsch Ltd., London 1970.

47. Mary Winterer Papatassos: *Doorway to Greece*, Lycabettus Press, Athens 1984.

48. Robert Wistrich: *Wer war wer im Dritten Reich*, Harnack Verlag, Munich 1983.

49. C. M. Woodhouse: *Modern Greece*, Faber and Faber, London 1986.

50. C. M. Woodhouse: *Apple of Discord*, W. B. O'Neill, Reston, Virginia, 1985.

51. C. M. Woodhouse: *Something Ventured*, Granada Publishing, St. Albans, Herts, 1982.

52. Marika Youla: *Kimena Gia Tin Ethniki Antistasi*, Verlag Aixmi, Lamia 1986.

Archives

1. Bundesarchiv, Militärarchiv, Freiburg i.B.: RH 19 VII/8, RH 19 VII/7, RH 20-12/139, RH 2/700, RH 2/698, RH 2/699, RH 2/701, RH 2/702, RH 2/703, RH20-12/153, RH 20-12/154, RW 40/163, RW 40/161, RW 40/162, RW 40/127 and others.

2. Bundesarchiv, Zentralnachweisstelle, Aachen.

3. Deutsche Dienststelle für die Benachrichtigung der nächsten Angehörigen von Gefallenen der ehemaligen deutschen Wehrmacht, Berlin.

4. Pionierschule und Fachschule des Heeres für Bautechnik, Munich.

5. Stato Maggiore Dell'Esercito, Ufficio Storico, Rome, Raccoglitore 1098A, 1093, 1200A, 1226, 1393 A, 1226, 1232.

7. Volksbund Deutsche Kriegsgräberfürsorge, Kassel

8. Zentralbibliothek der Bundeswehr, Düsseldorf.

The work of the
"Volksbund Deutsche Kriegsgräberfürsorge"
(German War Graves Commission)

This organisation takes care of 1,400,000 graves in 363 cemeteries in eighteen countries in Europe, North Africa and the Near East, for German soldiers who fell in the two World Wars. In over eighty countries in the world, there are graves of German soldiers. In the old Länder, the association also cares for cemeteries of Russian prisoners of war.

It commemorates the soldiers who fell in both World Wars and all those who lost their lives in the bombing and those who were persecuted for their race, political belief or their religion and died behind barbed wire and prison walls. There is a day of national mourning in November.

The association helps families to find the graves, it organises grave decoration and photos and even group travel for the families to the cemeteries. It tries to remind in particular the young people of the events of the war and to show them the cemeteries. It has held youth camps and over 120,000 young people have taken part since 1953.